Canning & Preserving

FOR

DUMMIES®

2ND EDITION

by Amelia Jeanroy and Karen Ward

WILEY

Wiley Publishing, Inc.

Canning & Preserving For Dummies®, 2nd Edition

Published by
Wiley Publishing, Inc.
111 River St.
Hoboken, NJ 07030-5774
www.wiley.com

Copyright © 2009 by Wiley Publishing, Inc., Indianapolis, Indiana

Published simultaneously in Canada

For general information on our other products and services, please contact our Customer Care Department within the U.S. at 877-762-2974, outside the U.S. at 317-572-3993, or fax 317-572-4002.

For technical support, please visit www.wiley.com/techsupport.

Wiley also publishes its books in a variety of electronic formats. Some content that appears in print may not be available in electronic books.

Library of Congress Control Number: 2009932704

ISBN: 978-0-470-50455-0

Manufactured in the United States of America

10 9 8 7 6 5 4 3 2 1

WILEY

About the Authors

Amy Jeanroy: Amy has been canning and preserving foods for 20 years. She is passionate about filling the pantry with useful, delicious foods, and creating healthy meals from her own small farm. Amy is the Herb Garden Guide for About.com and also writes a weekly farm newsletter that provides homemade recipes to help her readers store and use their summer bounty.

Karen Ward: The author of *Pickles, Peaches, and Chocolate*, Karen is a life-long home canner, home economist, and recipe developer. In addition to judging preserved food at the San Diego County Fair each year, Karen teaches canning and preserving to men and women of all ages. Karen has been a featured guest on many television shows, including QVC and HGTV's *Smart Solutions*. She is a founding member of the San Diego Chapter of Les Dames d'Escoffier International, a nonprofit organization mentoring women and providing scholarships in the culinary arts. Karen is a native-born Southern Californian. She makes her home in San Diego with her husband, Chris.

Dedication

From Amy: To my uncles, John and Paul, whose constant support and wisdom gave me the confidence to continue with my dreams.

Acknowledgments

From Amy: I would like to thank my entire editorial team at Wiley: Tracy Barr, who kept me motivated; Emily Nolan, who tested the recipes; and Elizabeth Kurtzman, who provided the illustrations. Thank you, everyone! Creating a book is truly a team effort.

Publisher's Acknowledgments

We're proud of this book; please send us your comments through our Dummies online registration form located at http://dummies.custhelp.com. For other comments, please contact our Customer Care Department within the U.S. at 877-762-2974, outside the U.S. at 317-572-3993, or fax 317-572-4002.

Some of the people who helped bring this book to market include the following:

Acquisitions, Editorial, and Media Development

Project Editor: Tracy Barr

Acquisitions Editor: Stacy Kennedy

Assistant Editor: Erin Calligan Mooney

Editorial Program Coordinator: Joe Niesen

Technical Editor and Recipe Tester: Emily Nolan

Nutritionist: Patricia Santelli

Illustrator: Elizabeth Kurtzman

Senior Editorial Manager: Jennifer Ehrlich

Editorial Supervisor and Reprint Editor: Carmen Krikorian

Editorial Assistant: Jennette ElNaggar

Art Coordinator: Alicia B. South

Cover Photos: © Elizabeth Watt Photography

Cartoons: Rich Tennant (www.the5thwave.com)

Composition Services

Project Coordinator: Katherine Crocker

Layout and Graphics: Christin Swinford, Christine Williams

Proofreaders: Melissa D. Buddendeck, Melanie Hoffman

Indexer: Potomac Indexing, LLC

Publishing and Editorial for Consumer Dummies

   Diane Graves Steele, Vice President and Publisher, Consumer Dummies

   Kristin Ferguson-Wagstaffe, Product Development Director, Consumer Dummies

   Ensley Eikenburg, Associate Publisher, Travel

   Kelly Regan, Editorial Director, Travel

Publishing for Technology Dummies

   Andy Cummings, Vice President and Publisher, Dummies Technology/General User

Composition Services

   Debbie Stailey, Director of Composition Services

Contents at a Glance

Recipes at a Glance

Vegetables, Canned

Vegetables, Dried

Vegetables, Frozen

Meats and Meals

Soups and Stocks

Jellies, Jams, and More

Chutneys, Relishes, and Pickles

Sauces, Salsas, Syrups, and Pastes

Snacks, Breads, and Pie Fillings

Juices and Drinks

Herb Mixes

Table of Contents

Introduction

· ·

*Y*ou're not alone if you've thought about canning and preserving your own food but haven't tried it because you're afraid it's too involved. Well, it's time to set aside your hesitation. Today's methods and procedures for home-canning, freezing, and drying food are simple and easy. Many of the techniques may be similar to those your grandmother used, but you'll find they've been perfected. In this book, you get all the information you need to can and preserve food safely.

About This Book

Welcome to the wonderful world of canning and preserving. This book presents four preserving methods — water-bath canning, pressure canning, freezing, and drying — in an easy-to-understand format and walks you step by step through each technique. You don't need any previous canning or preserving experience in order to start, or continue, your endeavor to become a first-class food preserver. Within these pages, you'll find information like the following:

- ✔ What to look for to make sure you're preserving the best, most fresh fruits and veggies.

- ✔ A list of canning supplies and equipment (complete with illustrations), as well as instructions on how to ensure your canning equipment is in good working order.

- ✔ What techniques help you preserve the best flavor in your foods and how to avoid spoilage and recognize it if it does occur.

- ✔ Illustrations of different techniques and equipment along with tips for making your canning and preserving journey fun and rewarding.

- ✔ A whole host of favorite recipes for your enjoyment.

Consider this book your guide to discovering simple ways to preserve all the foods your family loves, without any mystery or confusion along the way.

Conventions Used in This Book

The recipes in this book include preparation times, cooking times, processing times, and the yield you should expect from your efforts. Here are some details that apply to all of the recipes but aren't repeated each time:

- Use a vinegar with 5 percent acidity.
- Use pure salt with no additives. (Canning or pickling salt is best.)
- Cook all food in heavy-bottomed pots and pans.
- Use nonreactive equipment and utensils (items made from glass, stainless steel, or enamel-coated steel or iron).
- Use glass jars and two-piece caps approved for home-canning.
- Always use new lids for canning.
- Start counting your water-bath processing time when the water reaches a full, rolling boil.
- Begin counting your pressure-canner processing time after releasing air in the canner and achieving the required pressure.

Also, all temperatures are Fahrenheit. All recipes and processing times are developed for altitudes at sea level to 1,000 feet above sea level. (For higher altitudes, refer to the altitude adjustment charts for water-bath canning in Chapter 4 and for pressure canning in Chapter 9.)

Foolish Assumptions

In writing this book, we made some assumptions about you:

- You know your way around a kitchen. You're familiar with basic cooking techniques and food preparation methods.
- You've never canned or preserved food before or have relatively little experience with food preservation methods and want basic, easy-to-understand-and-follow instructions.
- If you have canned and preserved food before, it was long enough ago that you want to find out more about the newer, safer, and easier techniques that are recommended today.
- Perhaps most importantly, you want to stock your kitchen with more natural, healthier, homemade alternatives to standard supermarket fare.

How This Book Is Organized

This book is organized into parts. The first part gives you basic information about canning and preserving, filling you in on terminology, equipment, and food safety. The next four parts show you the techniques for different preserving methods. Each of these parts includes tried-and-true, tested recipes and preserving tips that offer you a lot of practice for each technique. Motivation for trying each technique won't be a problem.

Part 1: Getting Started

With so many misconceptions about canning and preserving, this book begins with an explanation of each food preservation method and dispels any fears you may have about each technique. This part is a good starting point if you're new to canning and preserving, or if you've been away from any of these techniques for a while. You'll find information on specialty equipment and utensils for each method. Don't overlook the chapter on food safety. It's important to know what dangers may occur — and how to recognize them — if you skip any processing step, make adjustments to your recipe, or change a processing method and time.

Part 11: Water-bath Canning

If you like sweet spreads, relishes, or pickled food, start with this part. Water-bath canning is the most popular food-preserving method and the easier of the two approved canning methods. This part leads you step by step through the process while explaining what foods are suitable for this preserving method. You can try dozens of recipes, from jam and jelly to chutney and relish.

Part 111: Pressure Canning

Pressure canning is the approved method for processing food that's naturally low in acid, like vegetables, meat, poultry, and seafood. These foods contain more heat-resistant and hard-to-destroy bacteria than food that's safely water-bath processed. This part carefully describes the procedure and steps for canning these foods, whether it's vegetables or meals of convenience.

Part IV: Freezing

In this part, you discover that your freezer is more than a place for leftovers and ice cream. Utilize this cold area for planning and preparing your meals with a minimum of time and effort. After reading this part, you'll understand why the proper freezer containers and packaging methods, combined with correct thawing practices, prevent damage to your food while preserving its quality, flavor, and color.

Part V: Drying and Storing

Drying, which preserves food by removing moisture, is the oldest and slowest method for preserving food, and this part explains how to dry a variety of fruits, vegetables, and herbs for future enjoyment. And you won't want to miss the instructions for making fruit leathers. Who doesn't like to unroll the dried sheets of puréed fruit? This is one time your kids can play with their food and get away with it.

Part VI: The Part of Tens

This part includes short chapters highlighting canning problems that you may encounter and fun places to shop online or by catalog to satisfy your canning and preserving needs.

Appendix

Near the back of the book, you find a metric equivalent chart that's a handy reference guide for converting any measurements.

Icons Used in This Book

The following four icons appear throughout this book and point out specific points or remind you of items you'll want to be sure not to miss.

This icon directs you to tips or shortcuts we've picked up over the years. The information here makes your work easier and more hassle free.

This icon means, "Okay, you've heard this stuff before, but the information is important and bears repeating."

When you see this icon, pay special attention. The information tells you about a potential problem and how to overcome or avoid it.

These bits of technical information are interesting, but you can skip them if you want to. Of course, the info contained in these paragraphs makes you seem like you've been canning and preserving since you've been walking.

Where to Go from Here

Although you can start in any portion of this book, don't skip Chapter 3. It describes safe processing methods and tells you how to identify spoiled food. If you have any doubts about canning and preserving safety, this chapter puts your fears at ease.

If you want to know about a particular food-preservation method, go to the part devoted to that method. Each one begins with a chapter that explains the technique. Review these initial chapters before selecting a recipe to make sure you have a decent idea what that particular food preservation method requires. If still can't decide where to start, review the recipes and start with one that sounds good to you! Then just back-track to the general techniques chapter as you need to. If you'd like to make the Dilly Beans recipe in Chapter 8, for example, check out Chapter 4 for the basics on water-bath canning. If you want to dry strawberries (you find the recipe in Chapter 17), check out Chapter 16 for general drying information.

And if you want to jump right in? Go the Recipes at a Glance page to find a recipe that sparks your interest.

Part I
Getting Started

The 5th Wave   By Rich Tennant

"I had the flu when I made up and canned that
sauce. The tang comes from a few squirts
of nasal decongestant."

In this part . . .

In Part I, you find out what benefits canning and preserving your own food can bring to your life. Discover what tools and supplies make the food preservation process run smoothly and which rumors you may have heard about canning are myths and which are true. The chapters here introduce you to the language of canning and preserving and explain how to do so safely so that you can begin to fill your pantry with delicious and healthy fare.

Chapter 1

A Quick Overview of Canning and Preserving

In This Chapter

▶ Discovering the world of canning and preserving

▶ Understanding the *whys* and *hows* of canning and preserving

▶ Preparing yourself for safely canning and preserving your foods

▶ Becoming a successful food canner and preserver

*O*ver the years, because of our busy lifestyles and the convenience of refrigeration and supermarkets, the art of canning and preserving has declined. Other than jams and jellies, many people started thinking of canning as sort of a novelty hobby. But today, many people have a renewed interest in learning this art. With the decline in the economy, more people are finding that canning and preserving foods is an inexpensive and easy way to have a full pantry.

This chapter gives you an overview of the four canning and preserving techniques presented in this book — water-bath canning, pressure canning, freezing, and drying — and explains the benefits, both practical and emotional, that canning and preserving your own foods can provide.

If you're new to canning and preserving, don't be overwhelmed or scared off by the rules. This book walks you through easy, step-by-step instructions for each technique. After you understand the basic procedures for a method, like water-bath canning, it's just a matter of concentrating on preparing your recipe.

Knowing the Benefits of Canning and Preserving Your Own Food

Canning and preserving are ways to protect food from spoilage so you can use it at a later time. Some preserving methods, like drying, date back to ancient times; others, like canning, are a little more recent. There's no doubt that being able to offer fresh-tasting, home-canned or -preserved foods to your family and friends throughout the year is definitely one of life's luxuries.

Whatever food-preservation method you choose (this book covers canning, freezing, and drying), your efforts will give you

- ✔ **A pantry full of fresh, homegrown foods.** Having a stocked pantry offers a cushion against the fluctuating cost of healthy foods. If you enjoy specialty foods from gourmet stores but dislike the high prices, home-canning is a safe and economical way to preserve large or small quantities of high-quality food.

- ✔ **Convenience:** You can build a pantry of convenience foods that fit into your busy lifestyle and that your family will enjoy.

- ✔ **Confidence in the ingredients that go into your food.** If you love fresh ingredients and like to know what goes into your food, doing your own canning and preserving is the answer.

- ✔ **Protection against rising food costs.** The whole idea of canning and preserving is to take advantage of fresh food when it's abundant. And abundant food generally means lower cost.

- ✔ **A sense of relaxation and accomplishment:** For many people working in the kitchen and handling food provides a sense of relaxation, and watching family and friends enjoy the products of your efforts gives you a great sense of accomplishment. Taking the time to select your recipe, choosing and preparing your food, and packaging and processing it for safety is fulfilling and a source of pride for you, the home-canner.

- ✔ **A good time:** Producing canned and preserved food in your kitchen is fun and easy — and who doesn't like fun?

The price of food has skyrocketed in the last few years. Food safety has become a concern for everyone. Canning is the answer to both the price dilemma and the desire to offer nutritious foods throughout the year. Home-canning and -preserving instantly rewards your efforts when you follow the proper steps for handling and processing your food.

Who's canning today?

Although home-canning and -preserving has skipped one or two generations, one thing is certain: It's on the rise. Men and women of all ages practice the art of home-canning. It no longer matters whether you live in the country or in the city or if you grow your own food. Fresh ingredients are available just about everywhere. Farmer's markets are commonplace in many cities and towns, making it easy to find the perfect foods to preserve for an affordable price.

Exact statistics regarding home-canning vary, but according to the largest manufacturer of home-canning products, Alltrista, approximately one out of four households in the United States cans food. Today, most home-canned products are used in the home where they're produced. In addition, a rising number of people are committed to eating locally, and these folks want to know what is in the foods they eat. By preserving their own foods, they can find the freshest food available and control what goes in their food.

Meeting Your Techniques: Canning, Freezing, and Drying

The techniques discussed in this book are safe for home use and produce superior results when you follow all the steps for each method. You compromise the quality and safety of your food if you make your own rules. An example of this is shortening your processing period or not timing it correctly. Either of these adjustments can cause food spoilage because the food doesn't heat long enough to destroy all of the microorganisms in it.

Review the basic techniques for your type of food preserving before you begin — and if you're already familiar with the techniques, review them annually just to refresh your memory. You'll experience fewer interruptions in your food-preserving process. Always do a trial run before canning. This ensures you have all your supplies and steps in order so that you can work quickly and efficiently.

You'll have no doubts about preparing safe home-canned and -preserved food after you discover what each method does, which method is best for different foods, the rules for the technique you choose, and safe food-handling techniques. The pages that follow introduce you to the ancient and modern-day techniques that will help you can and preserve with ease.

Put by or *putting up* are terms that describe canning years ago, before there was refrigeration. They meant, "Save something perishable for use later when you'll need it."

About canning food

Canning is the most popular preserving method used today. Don't let anyone tell you that home-canning is complicated and unsafe. It's simply not true. Canning is the process of applying heat to food that's sealed in a jar in order to destroy any microorganisms that can cause food spoilage. All foods contain these microorganisms. Proper canning techniques stop this spoilage by heating the food for a specific period of time and killing these unwanted microorganisms. Also, during the canning process, air is driven from the jar and a vacuum is formed as the jar cools and seals. This prevents microorganisms from entering and recontaminating the food.

Approved methods

Although you may hear of many canning methods, only two are approved by the United States Department of Agriculture (USDA). These are water-bath canning and pressure canning:

✔ **Water-bath canning:** This method, sometimes referred to as *hot water canning,* uses a large kettle of boiling water. Filled jars are submerged in the water and heated to an internal temperature of 212 degrees for a specific period of time. Use this method for processing high-acid foods, such as fruit, items made from fruit, pickles, pickled food, and tomatoes. Chapter 4 explains this method in detail.

✔ **Pressure canning:** Pressure canning uses a large kettle that produces steam in a locked compartment. The filled jars in the kettle reach an internal temperature of 240 degrees under a specific pressure (stated in pounds) that's measured with a dial gauge or weighted gauge on the pressure-canner cover. Use a pressure canner for processing vegetables and other low-acid foods, such as meat, poultry, and fish. For more information about pressure canning, see Chapter 9.

Don't confuse a pressure canner with a pressure cooker, which is used to cook food quickly. A pressure cooker does not have adequate room for both the canning jars and the water needed to create the right amount of pressure to preserve foods.

In both water-bath canning and pressure canning, you heat your filled jars of food to a high temperature in order to destroy microorganisms and produce an airtight, vacuum seal. The only way to reliably produce a safe canned product is to use the correct method for your type of food, follow your recipe instructions to the letter, and complete each processing step. For all the details you need about canning and a plethora of recipes, head to Parts II and Part III.

Canning methods to avoid

Older canning methods are unreliable and, for that reason, aren't used or recommended today for home-canning. Occasionally, these methods are "revived" as being faster and easier than water-bath or pressure canning, but using any of the following methods is like playing Russian roulette with your food safety. Just because your grandmother used one of the following methods doesn't make it safe to use today. If you see instructions that require you to use any of the following methods, do yourself a favor and pass by that recipe.

- ✔ **Oven method:** In this method, filled jars are placed in a hot oven. The method is unsafe because your food's internal temperature most likely won't become hot enough to destroy microorganisms and other bacteria that cause spoilage. There's just no guarantee that the food in the jars will reach the temperature you set your oven at. There's also a chance that your jars may explode from the sudden temperature change when your oven door is opened.

- ✔ **Open-kettle method:** In this method, food is cooked in an open pot and transferred to sterilized jars. The two-piece caps are quickly added in hopes of sealing the jars as the food cools. This process produces a low vacuum seal that may be broken as gas from spoiling food builds up in the jar. This occurs because your food isn't heated to destroy microorganisms. There's also a chance your food may become contaminated when transferring it into the jars.

- ✔ **Steam method:** This method uses a shallow, covered pan with a rack in the bottom. After the filled jars are placed in the pan, steam circulates around the jars. This method is unsafe because the jars aren't evenly heated and the steam isn't pressurized to superheat the food and destroy microorganisms. Don't confuse this method with pressure canning.

- ✔ **Microwave oven:** All microwave ovens heat differently. Because of this, there's no way to set standards for processing times that achieve a high temperature to penetrate the jars and destroy microorganisms that cause food spoilage.

- ✔ **Dishwasher:** Because there's no way to know the exact temperature of different dishwashers and because temperature fluctuates throughout the cleaning cycle, dishwasher canning is a no-no. You can't rely on it to produce a safely canned product. You can, however, use a dishwasher to wash your jars and let them sit in the hot dishwasher until you're ready to fill them.

- ✔ **Aspirin:** Don't laugh at this, but at one time, aspirin was used as a substitute for heat processing. It does contain a germicidal agent that acts as a preservative, but this agent doesn't destroy the enzyme that causes deterioration in food and food spoilage.

- ✔ **Wax or paraffin seal:** Using wax or paraffin was once thought of as a safe way to seal canned goods. It has been proven to be unreliable. and dangerous botulism spores can still develop.

About freezing food

Freezing foods is the art of preparing and packaging foods at their peak of freshness and plopping them into the freezer to preserve all that seasonal goodness. Freezing is a great way to preserve foods that can't withstand the high temperatures and long cooking of conventional canning methods.

The keys to freezing food are to make sure it's absolutely fresh, that you freeze it as quickly as possible, and that you keep it at a proper frozen temperature (0 degrees).

The quality won't get better just because you throw it in the freezer. Properly packaging food in freezer paper or freezer containers prevents any deterioration in its quality. Damage occurs when your food comes in contact with the dry air of a freezer. Although freezer-damaged food won't hurt you, it does make the food taste bad. Here are three things to help you avoid freezer burn:

- ✔ **Reduce exposure to air:** Wrap food tightly.
- ✔ **Avoid fluctuating temperatures.** Keep the freezer closed as much as possible. Know what you want to remove before opening the door.
- ✔ **Don't overfill your freezer.** An overly full freezer reduces air circulation and speeds freezer damage.

For information and instructions on freezing a variety of foods, go to Part IV.

About drying food

Drying is the oldest method known for preserving food. When you dry food, you expose the food to a temperature that's high enough to remove the moisture but low enough that it doesn't cook. Good air circulation assists in evenly drying the food.

An electric dehydrator is the best and most efficient unit for drying, or dehydrating, food. Today's units include a thermostat and fan to help regulate temperatures much better. You can also dry food in your oven or by using the heat of the sun, but the process will take longer and produce inferior results to food dried in a dehydrator. Go to Part V for drying instructions for fruits, vegetables, and herbs.

Key Tricks to Successful Canning and Preserving

Canning and preserving methods are simple and safe, and they produce food that's nutritious, delicious, and just plain satisfying to your taste buds. Becoming a successful food preserver takes time, effort, and knowledge of the rules. Follow these tips for achieving success as a home canner and preserver:

- ✔ **Start with the freshest, best products available.** Preserving doesn't improve food quality. If you put garbage in, you get garbage out.

- ✔ **Know the rules and techniques for your canning or preserving method before you start your work.** Don't try to learn a technique after you've started your processing.

- ✔ **Work in short sessions to prevent fatigue and potential mistakes.** Process no more than two items in one day, and work with only one canning method at a time.

- ✔ **Stay up to date on new or revised guidelines for your preserving method.** This book is a great start. You can also go to Web sites like www.freshpreserving.com, created by the makers of Ball canning supplies. Here you can find tips and directions for canning just about anything.

- ✔ **Use the correct processing method and processing time to destroy microorganisms.** The recipe will tell you what method to use, but it helps if you understand the difference between high- and low-acid foods and how the canning methods for each differ. Go to Chapter 3 for details.

- ✔ **Know the elevation you're working at.** Adjust your processing time or pressure when you're at an altitude over 1,000 feet above sea level. For accurate information on how to adjust for your altitude, refer to Chapter 4 for water-bath canning conversions and Chapter 9 for pressure canning conversions.

- ✔ **Put together a plan before you start your preserving session.** Read your recipe (more than once). Have the proper equipment and correct ingredients on hand to prevent last-minute shortages and inconvenient breaks (make a list of what you need and check off items as you gather them).

✔ **Test your equipment.** If you're using a pressure canner or an electric dehydrator, test out the equipment to ensure everything's working properly. And always check the seals on your jars.

✔ **Use recipes from reliable sources or ones that you've made successfully before.** Follow your recipe to the letter. Don't substitute ingredients, adjust quantities, or make up your own food combinations. Improvisation and safe food preservation aren't compatible. This also means you can't double your recipe. If you require more than what the recipe yields, make another batch. Always use the size jars that are recommended in the recipe as well. Trying to use a larger or smaller jar may throw off the yield and final result.

Now you're ready to take your food to its final destination in the preservation process. Whether you choose canning, freezing, or drying, proceed down your canning and preserving road with confidence.

Chapter 2

Gathering Your Canning and Preserving Gear

*H*ow many times have you heard the phrase, "Use the right tool for the job"? At no time is this truer than when you're canning and preserving. The majority of the items discussed in this chapter won't break the bank, but they'll make your canning and preserving tasks more efficient. The faster you process your fresh ingredients, the better the quality and flavor of your final product.

In this chapter, you find a list of the tools and utensils you need to complete your tasks. Some tools, like a jar lifter or a lid wand, are only used for canning. Other tools, like pots, pans, and knives, are used throughout the year for everyday tasks. Purchase good-quality tools and equipment; their quality and durability will pay for themselves many times over.

If your local stores aren't familiar with the canning and preserving items you're looking for or you're having trouble locating them, head to Chapter 22, where you can find a list of sources for canning and preserving supplies.

Assorted Basic Tools

The tools that make canning and preserving easier are many of the very same tools that are in most well-stocked kitchens. When a recipe recommends a tool for canning, there's a practical reason for doing so. Using the proper tool for the job decreases the chance of a jar failing to seal or being able to harbor bacteria. It can also reduce the chance of mishaps and injuries.

Key basic tools and utensils

If you're serious about any work in the kitchen, these basic tools are indispensable. Purchase the best quality you can afford. Good-quality items will grow old with you.

- ✔ **Knives:** You need three basic knives: a paring knife, a multipurpose knife with a 6-inch blade, and an 8-inch (some people prefer a 10-inch) chef's knife. When purchasing quality knives, look for two options: stamped or forged blades and blades made of stainless or high carbon steel (tempered steel knives are no longer the epitome of high quality cutlery). Ceramic is another high quality knife, but these high priced knives are easier to damage than their steel counterparts. Also, if you select knives that are balanced, the knife will do the work for you.

  Properly caring for your knives protects your investment. Keep your knives razor-sharp. Store them in a block or a magnetic knife storage strip so they don't touch each other. Hand-wash them (dishwashers are notorious for being hard on dishes, and knives take the brunt of banging around with the other silverware).

- ✔ **Measuring cups:** Accuracy in measuring ingredients is essential to achieve the correct balance of ingredients for canning. There are two types of measuring cups: those for measuring dry ingredients, like flour, sugar, and solid fats, and those for measuring liquid ingredients (see Figure 2-1).

  Liquid measuring cups are made from glass, plastic, or metal. With glass measuring cups, you can easily see the amount of liquid in the cup.

- ✔ **Measuring spoons (see Figure 2-2):** These come in graduated sizes from ⅛ teaspoon to 2 tablespoons. *Note:* Don't use adjustable measuring spoons for canning foods; they move too easily and could give the wrong measurement.

  To avoid having to stop and clean your measuring spoons whenever you measure the same amount of wet and dry ingredients, have two sets handy, one for dry ingredients and the other for wet ingredients.

Figure 2-1: Measuring cups for dry and liquid food products.

liquid measure cup

dry measure cups

✔ **Spoons:** You need at least a couple of cooking spoons made of nonreactive metal (like stainless steel) that won't change the taste of acidic foods they come in contact with. Some choices for nonreactive metals are stainless steel, anodized aluminum, glass, or enameled cast iron. You can also use an assortment of different-sized wooden spoons (see Figure 2-2).

✔ **Rubber spatulas (refer to Figure 2-2):** These are available in a variety of colors and sizes, from flat to spoon-shaped. Use heat-resistant ones for cooking items containing sugar. Check that the end does not easily come off the handle, a common problem with less-expensive spatulas.

✔ **Tongs:** Tongs are handy for all types of kitchen chores, especially moving large pieces of food into and out of hot water. Try the spring-loaded variety in different lengths. Don't overlook a locking mechanism. It keeps the tongs closed when you're not using them.

✔ **Ladle:** Use a ladle that's heatproof with a good pouring spout.

✔ **Potholders:** Protect your hands from hot items. Have twice the amount of potholders available that you think you'll need.

WARNING!

Potholders often get wet during canning. Have enough on hand so that you don't have to use wet potholders. Heat quickly transfers through a wet potholder (in the form of steam), causing a severe burn.

✔ **Kitchen towels and paper towels:** Use these for cleaning your jar rims and as a pad for your cooling jars.

Figure 2-2:
Miscellaneous kitchen tools: wooden spoon, box grater, timer, measuring spoons, rubber spatula, and lemon juicer.

✔ **Graters:** A box grater (refer to Figure 2-2) gives you four or more options for shredding and grating. A microplane grater (see Figure 2-3) is an updated version of a *rasp* (a woodworking tool) that's perfect for removing the zest from citrus fruit.

✔ **Zester (see Figure 2-3):** Before the microplane grater, a zester was the tool for removing citrus fruit *zest* (just the skin without the bitter white part). It's still an asset when you need a small amount of zest (a teaspoon or less), but for larger amounts, use a microplane grater.

✔ **Scissors:** Use scissors instead of knives to open food packages. Avoid cross-contaminating bacteria by washing your scissors after opening meats.

✔ **Timer (refer to Figure 2-2):** Choose a timer that's easy to read, easy to set, and loud enough to hear if you leave the room. Consider getting two to ensure accuracy.

✔ **Waterproof pens and markers:** Select ones that don't rub off.

✔ **Labels:** You can make labels from masking or freezer tape, customize your own on your home computer, or order small quantities from a company like My Own Labels (see Chapter 22).

✔ **Cutting board:** A good cutting board protects your knives while providing you with a movable work surface.

✔ **Candy thermometer:** A candy thermometer accurately registers the temperature of candy and sugar. In canning, it's used to check the temperature of cooked items. Some candy thermometers have marks indicating the gel point for jelly (220 degrees). Purchase a candy thermometer that's easy to read with a base to support the thermometer so the bulb portion doesn't touch the bottom of your pan. If this occurs, your temperature reading won't be accurate. Many come with a clip attached to keep the bulb off of the bottom.

Figure 2-3: Microplane grater and zester.

MICROPLANE GRATER

ZESTER

If you can, store a second thermometer in a handy location. If you accidentally break one while canning, you will have a backup.

The following items aren't absolutely mandatory, but they're certainly nice to have. If you don't already have these items in your kitchen, add them as you find the need for them. They don't take up a lot of room, and you'll find yourself constantly reaching for them when you can.

- ✔ **Vegetable peeler:** Use this for peeling carrots, potatoes, and apples.
- ✔ **Potato masher:** This makes quick work of smashing your cooked fruits or vegetables.
- ✔ **Lemon juicer (refer to Figure 2-2):** This tool works on any citrus fruit and allows you to extract the juice in a hurry. Just cut your fruit in half, insert the juicer point into the fruit, and press away.

    Measure your juice and keep seeds and pulp out at the same time by squeezing your fruit into a mesh strainer resting on the edge of a measuring cup.

- ✔ **Melon baller:** With a melon baller, you can easily remove the seeds from a halved cucumber without having the seeds end up all over your kitchen.
- ✔ **Corer:** This tool removes apple cores without damaging the fruit. This is a real timesaver when you're handling pounds of apples.
- ✔ **Cherry/olive pitter:** There's nothing better for removing cherry and olive pits. Purchase the size of pitter that holds your fruit size.

Pots, pans, mixing bowls, and more

You probably already have an assortment of pots, pans, and mixing bowls. If not, don't worry: You don't need to purchase everything at one time. Start with a good basic assortment and add pieces as you find a need for them.

- ✔ **Pots:** Pots have two looped handles (one on each side of the pot), range in size from 5 to 8 quarts, are deep, and allow ample space for the expansion of your food during a hard-rolling boil. A good-quality, heavy-bottomed pot provides even heat distribution for cooking jams, jellies, or other condiments.
- ✔ **Saucepans:** Saucepans range in size from 1 to 3 quarts. They have a long handle on one side of the pan and usually come with a fitted lid.
- ✔ **Mixing bowls:** Keep a variety of mixing bowl sizes in your kitchen. Look for sets in graduated sizes that stack inside each other for easy storage. Bowls made from glass and stainless steel are the most durable.

Purchase mixing bowls with flat, not curved, bases. They won't slide all over your kitchen counter while you work. When mixing vigorously, place a damp dishtowel under the bowl. This prevents the filled bowl from sliding.

✔ **Colander:** Colanders aren't just for draining pasta. They're perfect for washing and draining fruits and vegetables. Simply fill your colander with food and immerse it in a sink full of water. Remove the colander from the water and let your food drain while you move on to other tasks.

✔ **Wire basket:** A collapsible wire or mesh basket with a lifting handle makes blanching a breeze. Place your filled basket of food into your pot of boiling water. When the blanching time is up, lift the food-filled basket out of the boiling water.

Specialty equipment to make work easier

All the items in this list are indispensable for your canning chores. They all save you loads of time.

✔ **Food processor:** Purchase the best-quality food processor you can afford. It should be heavy and sturdy so that it doesn't bounce around on your kitchen counter as it's processing away. Figure 2-4 is one example of a food processor.

✔ **Food mill:** A food mill (see Figure 2-5) purées fruits and vegetables as it removes the peel and seeds. You accomplish this by manually cranking the blade, which forces the pulp through the mill. Look for a food mill that rests on the edge of your bowl or pot, which enables you to use one hand to stabilize the mill while you crank the blade with your other hand.

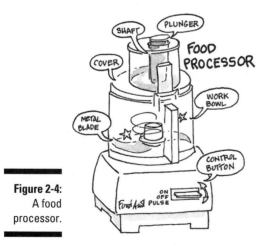

Figure 2-4:
A food
processor.

FOOD MILL

Figure 2-5:
Food mill.

✔ **Blender:** A blender purées fruits and vegetables in a hurry, but you need to remove the peel and seeds first. Be cautious of incorporating too much air into your food.

✔ **Food scale:** A food scale is essential when your canning recipe lists your fruit or vegetables by weight. The two most common types of food scales are spring and electronic. Examples of these are shown in Figure 2-6.

A food scale with metric quantity markings makes converting recipe ingredients a breeze.

✔ A *spring scale* (sometimes referred to as a manual scale) allows you to place a bowl on the scale and manually adjust the weight setting to 0 before weighing your food. After placing your food on the scale, read the indicator on the dial to determine the weight.

✔ An *electronic scale* is battery operated with a digital readout. It's more costly than a spring scale but easier to read. Look for one with a *tare feature.* This allows you to set the scale to 0 if you add a bowl to hold your food. If you have a choice, choose an electronic or digital scale.

SPRING SCALE

Figure 2-6:
Two types
of food
scales:
electronic
and spring.

ELECTRIC SCALE

✔ **Vacuum-sealing machines:** A vacuum sealer is the most efficient appliance around for removing air from food-storage bags. Use vacuum sealers for packaging dried foods or for storing raw or cooked foods in the freezer. Although it takes up room and can be costly, you'll realize its full value after you own one. New on the market are hand-held vacuum sealers. They can provide a less-expensive alternative to purchasing an electric version.

Canning Equipment

The equipment in this section is especially designed for canning, which means you'll use it during canning season but not much otherwise. Make sure you store these items in a safe, clean location. And be sure to look over every piece each time you use it to check for wear and tear.

Canning vessels

The kind of food you'll be canning determines the type of vessel you'll be using: a water-bath canner or a pressure canner. Refer to Chapters 4 and 9, respectively, for detailed information on using each of these vessels.

Water-bath canner

A water-bath canner, also referred to as a boiling-water canner, is a kettle used for processing high-acid foods (primarily fruits, jams, jellies, condiments, and pickled foods). The canner consists of a large enamelware or stainless-steel pot with a tight-fitting lid and a jar rack. Check out Chapter 4 for an illustration of a water-bath canner and instructions on how to use one.

Pressure canner

A pressure canner, sometimes referred to as a steam-pressure canner, is used for canning low-acid foods (primarily vegetables, meats, fish, and poultry) in an airtight container at a specific pressure. A weighted gauge or a dial gauge measures steam pressure in the canner. This ensures that the high temperature of 240 degrees is attained to safely process your food. Pressure canners and how to use them are described (and illustrated) in Chapter 9.

Canning tools

These tools are must-haves for water-bath or pressure canning. Safety in the kitchen is number one, and the right tools for handling hot, filled jars and other large canning equipment are indispensable.

Jar lifter

A jar lifter is one tool you don't want to be without. It's the best tool available for transferring hot canning jars into and out of your canning kettle or pressure canner. This odd-looking, rubberized, tonglike item (check out Figure 2-7) grabs the jar around the *neck* (the area just below the threaded portion at the top of the jar) without disturbing the screw band.

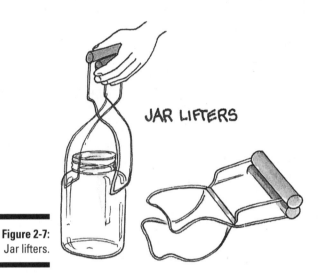

JAR LIFTERS

Figure 2-7:
Jar lifters.

Foam skimmer

A foam skimmer, shown in Figure 2-8, makes removing foam from the top of hot jelly, jam, or marmalade easy while leaving any pieces of fruit or rind in the hot liquid. (The openings in slotted spoons are too large to achieve quick and efficient foam removal.)

FOAM SKIMMER

Figure 2-8:
A foam
skimmer.

Home-canning jars

Over the years, many types of jars with many varieties of seals have been used for home-canning. The most commonly used jars bear the names of Ball and Kerr and are commonly referred to as Mason jars. They use a two-piece cap to produce a vacuum seal in the jar after heat processing.

To ensure safe home-canning today, use only jars approved for home-canning and made from tempered glass. *Tempering* is a treatment process for glass that allows the jars to withstand the high heat (212 degrees) of a water-bath canner, as well as the high temperature (240 degrees) of a pressure canner, without breaking.

Home-canning jars come in many sizes: 4-ounce, half-pint, 12-ounce, 1-pint, and 1-quart (see Figure 2-9). They offer two widths of openings: regular-mouth (about 2½ inches in diameter) and wide-mouth (about 3⅛ inches in diameter). Regular-mouth jars are used more frequently for jelly, jam, relish, or any other cooked food. Wide-mouth jars are mainly used for canning vegetables and pickles and meats, because it's easier to get the large pieces into the wide opening.

CANNING JARS

Figure 2-9:
Varieties
of canning
jars: wide-
mouth,
regular-
mouth, and
jelly jars.

Two-piece caps

Two-piece caps consist of a lid and a metal screw band (see Figure 2-10). They're made specifically for use with modern-day home-canning jars.

✔ **Lids:** The underside edge of the lid has a rubberlike sealing compound that softens when it's heated. This compound adheres to a clean jar rim and creates an airtight seal after the heat-processing period. Lids aren't reusable.

✔ **Screw bands:** The screw band holds the lid in place during the processing period and secures it in place when storing an opened jar in the refrigerator. After verifying that your cooled jars have successfully sealed (refer to Chapter 4), you remove the screw band before you store the canned food. The screw bands may be used many times as long as there are no signs of corrosion or rust and they aren't bent or dented.

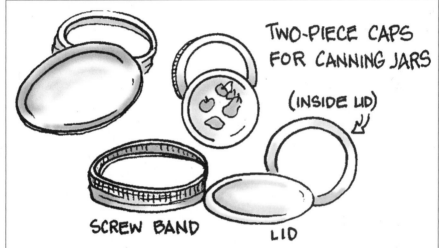

Figure 2-10: Two-piece caps: lids and screw bands.

TWO-PIECE CAPS FOR CANNING JARS

(INSIDE LID)

SCREW BAND

LID

Mason jars

If the most commonly used glass home-canning jars bear the names of Ball and Kerr, why do we call them Mason jars? The Mason jar is named for its creator, James Landis Mason. He designed and patented a unique glass jar that uses a screw-top lid to create an airtight seal for food. This easy-to-seal jar replaced the large stoneware vessels that had previously been used for food storage.

The tapered jars we use today were introduced after World War II. They use a two-piece cap consisting of a lid and a metal screw band that fits the threaded jar top. Today, all home-canning jars are generically referred to as Mason jars. Thank you, Mr. Mason, for making the task of home-canning easy with the use of screw-top closures.

Lid wand

A lid wand (see Figure 2-11) has a magnet on one end of a heat-resistant stick. With it, you can take a lid from hot water and place it on the filled-jar rim without touching the lid or disturbing the sealing compound.

Place your lids top to top and underside to underside to prevent them from sticking together in your pan of hot water. If they do stick together, dip them into a bowl of cold water to release the suction. Reheat them in the hot water for a few seconds before using them. Also offset the lids as you place them in the water. This keeps them fanned out and easier to pick up singly.

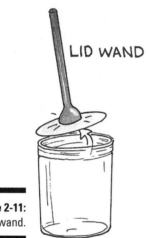

LID WAND

Figure 2-11:
A lid wand.

Thin plastic spatula

A thin, flexible plastic spatula is the right tool for releasing air bubbles between pieces of food in your filled jars (check out Figure 2-12). Buy a package of chopsticks for an inexpensive alternative.

Don't use a metal item or a larger object for this job because it may damage your food and crack or break your hot jar.

Figure 2-12:
A thin
plastic
spatula for
releasing air
bubbles.

PLASTIC SPATULA
FOR RELEASING AIR BUBBLES

Wide-mouth canning funnel

A wide-mouth funnel (see Figure 2-13) fits into the inside edge of a regular-mouth or a wide-mouth canning jar and lets you quickly and neatly fill your jars. This is an essential tool for canning.

Figure 2-13:
A wide-mouth canning funnel.

Jelly bag or strainer

A jelly bag is made for extracting juice from cooked fruit for making jelly. These bags aren't expensive, but if you'd rather not purchase one, make your own using a metal strainer lined with cheesecloth. Use a strainer that hangs on the edge of your pot or mixing bowl and doesn't touch the liquid. Head to Chapter 6 for instructions on making jelly.

Stoneware crocks

Stoneware crocks are available in sizes from 1 gallon to 5 gallons, usually without lids. They're nonreactive and are used for making pickles and olives. Make sure you use only crocks that are glazed on the interior and certified free of lead and *cadmium,* a form of zinc ore used in pigments or dyes.

Be wary of using secondhand stoneware crocks. These crocks were often made with leaded glaze that will leach into your foodstuff. Because you do not often know the history of used items, this is an item that is best purchased new and not secondhand.

Tools and Equipment for Freezing Food

Some of the items required for this simple form of food preservation are already in your kitchen. For a more detailed list, check out Chapter 13.

- **A freezer:** Usually, the freezer attached to your refrigerator is large enough for freezing food. But if you're serious about freezing lots of food, you may want to invest in a separate freezer unit.

- **Rigid containers:** These can be made of plastic or glass. Use only containers approved for the cold temperatures of a freezer. Plastic containers should be nonporous and thick enough to keep out odors and dry air in the freezer. Glass containers need to be treated to endure the low temperature of a freezer and strong enough to resist cracking under the pressure of expanding food during the freezing process.

- **Freezer bags:** Use bags made for freezing in sizes compatible with the amount of your food.

- **Freezer paper and wraps:** This laminated paper protects your food from freezer burn, which results when air comes in contact with your food while it's in the freezer. Tape this paper to keep the wrap tightly sealed. Heavy-duty aluminum foil is another great freezer wrap and requires no taping.

For extra protection against freezer damage, wrap food items in foil and place them in a freezer bag.

Tools and Equipment for Drying Food

Dehydrating food is a long, slow process of removing moisture from your food while exposing it to low heat. Here are some items you'll want to have for this process, which is explained in Chapter 16:

- **An electric dehydrator:** This machine dries your food in an enclosed chamber while it circulates warm air around your food.

- **A conventional oven:** If your oven maintains a low temperature and you can stand to be without it for up to 24 hours, use it for drying before making the investment in an electric food dehydrator.

✔ **Oven thermometer:** An oven thermometer tells you if your oven temperature is low enough to dry your food without cooking it (see Chapter 16 for detailed instructions for checking your oven's temperature).

✔ **Trays and racks:** These are used for holding your food while it's drying. They're included with an electric dehydrator. For oven-drying, use mesh-covered frames or baking sheets. For sun-drying, clean screens are necessary, along with clean cheesecloth to keep hungry bugs off the food as it dries.

Chapter 3

On Your Mark, Get Set, Whoa! The Road to Safe Canning and Preserving

. . . .

In This Chapter

▶ Putting your fears of home-canned food to rest

▶ Determining your processing method by your food's acidity

▶ Making the acquaintance of food-spoiling microorganisms and enzymes

▶ Recognizing the signs of food spoilage

. . . .

*T*he desire and determination to produce a delicious, safe-to-eat product without the risk of food poisoning is one thing longtime canners and people new to canning have in common. The canning and preserving techniques used today provide you with these results as long as you follow the proper steps and procedures for preparing, processing, and storing your food.

Before you begin your canning and preserving journey, take a stroll through this chapter, which introduces you to microorganisms, enzymes, and other potentially dangerous situations that cause food spoilage. You can also find info on how to prevent and identify food spoilage. The technical portion of this chapter shouldn't deter you from canning. Rest assured, after reading this information, you'll have no fear about preparing and serving your home-canned and -preserved food.

Dispelling Your Fears of Home-Canned and -Preserved Food

Preventing food spoilage is the key to safe canning. Over the years, home-canning has become safer and better. Scientists have standardized processing methods, and home-canners know more about using these methods. When you follow up-to-date guidelines exactly, you'll experience little concern about the quality and safety of your home-canned and -preserved foods.

The following sections offer some tips for handling, preparing, and processing your food.

Preparing your food properly

Use fresh, firm (not overripe) food. Wash and prepare your food well to remove any dirt and bacteria: Wash it in a large bowl filled with water and a few drops of detergent and then rinse it in a separate bowl of fresh water (see Figure 3-1). Can fruit and vegetables as soon as possible after they're picked.

No, you don't have to wash berries individually: Put them in a colander and submerge the colander, berries and all, in the wash bowl; then rinse them off with a running spray of water.

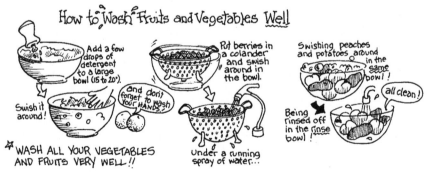

How to Wash Fruits and Vegetables Well

Add a few drops of detergent to a large bowl (15 to 20").

Swish it around!

And don't forget to wash your HANDS.

⚡ WASH ALL YOUR VEGETABLES AND FRUITS VERY WELL !!

Put berries in a colander and swish around in the bowl.

Under a running spray of water...

Swishing peaches and potatoes around in the same bowl!

all clean!

Being rinsed off in the rinse bowl!

Figure 3-1:
How to wash fruit and vegetables well.

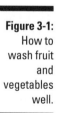

Packing your jars with care

How you fill the canning jars is also important:

- ✔ **Don't overpack foods.** Trying to cram too much food into a jar may result in underprocessing because the heat can't evenly penetrate the food.

- ✔ **Make sure your jars have the proper headspace.** *Headspace* is the air space between the inside of the lid and the top of your food or liquid in your jar or container (see Figure 3-2). Proper headspace is important to the safety of your preserved food because of the expansion that occurs as your jars are processed or your food freezes.

- ✔ **Make sure you release the air bubbles from the jar before sealing the lid.** No matter how carefully you pack and fill your jars, you'll always have some hidden bubbles.

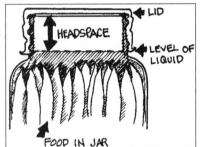

Figure 3-2:
Headspace.

The all-important headspace

When you're canning food, too little headspace in your canning jars restricts your food from expanding as it boils. Inadequate space for the expanding food may force some of it out of the jar and under the lid, leaving particles of food between the seal and the jar rim. If this occurs, your jar won't produce a vacuum seal.

Leaving too much headspace may cause discoloration in the top portion of your food. Excess headspace can keep your jar from producing a vacuum seal if the processing time isn't long enough to exhaust the excess air in the jar.

Always use the headspace stated in your recipe. If your recipe doesn't give you a headspace allowance, use these guidelines:

- ✔ For juice, jam, jelly, pickles, relish, chutney, sauces, and condiments, leave headspace of ¼ inch.

- ✔ For high-acid foods (fruits and tomatoes), leave headspace of ½ inch.

- ✔ For low-acid foods (vegetables, meats, fish, and poultry), leave head-space of 1 inch.

Headspace is also important when you're freezing food because frozen food expands during the freezing process. If you fail to leave the proper headspace in your freezer container, the lid may be forced off the container, or the container may crack or break. When your frozen food comes in direct contact with the air in your freezer, the quality of your food deteriorates and the food develops freezer burn (go to Chapter 13 for more on freezing food). On the other hand, too much air space allows excess air in your container. Even though your food doesn't come in direct contact with the air in the freezer, the excess space in the top of the container develops ice crystals. When your food thaws, the excess liquid reduces the food's quality.

If you don't trust yourself to eyeball the headspace, use a small plastic ruler (about 6 inches long) to measure the correct headspace in the jar.

Releasing air bubbles from your jars

The most important thing to do when you're filling your jars is to release trapped air bubbles between the food pieces. This may seem unimportant, but air bubbles can play havoc with your final product:

- **Jar seals:** Too much air in the jar from trapped air bubbles produces excessive pressure in the jar during processing. The pressure in the jar is greater than the pressure outside the jar during cooling. This imbalance interferes with the sealing process.

- **Liquid levels:** Air bubbles take up space. When there's trapped air between your food pieces before sealing the jars, the liquid level in the jar drops when the food is heated. (For releasing air bubbles, see Figure 3-3.) In addition, floating and discolored food results from packing your food without the proper amount of liquid in the jars. Snuggly packed food eliminates air and allows enough liquid to completely cover the food with proper headspace (refer to Figure 3-2).

Never skip the step of releasing air bubbles.

Choosing the right canning method and following proper procedures

Always use the correct processing method for your food. Process all high-acid and pickled food in a water-bath canner. Process all low-acid food in a pressure canner. To find out how to determine whether a food has a low or high acidity level, head to the next section. (You can find out about the different canning methods in Chapters 4 and 9.) In addition to choosing the right canning method, follow these steps to guard against food spoilage:

RELEASING AIR BUBBLES

USE A NONMETALLIC SPATULA TO PRESS BACK GENTLY ON THE CONTENTS. GO ALL THE WAY AROUND THE JAR.

Figure 3-3:
Releasing air bubbles from your filled jars.

- Don't experiment or take shortcuts. Use only tested, approved methods.

- Never use an outdated recipe. Look for a newer version. Do not update the directions yourself. Check the publishing date at the beginning of the recipe book. If it is more than 5 years old, find a newer version.

- If your elevation is higher than 1,000 feet above sea level, make the proper adjustments in processing time and pressure for your altitude. See the section "Adjusting your altitude" for information on altitudes and processing times.

- If you're pressure canning, allow your pressure canner to depressurize to 0 pounds pressure naturally; don't take the lid off to accelerate the process.

- Allow your processed jars to cool undisturbed at room temperature.

- Process your filled jars for the correct amount of time and, if you're pressure canning, at the correct pressure (both will be stated in your recipe). Make adjustments to your processing time and pressure for altitudes over 1,000 feet above sea level.

- Test each jar's seal and remove the screw band before storing your food.

Checking your equipment

To prevent spoilage, your equipment must be in good shape and working properly:

- ✔ Have the pressure gauge and seal on your pressure canner tested every year for accuracy. (Weighted gauges don't require testing.) This is often offered for free at your local extension office.

- ✔ Use jars and two-piece caps made for home-canning. Discard any jars that are cracked or nicked.

- ✔ Never use sealing lids a second time. Always use new lids. The sealant on the underside of the lid is good for only one processing. If your jars do not seal the first time, always replace the lid with a fresh one. There may be a problem with the sealant, despite starting with a new lid.

Knowing the Acidity Level of Your Food

Knowing the acidity level of the food you're processing is important because the *pH,* the measure of acidity, determines which canning method you use: water-bath or pressure canning. For canning purposes, food is divided into two categories based on the amount of acid the food registers:

- ✔ **High-acid** foods include fruits and pickled foods. (For detailed information on identifying and processing high-acid food, refer to Chapter 4.) Foods in this group have a pH of 4.6 or lower. Processing them in a water-bath canner destroys harmful microorganisms.

  Tomatoes are considered a low-high acid food. With all of the new varieties of tomatoes, it is now recommended that the home canner add an acid to the canning process, to ensure that the proper acidity is reached every time.

- ✔ **Low-acid** foods, primarily vegetables, meat, poultry, and fish, contain little natural acid. Their pH level is higher than 4.6. (Check out Chapter 9 for detailed information on identifying and processing low-acid food.) Process these foods in a pressure canner, which superheats your food and destroys the more heat-resistant bacteria, like botulism.

If you want to feel like you're back in science class all over again, you can buy litmus paper at teacher- or scientific-supply stores and test the acidity level of your food yourself. Also referred to as pH paper, litmus paper is an acid-sensitive paper that measures the acid in food. When you insert a strip of pH paper into your prepared food, the paper changes color. You then compare the wet strip to the pH chart of colors that accompanies the litmus paper.

The *pH,* or potential of hydrogen, is the measure of acidity or alkalinity in food. The values range from 1 to 14. Neutral is 7. Lower values are more acidic, while higher values are more alkaline. The lower the pH value in your food, the more acidic it is.

Avoiding Spoilage

Food spoilage is the unwanted deterioration in canned or preserved food that makes your food unsafe for eating. Ingesting spoiled food causes a wide range of ailments, depending on the type of spoilage and the amount of food consumed. Symptoms vary from mild, flulike aches and pains to more-serious illnesses or even death.

But having said that, the potential for spoiled food shouldn't stop you from canning. When you understand the workings of these microscopic organisms and enzymes, you'll know why using the correct processing method for the correct amount of time destroys these potentially dangerous food spoilers. And you'll have nothing to worry about.

Meeting the spoilers

Mold, yeast, bacteria, and enzymes are the four spoilers. *Microorganisms* (mold, yeast, and bacteria) are independent organisms of microscopic size. *Enzymes* are proteins that exist in plants and animals. When any one or more of the spoilers have a suitable environment, they grow rapidly and divide or reproduce every 10 to 30 minutes! With this high-speed development, it's obvious how quickly food can spoil. Some of these create spoilage that can't be seen with the naked eye (like botulism), while others (like mold) make their presence known visually.

Living microorganisms are all around — in your home, in the soil, and even in the air you breathe. Sometimes microorganisms are added to food to achieve a fermented product, like beer or bread (for leavening). They're also important for making antibiotics. The point? Not all microorganisms are bad, just the ones that cause disease and food spoilage.

Mold

Mold is a fungus with dry spores. Poorly sealed jars of high-acid or pickled foods are perfect locations for these spores to set up housekeeping. After the spores float through the air and settle on one of their favorite foods, they start growing. At first you see what looks like silken threads, then streaks of color, and finally fuzz, which covers the food. Processing high-acid and pickled food in a water-bath canner destroys mold spores.

Don't eat food that's had fuzz scraped off of it. This was thought safe at one time but not anymore. Mold contains carcinogens that filter into the remaining food. Although the food appears to be noninfected, ingesting this food can cause illness.

Yeast

Yeast spores grow on food like mold spores. They're particularly fond of high-acid food that contains lots of sugar, like jam or jelly. They grow as a dry film on the surface of your food. Prevent yeast spores from fermenting in your food by destroying them in a water-bath canner.

Bacteria

Bacteria are a large group of single-celled microorganisms. Common bacteria are staphylococcus and salmonella. Botulism, the one to be most concerned with in canning, is the most dangerous form of bacteria and can be deadly. It's almost undetectable because it's odorless and colorless. Botulism spores are stubborn and difficult to destroy.

Botulism spores hate high-acid and pickled foods, but they love low-acid foods. When you provide these spores with an airless environment containing low-acid food, like a jar of green beans, the spores produce a toxin in the food that can kill anyone who eats it. The only way to destroy them in low-acid food is by pressure canning.

For safety's sake, before eating any home-canned, low-acid food, boil it for 15 minutes from the point of boiling at altitudes of 1,000 feet or lower. For altitudes above 1,000 feet, add 1 additional minute for each 1,000 feet of elevation.

Boiling does *not* kill the botalism bacteria. Symptoms from ingesting botulism-infected food occur within 12 to 36 hours after eating it. Symptoms include double vision and difficulty swallowing, breathing, and speaking. Seek medical attention immediately if you believe you've eaten infected food. Antitoxins are available to treat this poisoning, but the sooner, the better.

Enzymes

Enzymes are proteins that occur naturally in plants and animals. They encourage growth and ripening in food, which affects the flavor, color, texture, and nutritional value. Enzymes are more active in temperatures of 85 to 120 degrees than they are at colder temperatures. They're not harmful, but they can make your food overripe and unattractive while opening the door for other microorganisms or bacteria.

An example of enzymes in action occurs when you cut or peel an apple. After a few minutes, the apple starts to brown. Stop this browning by treating the cut apple with an antioxidant solution (see Chapter 5). Other methods for halting the enzymatic action in your food are blanching and hot packing.

Adjusting your altitude

Properly processing your home-canned foods destroys microorganisms. Knowing your altitude is important because the boiling point of water and pressure in a pressure canner changes at altitudes over 1,000 feet above sea level. This occurs because the air is thinner at higher elevations. With less air resistance, water boils at a temperature below 212 degrees.

To produce food free from microorganisms at higher elevations, adjust your processing time and pressure to compensate for your altitude. Use the altitude adjustment charts in Chapter 4 (for water-bath canning) and in Chapter 9 (for pressure canning). These adjustments ensure that your food is heated to the correct temperature for destroying microorganisms.

If you don't know the elevation of your city, check with your city offices, your public library, or your state or county cooperative extension service listed in your local telephone directory. Or check out `http://national4-hhead quarters.gov/extension/index.html` on the Internet. Just enter your city and state in the box at the bottom of the page, click Submit, and scroll down to find the elevation of your city.

Detecting Spoiled Foods

No one can't promise you that your home-canned foods will always be free from spoilage, but you can rest assured that your chances for spoiled food are greatly reduced when you follow the precise guidelines for each preserving method. If you suspect, for any reason, that your food is spoiled or just isn't right, don't taste it. Also, just because your food doesn't look spoiled, doesn't mean that it's not.

The best way to detect food spoilage is by visually examining your jars. Review the following checklist. If you can answer "true" for each of the following statements, your food should be safe for eating:

- The food in the jar is covered with liquid, is fully packed, and has maintained the proper headspace.
- The food in the jar is free from moving air bubbles.
- The jars have good, tight seals.
- The food has maintained a uniform color.
- The food isn't broken or mushy.
- The liquid in the jar is clear, not cloudy, and free of sediment.

After your food has passed the previous checklist, examine your jars more closely. If you discover any spoilage during any step of this process, don't continue your search, but properly dispose of your product.

1. **Hold the jar at eye level.**

2. **Turn and rotate the jar, looking for any seepage or oozing from under the lid that indicates a broken seal.**

3. **Examine the food surface for any streaks of dried food originating at the top of the jar.**

4. **Check the contents for any rising air bubbles or unnatural color.**

   The food and liquid should be clear, not cloudy.

5. **Open the jar.**

   There shouldn't be any spurting liquid.

6. **Smell the contents of the jar.**

   Take note of any unnatural or unusual odors.

7. **Look for any cottonlike growth, usually white, blue, black, or green, on the top of your food surface or on the underside of the lid.**

Spoiled low-acid food may exhibit little or no visual evidence of spoilage. Treat any jars that are suspect as if they contained botulism toxins. Follow the detailed instructions for responsibly disposing of spoiled, low-acid food in Chapter 9. Never use or taste any canned food that exhibits signs of spoilage or that you suspect is spoiled.

Removing the screw bands from your cooled, sealed jars before storing them allows you to easily detect any broken seals or food oozing out from under the lid that indicates spoilage.

Part II
Water-bath Canning

"The kids mixed up the canning labels with the photo album labels. Just hand me a jar of Aunt Thelma so I can finish this pie before Peaches and Pickles get here."

In this part . . .

This part tells you all you need to know about the most
popular method of canning: water-bath canning. Some
of the products, like jam, jelly, marmalade, relish, and
salsa may be familiar to you, while others, like chutney,
conserves, and pickled vegetables, may be new. Packed
with easy-to-follow instructions for canning a wide variety
of fruits, jellies, and more, this part sends you well on
your way to a pantry stocked with healthy and delicious
items.

Chapter 4

Come On In, the Water's Fine! Water-bath Canning

● ●

In This Chapter

▶ Discovering water-bath canning

▶ Recognizing high-acid foods

▶ Stepping up to high-altitude canning

▶ Knowing the proper processing procedures

● ●

*W*ith water-bath canning you essentially use a special kettle to boil filled jars for a certain amount of time. Common foods for water-bath canning include fruits and tomatoes, as well as jams, jellies, marmalades, chutneys, relishes, pickled vegetables, and other condiments.

You're probably wondering whether water-bath canning is safe for canning food at home. Rest assured: The answer is a most definite "Yes!" — provided that you follow the instructions and guidelines for safe canning.

In this chapter, you discover which foods are safely processed in a water-bath canner and step-by-step instructions for completing the canning process. In no time, you'll be turning out sparkling jars full of homemade delicacies to dazzle and satisfy your family and friends.

Water-bath Canning in a Nutshell

Water-bath canning, sometimes referred to as the *boiling-water method,* is the simplest and easiest method for preserving high-acid food, primarily fruit, tomatoes, and pickled vegetables.

To water-bath can, you place your prepared jars in the a *water-bath canner,* a kettle especially designed for this canning method (see the section "Key equipment for water-bath canning" for more on the canner and other necessary equipment); bring the water to a boil; and then maintain that boil for a certain number of minutes, determined by the type of food and the size of the jar. Keeping the water boiling in your jar-filled kettle throughout the processing period maintains a water temperature of 212 degrees. This constant temperature is critical for destroying mold, yeast, enzymes, and bacteria that occur in high-acid foods.

 Water-bath canning is one of the two recommended methods for safely home-canning food (the other method is pressure canning, covered in Chapter 9). Although each processing method uses different equipment and techniques, the goal is the same: to destroy any active bacteria and microorganisms in your food, making it safe for consumption at a later time. This is accomplished by raising the temperature of the food in the jars and creating a vacuum seal.

 Water-bath canning and pressure-canning methods aren't interchangeable because the temperature of a water bath only reaches 212 degrees while the temperature of a pressure canner reaches 240 degrees, the temperature necessary to safely process low-acid foods. For more on pressure canning, go to Chapter 9.

Foods you can safely water-bath can

You can safely water-bath can only high-acid foods — those with a pH factor (the measure of acidity) of 4.6 or lower. So just what is a high-acid food? Either of the following:

- ✔ **Foods that are naturally high in acid:** These foods include most fruits.

- ✔ **Low-acid foods that you add acid to, thus converting them into a high-acid food.** *Pickled vegetables* fall into this category, making them safe for water-bath canning. You may change the acid level in low-acid foods by adding an acid, such as vinegar, lemon juice, or *citric acid,* a white powder extracted from the juice of acidic fruits such as lemons, limes, or pineapples. Some examples of altered low-acid foods are pickles made from cucumbers, relish made from zucchini or summer squash, and green beans flavored with dill. Today, tomatoes tend to fall into this category. They can be water-bath canned, but for safety's sake you add a form of acid to them.

 If your recipe doesn't tell you which processing method (water-bath canning or pressure canning) is appropriate for your food, don't guess. Instead, use litmus paper to test the pH level of your food (see Chapter 3). If your food has a pH of 4.6 or lower, use the water-bath canning method; if it has a pH of 4.7 or higher, use the pressure-canning method.

Key equipment for water-bath canning

Just as you wouldn't alter the ingredients in a recipe or skip a step in the canning process, you don't want to use the wrong equipment when you're home-canning. This equipment allows you to handle and process your filled jars safely.

The equipment for water-bath canning is less expensive than the equipment for pressure canning (check out Chapter 9 to see what equipment pressure canning requires). Water-bath canning kettles cost anywhere from $25 to $45. In some instances, you may purchase a "starter kit" that includes the canning kettle, the jar rack, a jar lifter, a wide-mouth funnel, and jars for about $50 to $60. (If you don't have a supplier near you, check out Chapter 22.)

Following is a list of the equipment you must have on hand, no exceptions or substitutions, for safe and successful water-bath canning:

✔ **A water-bath canner:** The water-bath canner consists of a large kettle, usually made of porcelain-coated steel or aluminum, that holds a maximum of 21 to 22 quarts of water, has a fitted lid, and uses a rack (see the next item) to hold the jars (see Figure 4-1). Do not substitute a large stock pot for a water-bath canner. It is important for the jars to be sitting off the bottom of the canner, and there are racks that fit this purpose, included in your canner kit.

Although aluminum is a *reactive metal* (a metal that transfers flavor to food coming in direct contact with it), it's permitted for a water-bath canner because your sealed jar protects the food from directly touching the aluminum.

WATER-BATH CANNING KETTLE

Figure 4-1: A water-bath canning kettle with the rack hanging on the edge of the kettle.

RACK

LID

BASE

- ✔ **A jar rack:** The jar rack for a water-bath canner is usually made of stainless steel and rests on the bottom of your canning kettle. It keeps your jars from touching the bottom of the kettle, or each other, while holding the filled jars upright during the water-bath processing period. The rack has lifting handles for hanging it on the inside edge of your canning kettle (refer to Figure 4-1), allowing you to safely transfer your filled jars into and out of your kettle.

- ✔ **Canning jars:** Canning jars are the only jars recommended for home-canning. Use the jar size recommended in your recipe. For more on canning jars, refer to Chapter 2.

- ✔ **Two-piece caps (lids and screw bands):** These lids and screw bands, explained in detail in Chapter 2, create a vacuum seal after the water-bath processing period, preserving the contents of the jar for use at a later time. This seal protects your food from the reentry of microorganisms.

The older-style rubber rings are no longer recommended. Although they are sometimes still available secondhand, the seal is no longer dependable enough to result in a safe product. You can find these rubber rings in some specialty canning stores; however, due to their novelty, they are very expensive and sold in small quantities. Reserve this type of canning jar and kitschy design for your fun food gifts, not canning for a family's pantry.

In addition to the must-have items listed in the preceding, you may also want the following things. These items aren't critical to the outcome of your product, but you'll discover a more streamlined, efficient level of work if you use them (you can find out more about these and other helpful but not necessary tools in Chapter 2):

- ✔ **A teakettle or saucepan** filled with boiling water to use as a reserve.

- ✔ **A ladle and wide-mouth funnel** to make transferring food into your jars easier. The funnel also keeps the rims of the jars clean, for a better seal.

- ✔ **A lid wand** so that you can transfer your lids from the hot water to the jars without touching them and a jar lifter so that you can safely and easily lift canning jars in and out of your canning kettle.

- ✔ **A thin plastic spatula** to use for releasing air bubbles in the jar.

The Road to Your Finished Product

Every aspect of the canning procedure is important, so don't skip anything, no matter how trivial it seems. When your food and canning techniques are in perfect harmony and balance, you'll have a safely processed product for use at a later time.

The following sections guide you through the step-by-step process for creating delicious, high-quality, homemade treats for your family and friends.

Always practice proper kitchen sanitation and cleanliness, carefully handle your food, and follow your recipe to the letter. Don't alter your recipe or skip any processing step.

Step 1: Getting your equipment ready

The first thing you do when canning is to inspect your equipment and get everything ready so that when you're done preparing the food (Step 2 in the canning process), you can fill your jars immediately.

Inspect your jars, lids, and screw bands

Always review the manufacturer's instructions for readying your jars, lids, and screw bands. Then inspect your jars, lids, and screw bands for any defects as follows:

- ✓ **Jars:** Check the jar edges for any nicks, chips, or cracks in the glass, discarding any jars with these defects. If you're reusing jars, clean any stains or food residue from them and then recheck them for any defects.

- ✓ **Screw bands:** Make sure the bands aren't warped, corroded, or rusted. Test the roundness of the band by screwing it onto a jar. If it tightens down smoothly without resistance, it's useable. Discard any bands that are defective or *out of round* (bent or not completely round).

  You can reuse screw bands over and over, as long as they're in good condition. And because you remove them after your jars have cooled, you don't need as many bands as jars.

- ✓ **Lids:** All lids must be new. Lids aren't reusable. Check the sealant on the underside of each lid for evenness. Don't use scratched or dented lids. Defective lids won't produce a vacuum seal. Don't buy old lids from secondhand stores. Older lids will not seal properly.

Wash your jars, lids, and screw bands

After examining the jars for nicks or chips, the screw bands for proper fit and corrosion, and the new lids for imperfections and scratches, wash everything in warm, soapy water, rinsing the items well and removing any soap residue. Discard any damaged or imperfect items.

Get the kettle water warming

Fill your canning kettle one-half to two-thirds full of water and begin heating the water to simmering. Remember that the water level will rise considerably as you add the filled jars. Be sure to not overfill at this point.

Heat extra water in a teakettle or saucepan as a reserve. You want to make sure that the jars are covered with at least 1 to 2 inches of water. By adding preheated water, you don't have to wait for the entire canner to reheat before continuing.

Keeping your equipment and jars hot while you wait to fill them

While you're waiting to fill your jars, submerge the jars and lids in hot, not boiling, water, and keep your screw bands clean and handy as follows:

- ✔ **Jars:** Submerge them in hot water in your kettle for a minimum of 10 minutes. Keep them there until you're ready to fill them.
- ✔ **Lids:** Submerge them in hot, not boiling, water in a saucepan. Keeping them separate from your jars protects the lid sealant.
- ✔ **Screw bands:** These don't need to be kept hot, but they do need to be clean. Place them where you'll be filling your jars.

Step 2: Readying your food

Always use food of the highest quality when you're canning. If you settle for less than the best, your final product won't have the quality you're looking for. Carefully sort through your food, discarding any bruised pieces or pieces you wouldn't eat in the raw state.

Follow the instructions in your recipe for preparing your food, like removing the skin or peel or cutting it into pieces.

Similarly, prepare your food exactly as instructed in your recipe. Don't make any adjustments in ingredients or quantities of ingredients. Any alteration may change the acidity of the product, requiring pressure canning (see Chapter 9) instead of water-bath canning to kill microorganisms.

If your recipe states something specifically, it's there for a reason. If you don't follow the recipe instructions to the letter, your final results won't be what the recipe intended.

Step 3: Filling your jars

Add your prepared food (cooked or raw) and hot liquid to your prepared jars as soon as they're ready. Follow these steps:

1. **Transfer your prepared food into the hot jars, adding hot liquid or syrup if your recipe calls for it, and being sure to leave the proper headspace.**

   Use a wide-mouth funnel and a ladle for quickly filling your jars. You'll eliminate a lot of spilling and have less to clean from your jar rims. It also helps cleanup and prevents slipping if you place your jars on a clean kitchen towel before filling.

2. **Release any air bubbles with a nonmetallic spatula or a tool to free air bubbles. Add more prepared food or liquid to the jar after releasing the air bubbles to maintain the recommended headspace.**

   Before applying the two-piece caps, always release air bubbles and leave the headspace specified in your recipe. These steps are critical for creating a vacuum seal and preserving your food.

3. **Wipe the jar rims with a clean, damp cloth.**

   If there's one speck of food on the jar rim, the sealant on the lid edge won't make contact with the jar rim and your jar won't seal.

4. **Place a hot lid onto each jar rim, sealant side touching the jar rim, and hand-tighten the screw band.**

   Don't overtighten because air needs to escape during the sealing process.

Step 4: Processing your filled jars

With your jars filled, you're ready to begin processing. Follow these steps:

1. **Place the jar rack in your canning kettle, suspending it with the handles on the inside edge of the kettle.**

2. **Place the filled jars in the jar rack, making sure they're standing upright and not touching each other.**

   Although the size of your kettle seems large, don't be tempted to pack your canner with jars. Only place as many jars as will comfortably fit yet still allow water to move freely between them. And always process jars in a single layer in the jar rack.

Never process half-pint or pint jars with quart jars because the larger amount of food in quart jars requires a longer processing time to kill any bacteria and microorganisms. If your recipe calls for the same processing times for half-pint and pint jars, you may process those two sizes together.

3. **Unhook the jar rack from the edge of the kettle, carefully lowering it into the hot water, and add water if necessary.**

   Air bubbles coming from the jars are normal. If your jars aren't covered by at least 1 inch of water, add boiling water from your reserve. Be careful to pour this hot water between the jars, instead of directly on top of them, to prevent splashing yourself with hot water.

   Make sure the tops of the submerged jars are covered with 1 to 2 inches of hot water. Add additional water from your reserve teakettle or saucepan to achieve this level.

4. **Cover the kettle and heat the water to a full, rolling boil, reducing the heat and maintaining a gentle, rolling boil for the amount of time indicated in the recipe.**

   Start your processing time after the water boils. Maintain a boil for the entire processing period.

   If you live at an altitude above 1,000 feet above sea level, you need to adjust your processing time. Check out "Adjusting Your Processing Times at High Altitudes" later in this chapter for details.

Step 5: Removing your filled jars and testing the seals

After you complete the processing time, immediately remove your jars from the boiling water with a jar lifter and place them on clean, dry, kitchen or paper towels away from drafts, with 1 or 2 inches of space between the jars — don't attempt to adjust the bands or check the seals — and allow them to cool completely. The cooling period may take 12 to 24 hours. Do not try to hurry this process by cooling the jars in any way. This may result in unsealed jars or cracked glass.

After your jars have completely cooled, test your seals by pushing on the center of the lid (see Figure 4-2). If the lid feels solid and doesn't indent, you have a successful vacuum seal. If the lid depresses in the center and makes a popping noise when you apply pressure, the jar isn't sealed. Immediately refrigerate unsealed jars, using the contents within two weeks or as stated in your recipe.

TEST THE SEAL
BY DEPRESSING
THE CENTER OF
THE LID OF THE
COMPLETELY
COOLED JAR.

Figure 4-2:
Testing your
jar seal.

Reprocessing unsealed jars

Jars may not seal for several reasons: You may have miscalculated the processing time, pieces of food may not have been cleaned from the jar rim, you may have left an improper amount of headspace, or the sealant on the lids may have been defective. The safest and easiest method for treating processed jars that didn't seal is to refrigerate the jar immediately and use the product within two weeks.

If you want to reprocess jars that didn't seal, you can do that. But keep in mind that reprocessing your food takes almost as much time as making the recipe from the beginning. The only time to consider reprocessing jars is if every jar in the kettle doesn't seal.

To reprocess unsealed jars, follow these steps:

1. **Remove the lid and discard it.**

2. **Check the edge of the jar for damage.**

   If the jar is damaged, discard the food in case a broken piece of glass fell into the food.

3. **Discard any damaged jars.**

4. **Reheat the food.**

5. **Follow the step-by-step instructions in this chapter for filling your jars, releasing air bubbles, and processing your sterilized, filled jars.**

6. **Reprocess the filled jars for the recommended time for your recipe.**

7. **Check the seal after your jars have completely cooled.**

Step 6: Storing your canned food

After you've tested the seal and know that it's good (see the preceding section), it's time to store your canned food. To do that, follow these steps:

1. **Remove the screw bands from your sealed jars.**
2. **Wash the sealed jars and the screw bands in hot, soapy water.**

   This removes any residue from the jars and screw bands.
3. **Label your filled jars, including the date processed.**
4. **Store your jars, without the screw bands, in a cool, dark, dry place.**

Adjusting Your Processing Times at High Altitudes

When you're canning at an altitude higher than 1,000 feet above sea level, you need to adjust your processing time (see Table 4-1). Because the air is thinner at higher altitudes, water boils below 212 degrees. As a result, you need to process your food for a longer period of time to kill any microorganisms that can make your food unsafe.

If you live higher than 1,000 feet above sea level, follow these guidelines:

- ✓ **For processing times of less than 20 minutes:** Add 1 additional minute for each additional 1,000 feet of altitude.

- ✓ **For processing times of more than 20 minutes:** Add 2 additional minutes for each 1,000 feet of altitude.

Table 4-1 High-Altitude Processing Times for Water-bath Canning

Altitude (in feet)	For Processing Times Less Than 20 Minutes	For Processing Times Greater Than 20 Minutes, Add This
1,001–1,999	Add 1 minute	Add 2 minutes
2,000–2,999	Add 2 minutes	Add 4 minutes
3,000–3,999	Add 3 minutes	Add 6 minutes
4,000–4,999	Add 4 minutes	Add 8 minutes

Altitude (in feet)	For Processing Times Less Than 20 Minutes	For Processing Times Greater Than 20 Minutes, Add This
5,000–5,999	Add 5 minutes	Add 10 minutes
6,000–6,999	Add 6 minutes	Add 12 minutes
7,000–7,999	Add 7 minutes	Add 14 minutes
8,000–8,999	Add 8 minutes	Add 16 minutes
9,000–9,999	Add 9 minutes	Add 18 minutes
Over 10,000	Add 10 minutes	Add 20 minutes

If you don't know your altitude level, you can get this information from many sources. Try contacting your public library, a local college, or the cooperative extension service in your county or state. Check your local phone book for contact numbers. Or check out `http://national4-hheadquarters.gov/Extension/index.html`. Just find your state on the map and then your location on the individual state's site.

Chapter 5

Simply Fruit

Canning fresh fruit is a great way to preserve large quantities of ripe fruit in a short period of time. Buying fruit when it is in season saves money, and you can be assured of the best-flavored fruit. Canning fruit is easy to do: Just fill your jars with fruit and hot liquid and then process them! With canned fruit readily available, you have an easy snack or a quick side dish.

This chapter explains the importance of using freshly picked, perfectly ripe fruit and keeping your fruit looking and tasting its best. In addition to the instructions for canning a variety of popular fruits, you'll also find tomatoes in this chapter. Often considered a vegetable, they are actually a fruit, and can be canned using the same technique.

Picking and Preparing Your Fresh Fruit

When selecting your fruit, think fresh, fresh, fresh! The best fruit for canning is freshly picked, ripe fruit. You're lucky if you grow your own fruit or have a friend who shares hers with you. Some growers offer a "pick your own" option in their growing area for a fee. (Ask growers at farmer's markets or check your local phone directory for locations in your area.) You'll need to bring your own containers for the fruit.

Fruit from your supermarket isn't the best choice because it's often picked before it's fully ripened in order to compensate for the time it takes to get the fruit from the field to the store shelf. Don't boycott your supermarket, just be finicky when selecting your fruit for canning.

The sooner you process your picked fruit, the better the texture and flavor of your final product. Your fruit can wait a few hours or overnight before you process it, but be sure to refrigerate it until you're ready.

Almost all fresh fruits can well with these exceptions: bananas, lemons, limes, melons, persimmons, and strawberries.

Identifying the proper degree of ripeness

How do you know if your fruit is ripe? *Ripe* fruit is defined as being fully developed, or mature, and ready for eating. If you grow your own fruit, you can check its development and maturity daily.

To check the fruit's ripeness

> ✔ **Hold the fruit in the palm of your hand and apply gentle pressure with your thumb and fingers.** The fruit should be firm to the touch. If there's an impression in the fruit that doesn't bounce back, the fruit is overripe. If it's hard as a rock, it's underripe. Neither should be canned. If you're picking your fruit for canning, you can perform the same test, with a slight difference: Do it while the fruit's still attached to the tree.
>
> ✔ **Smell the fruit.** Ripe fruit has a rich, full fruit aroma. A peach should smell like a peach; an apple should smell like an apple. The fragrance should be strong enough to entice you to devour the fruit on the spot.

Always use fruit picked directly from the bush or tree. Fruit collected from the ground (referred to as *dropped fruit* or *ground fruit*) is an indication that the fruit is overripe. Don't use it for canning.

Cutting and peeling: Necessary or not?

When you can fruit, should you leave the skin on or take it off? Depends on the recipe. Sometimes leaving the skin on your fruit is optional. Other times, the peel must be removed. Always follow your recipe for specific guidelines.

Similarly, you may wonder whether cutting your fruit is necessary. The answer here depends on the fruit. The fruit you select dictates using it whole or cutting it into pieces. For example, fitting whole apples into a canning jar is difficult, but peeled apples cut into slices easily pack into a jar. You leave small fruit, like berries, whole.

Deterring discoloration

There's probably nothing more unattractive than a piece of perfectly ripe cut fruit that's _oxidized_ or _discolored,_ dark or brown. Discoloration primarily occurs in apples, apricots, nectarines, peaches, and pears but may occur in other fruits.

You can protect your fruit from oxidation by slicing it directly into one of the following _antioxidant solutions,_ a liquid to keep your fruit from darkening:

- **An ascorbic acid or citric solution:** Make a solution with 1 teaspoon of lemon or lime juice in 1 cup of cold water, or use a commercial product, like Ever-Fresh or Fruit-Fresh, available in most supermarkets. When using one of these products, follow the instructions on the container.

   Ascorbic acid or citric acid is simply vitamin C. It doesn't change the fruit flavor. It's sold in powder form and is usually found in drugstores.

- **Vinegar, salt, and water:** Make this solution with 2 tablespoons of vinegar (5 percent acidity), 2 tablespoons of salt (pickling or kosher), and 1 gallon of cold water. Don't leave your fruit in this solution longer than 20 minutes because the solution extracts nutrients from your fruit and changes its flavor.

After its dip in your antioxidant solution, you just rinse and drain your fruit before packing it into your prepared jars.

Raw pack and hot pack

Raw pack and _hot pack_ refer to two methods of getting the product into the jars. Generally, both methods can be used for either water-bath canning (covered in Chapter 4) or pressure canning (covered in Chapter 9). Whether you use one or the other is determined by the texture of the food and its tendency (or not) to not fall apart from a lot of cooking. Whether you raw-pack or hot-pack also affects the processing times of the foods. Always refer to your recipe for guidance.

- **Raw pack:** A raw pack is the preferred method for fruits that become delicate after cooking, such as peaches and nectarines. This method is what it says: packing raw fruit into hot jars.

✔ **Hot pack:** Hot packing heats your fruit in a hot liquid before packing it into your prepared jars. The advantages of hot packing over raw packing include fitting more fruit into the jars because the fruit's softer and more pliable, using fewer jars because you can fit more fruit into the jars, and spending less time waiting for the water in your kettle to boil because the filled jars are hot in the middle.

With a few exceptions, most fresh fruits may be packed raw or hot. Always start with clean, ripe fruit and follow your recipe instructions.

Lining your jars with liquid

You always add liquid when canning fresh fruit. Your options are boiling water, sugar syrup, or fruit juice. Determining which liquid you use is up to you, but consider the final use for your canned fruit. For instance, if you're using your canned berries in a fruit cobbler, boiling water may be the better choice because you'll add sugar to the cobbler. If you'll be eating your canned fruit out of the jar, use a sugar syrup or fruit juice.

After adding the hot liquid to your filled jars, you release any trapped air bubbles in the jar. If the headspace drops after releasing the air bubbles, add more liquid to maintain the proper headspace (refer to Chapter 3 for information about headspace). If the fruit level drops, you need to add fruit.

Sugar syrups

Sugar syrup is simply a mixture of sugar and water. It adds flavor to your canned fruit, preserves its color, and produces a smooth, firm texture. Other sweeteners, such as honey, may be added in addition to or without the sugar.

Use these guidelines for making your sugar-syrup choice:

✔ **Super-light syrup:** This syrup adds the least amount of calories. The sweetness level is the closest to the natural sugar level in most fruits.

✔ **Extra-light syrup:** Use this syrup for a sweet fruit, such as figs.

✔ **Light syrup:** This is best with sweet apples and berries.

✔ **Medium syrup:** This syrup complements tart apples, apricots, nectarines, peaches, and pears.

✔ **Heavy syrup:** Use this with sour fruit, such as grapefruit.

Sugar syrup recipe alternatives

Although syrup of sugar and water is the most common liquid used when canning fresh fruit, you may use honey in place of or in addition to granulated sugar. Use a mild-flavored honey that won't detract from the natural flavor of your fruit. Here are some suggestions:

Type of Syrup	Sugar	Honey	Water	Syrup Yield
Light	1 cup	1 cup	4 cups	5½ cups
Light	None	1 cup	3 cups	4 cups
Medium	2 cups	1 cup	4 cups	6 cups
Medium	None	2 cups	2 cups	4 cups

Combine the syrup ingredients in a saucepan over medium heat, stirring the syrup to dissolve the sugar and/or the honey. After the liquid boils, keep it hot or refrigerate it up to two days. If you refrigerate your syrup, reheat it to a boil before adding it to your filled jars.

Remember: Honey and canned goods made with honey should never be fed to children under 1 year of age due to the danger of infant botulism.

Table 5-1 offers you five concentrations of sugar syrup. Allow ½ to ¾ cup of liquid for each filled pint jar and 1½ cups of liquid for each filled quart jar of fruit. Bring your syrup ingredients to a boil in a saucepan over high heat; stir to dissolve the sugar.

Table 5-1	Sugar Syrup Concentrations		
Syrup Strength	**Granulated Sugar**	**Water**	**Approximate Yield**
Super-light	¼ cup	5¾ cups	6 cups
Extra-light	1¼ cups	5½ cups	6 cups
Light	2¼ cups	5¼ cups	6½ cups
Medium	3¼ cups	5 cups	7 cups
Heavy	4¼ cups	4¼ cups	7 cups

Always prepare your hot liquid before you prepare your fruit. The liquid should be waiting for you; you shouldn't be waiting for your liquid to boil.

Water or fruit juice

Packing fresh fruit in boiling water or fruit juice produces fruit with a soft texture. Two good choices for fruit juices are unsweetened pineapple juice or white grape juice. Use water you like to drink, without minerals and not the sparkling variety.

Always use the hot-pack method (see the section "Raw pack and hot pack" earlier in this chapter) when using water or unsweetened fruit juice for your canning liquid.

Fresh Fruit Canning Guidelines

The following sections list foods that are commonly grown in home gardens. The quantity guide for each fruit fills a 1-quart jar. If you're using pint jars, cut the quantity in half.

The recipes in the following sections use the water-bath canning method. For detailed instructions on water-bath canning, filling and processing your jars, and releasing air bubbles, refer to the step-by-step guidelines in Chapter 4. And for a more extensive list of fruits, refer to the *Complete Guide to Home Canning and Preserving,* Second Revised Edition, by the United States Department of Agriculture.

Apples

Choose apples suitable for eating or making pies. Prep is easy: Just peel and core the apples and then cut them into slices or quarters. To prevent discoloration, treat the fruit with an antioxidant (refer to "Deterring discoloration," earlier in this chapter).

Canned Apples

Canned apples are wonderful for apple crisp, breads, and other recipes calling for slices
or chunks of fruit. Use any crisp, tart apple that ripens in the fall. Summer-ripened
apples tend to be softer and won't hold up well to canning. Try making them with a light
sugar syrup for a fresh-tasting treat.

Preparation time: *15 minutes*

Processing time: *20 minutes*

Yield: *8 pints or 4 quarts*

12 pounds apples   *Sugar syrup, light*

1 Prepare your canning jars and two-piece caps (lids and screw bands) according to the
manufacturer's instructions. Keep the jars and lids hot. (For detailed instructions on
preparing your jars, see Chapter 4.)

2 Wash, core, and peel your apples; then slice them into ¼-inch pieces or cut them into
even chunks. Meanwhile, bring the sugar syrup to a boil.

3 Pack apples firmly into hot jars and pour boiling hot sugar syrup over the apples, leaving
½-inch headspace. Wipe the jar rims; seal the jars with the two-piece caps, hand-
tightening the bands.

4 Process the filled jars in a water-bath canner for 20 minutes for pints and quarts from
the point of boiling.

5 Remove the jars from the canner with a jar lifter. Place them on a clean kitchen towel
away from drafts. After the jars cool completely, test the seals (see Chapter 4). If you
find jars that haven't sealed, refrigerate them and use them within two weeks.

Vary It! *For a sweeter canned apple, try a medium syrup instead.*

Per ½-cup serving: *Calories 137 (From fat 4); Fat 0g (Saturated 0g); Cholesterol 0mg; Sodium 0mg; Carbohydrates
36g (Dietary fiber 3g); Protein 0g.*

Apple Pie Filling

Get a quick start to your piemaking by creating apple pie filling ahead of time. To thicken this filling to just the right consistency, add a tablespoon of flour to the filled pie before adding the top crust.

Preparation time: *15 minutes*

Cooking time: *45 minutes*

Processing time: *Pints, 25 minutes*

Yield: *6 pints*

6 pounds apples	*½ teaspoon nutmeg*
2 cups sugar	*2 tablespoons lemon juice*
2 teaspoons cinnamon	

1 Peel and slice or cube the apples. Place the apples and the other ingredients into a heavy pan. Allow the mixture to stand about 30 minutes or until it becomes juicy.

2 While the apples are standing, prepare your canning jars and two-piece caps (lids and screw bands) according to the manufacturer's instructions. Keep the jars and lids hot. (For detailed instructions on preparing your jars, see Chapter 4.)

3 Cook the apple mixture over medium heat until the apples are softened, about 7 minutes.

4 Ladle the pie filling into the pint jars, leaving ¼-inch headspace. Release any air bubbles with a nonreactive utensil (refer to Chapter 3). Wipe the jar rims; seal the jars with the two-piece caps, hand-tightening the bands.

5 Process the filled jars in a water-bath canner for 25 minutes from the point of boiling.

6 Remove the jars from the canner with a jar lifter. Place them on a clean kitchen towel away from drafts. After the jars cool completely, test the seals (see Chapter 4). If you find jars that haven't sealed, refrigerate them and use them within two weeks.

Vary It! *Substitute or add to the spices listed to create the pie your family likes.*

Per ½-cup serving: *Calories 121 (From fat 3); Fat 0g (Saturated 0g); Cholesterol 0mg; Sodium 0mg; Carbohydrates 31g (Dietary fiber 2g); Protein 0g.*

Applesauce

A true family favorite, you can use this sauce in breads and cakes. It is a smooth, sweet version with a pretty rose color that results from cooking the apples in their skins. For a richer flavor, use a variety of apples.

Preparation time: *15 minutes*

Cooking time: *1 hour*

Processing time: *20 minutes*

Yield: *4 quarts*

10 pounds apples, cut in half	*2½ cups sugar*

1 Prepare your canning jars and two-piece caps (lids and screw bands) according to the manufacturer's instructions. Keep the jars and lids hot. (For detailed instructions on preparing your jars, see Chapter 4.)

2 Cut the apples in half (don't peel or core them) and place them in a 12-quart pot. Add enough water to cover the bottom of the pot and to keep the apples from scorching. Cook the apples over medium heat until they're soft, about 20 minutes. Press the softened apples through a food mill or sieve to remove the skins and seeds.

3 Return the apple purée to the pot and add the sugar. Bring the mixture to a boil, stirring often to prevent scorching.

4 Ladle the hot applesauce into your prepared jars, leaving ½-inch headspace. Release any air bubbles with a nonreactive utensil (refer to Chapter 3). Wipe the jar rims; seal the jars with the two-piece caps, hand-tightening the bands.

5 Process the filled jars in a water-bath canner for 20 minutes from the point of boiling.

6 Remove the jars from the canner with a jar lifter. Place them on a clean kitchen towel. After the jars cool completely, test the seals (see Chapter 4). If you find jars that haven't sealed, refrigerate them and use them within two weeks.

Vary It! *Try adding cinnamon and cloves for a spicy version.*

Tip: *To help prevent scorching, use a stovetop heat diffuser under the pot.*

*Per ½-**cup serving:** Calories 129 (From fat 3); Fat 0g (Saturated 0g); Cholesterol 0mg; Sodium 0mg; Carbohydrates 34g (Dietary fiber 2g); Protein 0g.*

Apricots, nectarines, and peaches

Peaches are a wonderful fruit, and by canning them yourself you can save a lot of money. Use a light syrup so that you can enjoy the full flavor of the peach. Trust us: Home-canned peaches are much nicer than the heavy sweetness you find in store-canned varieties.

Nectarines and apricots are just as tasty as peaches and have the benefit of not needing to be peeled, making them even easier to can. For a quick guide to peeling fruit, see Figure 5-1.

Apricots make a sunny-flavored addition to the winter meals. They make a great substitute for apples in an apple crisp recipe, too — you'll love the results!

Canned Apricots, Nectarines, and Peaches

Consider this recipe a three-for: You follow the same steps and cooking times for all three of these luscious fruits. The only difference is in the prep step: Whereas you have to peel peaches, you leave the peel on apricots and nectarines.

Preparation time: *15 minutes*

Processing time: *Pints, 25 minutes; quarts, 30 minutes*

Yield: *8 pints or 4 quarts*

10 pounds apricots or 10 pounds nectarines or 12 pounds peaches	*Sugar syrup, light*

1 Prepare your canning jars and two-piece caps (lids and screw bands) according to the manufacturer's instructions. Keep the jars and lids hot. (For detailed instructions on preparing your jars, see Chapter 4.)

2 Wash your fruit. To prepare peaches, peel them; then cut them in half and remove the pits (see Figure 5-1). To prepare nectarines or apricots, simply cut them in half and remove the pits. Meanwhile, bring the sugar syrup to a boil.

3 Pack the fruit firmly into hot jars and pour boiling hot sugar syrup over fruit, leaving ½-inch headspace. Release any air bubbles with a nonreactive utensil (refer to Chapter 3). Wipe the jar rims; seal the jars with the two-piece caps, hand-tightening the bands.

4 Process the filled jars in a water-bath canner for 25 minutes (pints) or 30 minutes (quarts) from the point of boiling.

5 Remove the jars from the canner with a jar lifter. Place them on a clean kitchen towel away from drafts. After the jars cool completely, test the seals (see Chapter 4). If you find jars that haven't sealed, refrigerate them and use them within two weeks.

Vary It! To make a sweeter canned fruit, use a medium syrup.

Tip: To make peaches easy to peel, blanch them to loosen the skin: Dip them in boiling water for 30 seconds and then dip them in cold water.

Per ½-cup serving apricots: Calories 118 (From fat 5); Fat 1g (Saturated 0g); Cholesterol 0mg; Sodium 2mg; Carbohydrates 29g (Dietary fiber 3g); Protein 2g.

Per ½-cup serving nectarines: Calories 118 (From fat 5); Fat 1g (Saturated 0g); Cholesterol 0mg; Sodium 0mg; Carbohydrates 29g (Dietary fiber 2g); Protein 1g.

Per ½-cup serving peaches: Calories 88 (From fat 1); Fat 0g (Saturated 0g); Cholesterol 0mg; Sodium 4mg; Carbohydrates 23g (Dietary fiber 2g); Protein 1g.

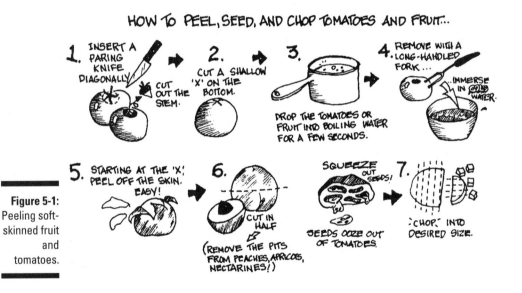

Figure 5-1:
Peeling soft-skinned fruit and tomatoes.

Berries (except strawberries)

Canned berries have so many uses! You can use them to make smoothies or pies and as a sweet addition to your oatmeal. If your pantry is like ours, your berries will be the first things used up,

For canning, you want perfect, not soft or mushy, berries. Leave them whole. Wash and drain the berries (handling them as little as possible); remove any stems or hulls.

Strawberries don't can well. During the processing, they turn mushy and lose their taste and red color. They do, however, freeze very well. See Chapter 13 for complete instructions.

Depending on the type of berry, you'll use either the raw or hot pack method:

- ✔ **Raw pack:** Raw packing is best for soft berries, like blackberries, boysenberries, and raspberries.

- ✔ **Hot pack:** Use this method for firmer berries, such as blueberries, cranberries, and huckleberries.

Canned Raspberries

With soft berries, like raspberries, boysenberries, and blackberries, you don't have to cook the berries before canning. Simply place them in your canning jars and pour hot syrup over them. This recipe explains how to can raspberries, but you can use it to can any other soft berry the same way.

Preparation time: *15 minutes*

Processing time: *Pints, 15 minutes; quarts, 20 minutes*

Yield: *8 pints or 4 quarts*

12 pounds raspberries   *Sugar syrup, light*

1 Prepare your canning jars and two-piece caps (lids and screw bands) according to the manufacturer's instructions. Keep the jars and lids hot. (For detailed instructions on preparing your jars, see Chapter 4.)

2 Wash the berries gently in cold water to firm them and remove any stems or hulls. Meanwhile, bring the sugar syrup to a boil.

3 Pack berries loosely into your prepared jars and pour boiling hot sugar syrup over them, leaving ½-inch headspace. Release any air bubbles with a nonreactive utensil (refer to Chapter 3), adding more sugar syrup as necessary to maintain the proper headspace. Wipe the jar rims; seal the jars with the two-piece caps, hand-tightening the bands.

4 Process the filled jars in a water-bath canner for 15 minutes (pints) or 20 minutes (quarts) from the point of boiling.

5 Remove the jars from the canner with a jar lifter. Place them on a clean kitchen towel away from drafts. After the jars cool completely, test the seals (see Chapter 4). If you find jars that haven't sealed, refrigerate them and use them within two weeks.

Vary It! For sweeter canned berries, use medium syrup.

Per ½-cup serving: Calories 138 (From fat 8); Fat 1g (Saturated 0g); Cholesterol 0mg; Sodium 0mg; Carbohydrates 34g (Dietary fiber 12g); Protein 2g.

Canned Blueberries

To can hard berries (like blueberries and cranberries), you follow the same general steps you do for soft berries, with one exception: Instead of packing the jars and adding sugar syrup, you boil the berries and sugar together before filling the jars. This recipe shows you how to can blueberries. Follow the same directions for any other type of hard berry.

Preparation time: 20 minutes

Processing time: Pints, 15 minutes; quarts, 20 minutes

Yield: 8 pints or 4 quarts

10 pounds blueberries   Boiling water

Sugar syrup, light

1 Prepare your canning jars and two-piece caps (lids and screw bands) according to the manufacturer's instructions. Keep the jars and lids hot. (For detailed instructions on preparing your jars, see Chapter 4.)

2 Wash the berries gently in cold water to firm them and remove any stems or hulls.

3 Measure the berries into a saucepan and add ½ cup sugar for each quart of berries. Bring the mixture to a boil over medium-high heat and stir occasionally to prevent sticking. In a large pot, bring water for your reserve to a boil.

4 Ladle the hot berries and liquid into your prepared jars, adding boiling water if there isn't enough liquid to fill the jars, leaving ½-inch headspace. Release any air bubbles with a nonreactive utensil (refer to Chapter 3), adding more berries and water as necessary to maintain the proper headspace. Wipe the jar rims; seal the jars with the two-piece caps, hand-tightening the bands.

5 Process the filled jars in a water-bath canner for 15 minutes (pints) or 20 minutes (quarts) from the point of boiling.

6 Remove the jars from the canner with a jar lifter. Place them on a clean kitchen towel away from drafts. After the jars cool completely, test the seals (see Chapter 4). If you find jars that haven't sealed, refrigerate them and use them within two weeks.

Vary It! For sweeter canned berries, use medium syrup.

Per ½-cup serving: Calories 124 (From fat 3); Fat 0g (Saturated 0g); Cholesterol 0mg; Sodium 2mg; Carbohydrates 32g (Dietary fiber 6g); Protein 1g.

Pears

All varieties of pears can well, so use your favorite variety. After cutting and peeling the pears, treat your fruit with an antioxidant to prevent discoloring (refer to the "Deterring discoloration" section of this chapter).

Canned Pears

Pears are great fun to have on the pantry shelf. Try canned pears in place of apples in any recipe calling for cooked fruit.

Preparation time: *15 minutes*

Processing time: *Pints, 20 minutes; quarts, 25 minutes*

Yield: *8 pints or 4 quarts*

12 pounds pears   Sugar syrup, light

1 Prepare your canning jars and two-piece caps (lids and screw bands) according to the manufacturer's instructions. Keep the jars and lids hot. (For detailed instructions on preparing your jars, see Chapter 4.)

2 Wash, peel, and core the pears. Slice the pears into ¼-inch pieces or cut them into even-sized chunks. Bring your sugar syrup to a boil.

3 Pack the pears firmly into the hot jars and pour the boiling hot sugar syrup over them, leaving ½-inch headspace. Release any air bubbles with a nonreactive utensil (refer to Chapter 3), adding more sugar syrup as necessary to maintain the proper headspace. Wipe the jar rims; seal the jars with the two-piece caps, hand-tightening the bands.

4 Process the filled jars in a water-bath canner for 20 minutes (pints) or 25 minutes (quarts) from the point of boiling.

5 Remove the jars from the canner with a jar lifter. Place them on a clean kitchen towel away from drafts. After the jars cool completely, test the seals (see Chapter 4). If you find jars that haven't sealed, refrigerate them and use them within two weeks.

Per ½-cup serving: Calories 79 (From fat 0); Fat 0g (Saturated 0g); Cholesterol 0mg; Sodium 2mg; Carbohydrates 21g (Dietary fiber 1g); Protein 0g.

Rhubarb

Rhubarb looks like red celery but isn't related to celery. It can be mixed with strawberries for a pie filling and is delectable when combined with tart apples. Because of its tart taste, rhubarb is always canned with sugar and makes a great pie filling.

Rhubarb leaves are toxic. Always remove and discard any leaves from the stalks before preparing your rhubarb.

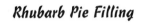

Rhubarb Pie Filling

Everyone loves rhubarb pie. If you make the filling ahead of time, in the winter you can just open a jar and fill your pie crust. Delicious!

Preparation time: *15 minutes plus 4 hours standing time*

Processing time: *15 minutes*

Yield: *6 quarts*

12 pounds rhubarb	*6 cups sugar, or to taste*

1 Wash, trim, and remove the leaves from the rhubarb. Cut the stalks into ½-inch pieces. Place the rhubarb pieces in a 6-quart pan. Add sugar to the cut pieces and let them stand for 4 hours to draw out the juice. Taste the mixture with a clean spoon to check that it is sweet enough. If not, add more suger, to taste.

2 Prepare your canning jars and two-piece caps (lids and screw bands) according to the manufacturer's instructions. Keep the jars and lids hot. (For detailed instructions on preparing your jars, see Chapter 4.)

3 When the standing time is complete, heat the rhubarb and sugar mixture to boiling over high heat.

4 Pack the hot rhubarb mixture into your canning jars, leaving ½-inch headspace. Release any air bubbles with a nonreactive utensil (refer to Chapter 3), adding more of the rhubarb mixture as necessary to maintain the proper headspace. Wipe the jar rims; seal the jars with the two-piece caps, hand-tightening the bands.

5 Process the filled quart jars in a water-bath canner for 20 minutes from the point of boiling.

6 Remove the jars from the canner with a jar lifter. Place them on a clean kitchen towel away from drafts. After the jars cool completely, test the seals (see Chapter 4). If you find jars that haven't sealed, refrigerate them and use them within two weeks.

Per ½-cup serving: Calories 115 (From fat 2); Fat 0g (Saturated 0g); Cholesterol 0mg; Sodium 4mg; Carbohydrates 29g (Dietary fiber 2g); Protein 1g.

Rhubarb Sauce

Rhubarb sauce is a nice change from applesauce. Surprise your family with this tart and tasty side dish!

Preparation time: 45 minutes plus 4 hours standing time

Processing time: 20 minutes

Yield: 8 pints or 4 quarts

8 pounds rhubarb   *8 cups sugar, or to taste*

1 Wash, trim, and remove the leaves from the rhubarb. Cut the stalks into ½-inch pieces. Place the rhubarb pieces in a 6-quart pot and add the sugar. Let the rhubarb-sugar mixture stand for 4 hours to draw out the juice.

2 Prepare your canning jars and two-piece caps (lids and screw bands) according to the manufacturer's instructions. Keep the jars and lids hot. (For detailed instructions on preparing your jars, see Chapter 4.)

3 Heat the rhubarb and sugar mixture to boiling over high heat and cook the mixture until it's slightly chunky (about 30 minutes) or until the rhubarb is the consistency you desire.

4 Ladle the boiling hot rhubarb sauce into your prepared jars, leaving 1-inch headspace. Release any air bubbles with a nonreactive utensil (refer to Chapter 3), adding more rhubarb sauce as necessary to maintain the proper headspace. Wipe the jar rims; seal the jars with the two-piece caps, hand-tightening the bands.

5 Process the filled jars in a water-bath canner for 20 minutes (both pints and quarts) from the point of boiling.

6 Remove the jars from the canner with a jar lifter. Place them on a clean kitchen towel away from drafts. After the jars cool completely, test the seals (see Chapter 4). If you find jars that haven't sealed, refrigerate them and use them within two weeks.

Per ½-cup serving: Calories 211 (From fat 2); Fat 0g (Saturated 0g); Cholesterol 0mg; Sodium 4mg; Carbohydrates 54g (Dietary fiber 2g); Protein 1g.

Tackling Tomatoes

Tomatoes are misunderstood. Are they a fruit or a vegetable? By definition, a *fruit* is a sweet, edible plant containing seeds inside a juicy pulp — which defines tomatoes perfectly. Each tomato variety has its own color, flavor, and texture. Roma or paste tomatoes and slicing varieties are all used for canning. Paste varieties simply have less juice and, therefore, require less cooking to remove excess water for paste and thick sauces. You can use both interchangeably, but cooking times will vary.

Not all tomato varieties are suitable for canning due to their lack of taste and mass-production genetics. Stick with those that boast good canning results on the plant's tag or use a proven Heirloom variety. Some varieties that work well include Ace, Amish paste, Homestead 24, and Rutgers.

As always, choose nice, ripe, unblemished tomatoes. And to ensure the proper acidity level for your variety (4.6 or lower), add an acid, like bottled lemon juice or powdered citric acid: Add 2 tablespoons lemon juice per quart jar or 1 tablespoon lemon juice per pint. If you're using citric acid, add ½ teaspoon per quart and ¼ teaspoon per pint.

Just what do tomatoes taste like?

Tomatoes were the first thing I (Amy) ever remember canning. My grandmother would have me stand on a milk crate, and I would help her peel off the skins and add more ice to the water when it was needed.

My grandmother made canning and preserving seem second nature. She never rushed, but always kept moving. Before you knew it, there were dozens of jars of bright, red tomatoes sitting on the shelf.

I owe my addiction to canning to my grandmother's talent and my grandfather's taste for homemade foods. To me, canned tomatoes taste like sunshine, happy memories, and love.

Canned Tomatoes

With the abundance of tomatoes in the summer months, can some for winter eating. Tomatoes, after all, are the best-tasting and easiest produce to keep. Try adding a jar of tomatoes to bow tie pasta and butter for a filling and delicious wintertime treat.

Preparation time: *15 minutes*

Processing time: *Pints, 35 minutes; quarts, 45 minutes*

Yield: *6 pints or 4 quarts*

12 pounds whole tomatoes

Bottled lemon juice or citric acid

Canning salt (optional)

Boiling water

1 Prepare your canning jars and two-piece caps (lids and screw bands) according to the manufacturer's instructions. Keep the jars and lids hot. (For detailed instructions on preparing your jars, see Chapter 4.)

2 Wash and peel the tomatoes. (To make peeling tomatoes easier, blanch them first to loosen the skins: Dip them in boiling water for 30 seconds and then into cold water.) After peeling, cut the larger tomatoes into halves or quarters.

3 Place the tomatoes into your prepared canning jars, pressing them to release their juice. (Use a canning funnel to keep the rims clean.) To each pint jar, add 1 tablespoon lemon juice or ¼ teaspoon citric acid and, if desired, ½ teaspoon salt. To each quart jar, add 2 tablespoons lemon juice or ½ teaspoon citric acid and, if desired, 1 teaspoon salt. If there's not enough juice to cover the tomatoes, add boiling water to the jars, leaving ½-inch headspace. Release any air bubbles with a nonreactive utensil (refer to Chapter 3), adding more tomatoes as necessary to maintain the proper headspace. Wipe the jar rims; seal the jars with the two-piece caps, hand-tightening the bands.

4 Process the filled jars in a water-bath canner for 35 minutes (pints) or 45 minutes (quarts) from the point of boiling.

5 Remove the jars from the canner with a jar lifter. Place them on a clean kitchen towel away from drafts. After the jars cool completely, test the seals (see Chapter 4). If you find jars that haven't sealed, refrigerate them and use them within two weeks.

Tip: *Use wide-mouth pints or quart jars for ease in filling. Although not necessary, they will make the entire process go faster and with less mess.*

Per ½-cup serving: *Calories 44 (From fat 6); Fat 1g (Saturated 0g); Cholesterol 0mg; Sodium 19mg; Carbohydrates 10g (Dietary fiber 2g); Protein 2g.*

Tomato Paste

Tomato paste is packed with flavor, and if you're overrun with tomatoes, this recipe is the answer because it uses *a lot* of fruit! You can use this thick paste as-is for pizza (it's only slightly less thick than store bought but just as rich and fabulous); simply add your seasonings right on top. Your family will love the extra tomato taste. You can also add this paste to soups for amazing flavor and extra vitamins. For this recipe, use paste or plum tomatoes, which have much less extra water to cook off. This thick, rich sauce is canned in half-pint jars.

Preparation time: *15 minutes*

Cooking time: *1 hour, and then 3 hours more*

Processing time: *30 minutes*

Yield: *16 half-pints*

16 pounds plum or paste tomatoes, cubed

3 cups sweet pepper, chopped

2 bay leaves

2 tablespoons salt

3 cloves garlic

Bottled lemon juice or citric acid

1 Combine all ingredients in a 6-quart pot and cook slowly over medium heat for 1 hour, stirring frequently to prevent sticking. Remove the bay leaves and press the mixture through a food mill or sieve. Return the mixture to the pot and continue to cook for another 3 hours over medium-low heat, stirring often.

2 Prepare your canning jars and two-piece caps (lids and screw bands) according to the manufacturer's instructions. Keep the jars and lids hot. (For detailed instructions on preparing your jars, see Chapter 4.)

3 Pour the hot mixture into your canning jars, leaving ¼-inch headspace. Add ½ tablespoon lemon juice or ⅛ teaspoon citric acid to each half-pint jar. Release any air bubbles with a nonreactive utensil (refer to Chapter 3), adding more of the mixture as necessary to maintain the proper headspace. Wipe the jar rims; seal the jars with the two-piece caps, hand-tightening the bands.

4 Process the filled half-pint jars in a water-bath canner for 30 minutes from the point of boiling.

5 Remove the jars from the canner with a jar lifter. Place them on a clean kitchen towel away from drafts. After the jars cool completely, test the seals (see Chapter 4). If you find jars that haven't sealed, refrigerate them and use them within two weeks.

Tip: To check for sauce thickness, put a spoonful of sauce onto the center of a plate. Wait for 60 seconds and see if water seeps from it. If so, cook for 30 minutes more and recheck.

Per ½-cup serving: Calories 48 (From fat 6); Fat 1g (Saturated 0g); Cholesterol 0mg; Sodium 455mg; Carbohydrates 11g (Dietary fiber 2g); Protein 2g.

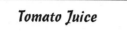

Tomato Juice

Tomato juice makes a nice change from traditional fruit juices. And because tomato juice is a great tenderizer and adds a wonderful flavor to gravy, you can also use it to cook tough pieces of meat.

Preparation time: *1 hour*

Processing time: *Pints, 40 minutes; quarts, 45 minutes*

Yield: *14 pints or 7 quarts*

25 pounds tomatoes   Lemon juice or citric acid

1 Prepare your canning jars and two-piece caps (lids and screw bands) according to the manufacturer's instructions. Keep the jars and lids hot. (For detailed instructions on preparing your jars, see Chapter 4.)

2 Wash and core tomatoes. Roughly chop them into chunks. Place the tomatoes in a large pot and bring them to simmer over medium heat, stirring frequently to prevent scorching. Cook the tomatoes until they're soft, about 25 to 30 minutes.

3 Strain the tomatoes through a food mill to separate the juice from the skins and seeds. Return the juice to the pot and bring it to a simmer over medium heat. Allow it to simmer 5 minutes.

4 Ladle the hot juice into your canning jars. To each quart jar, add 2 tablespoons of lemon juice or ½ teaspoon citric acid. To each pint jar, add 1 tablespoon lemon juice or ¼ teaspoon citric acid. Leave ½-inch headspace. Release any air bubbles with a nonreactive utensil (refer to Chapter 3), adding more juice as necessary to maintain the proper headspace. Wipe the jar rims; seal the jars with the two-piece caps, hand-tightening the bands.

5 Process the filled jars in a water-bath canner for 40 minutes (pints) or 45 minutes (quarts) from the point of boiling.

6 Remove the jars from the canner with a jar lifter. Place them on a clean kitchen towel away from drafts. After the jars cool completely, test the seals (see Chapter 4). If you find jars that haven't sealed, refrigerate them and use them within two weeks.

Per ½-cup serving: Calories 35 (From fat 0); Fat 0g (Saturated 0g); Cholesterol 0mg; Sodium 16mg; Carbohydrates 7g (Dietary fiber 2g); Protein 3g.

Chapter 6

Sweet Spreads: Jams, Jellies, Marmalades, and More

Sweet spreads are our most favorite items to can. Think outside of the box for ways to serve your homemade creations. For some of our favorite serving ideas, check out the introductory notes in the recipes. We hope you'll come up with even more ideas. You can make combinations of ingredients that aren't commercially available. Sweet spreads aren't just for toast anymore!

In this chapter, we include a variety of our favorite recipes with unique flavor combinations. The recipes utilize a variety of preparation techniques that take you step by step through each process. In addition to fresh fruit, some recipes use frozen fruit and fruit juice.

Understanding Your Sweet Spreads

Making sweet spreads is basic chemistry, using exact proportions of fruit and sugar, cooking the two, and sometimes adding acid or pectin. Don't worry if chemistry wasn't your strong suit in school. Good recipes do the homework for you. Your responsibility is to follow the recipe exactly, using the correct ingredients and measuring them accurately.

Never double a sweet spread recipe or adjust the sugar amount. Recipes are balanced to achieve a specific consistency and texture. Any alteration or adjustment to the recipe upsets the perfect chemical balance and adversely affects your spread by producing inferior results. If you want more of the same recipe, make it twice. If you would like to use less sugar, find another recipe that uses your desired amount.

Sweet spreads, generically referred to as *preserves,* come in many forms and textures. The various types of sweet spreads are as follows:

- **Jam:** Jam is a combination of fruit (crushed or chopped), sugar, and sometimes pectin and acid, cooked until the pieces of fruit are soft and almost lose their shape. Common uses for jam include bread spreads, cookie and pastry fillings, and a topping for cheesecake.

- **Jelly:** This mixture combines fruit juice, sugar, and sometimes pectin. It's transparent with a bright color and should be firm, yet jiggly. If you use fresh fruit, you may be instructed to strain it. Use jelly as a bread spread or as a filling for cakes and cookies.

- **Marmalade:** These are soft jellies with pieces of fruit rind, usually citrus fruit, suspended in them. In addition to bread spread, marmalades are great as a glaze on a baked ham (use your favorite flavor!).

- **Preserves:** In addition to the generic term representing all sweet spreads, preserves have a definition of their own. They contain cooked fruit, sugar, and sometimes pectin and have a jamlike consistency, but with whole or large pieces of fruit. The fruit maintains its shape during the cooking process.

- **Butter:** This smooth, thick spread is made from fruit purée and sugar cooked for a long period of time. The results are a thick spread. Butters normally use less sugar than other sweet spreads and may have spices added to enhance the flavor of the fruit.

- **Conserves:** These usually contain two fruits mixed with sugar and nuts and cooked to achieve a consistency similar to jam. Traditionally, conserves were used as a spread on biscuits and crumpets.

Choosing Fruit for Sweet Spreads

Always select the freshest fruit available to you. Everyone has his or her favorite. Know when your favorites are in season for the best selection, the highest quality, and, usually, the most reasonable pricing. (For detailed information on selecting fresh fruits, check out Chapter 5.)

Local growers are good indicators of the types of fruit grown in your area. Check out your local farmer's markets and ask the sellers about their fruit. People love to talk about their passion, and who better to learn from than the person who grows the food you're buying? Ask questions about the fruit you see, how they determine ripeness, and how a particular fruit tastes. If they're not passing out samples, they'll probably be happy to cut you a taste.

Carry copies of your favorite recipes when you're visiting local growers or farmer's markets. That way, you'll always buy the right amount of fruit for your favorite recipe.

Getting Up to Speed with Fruit Pectin

Pectin is a natural, water-based substance that's present in ripe fruit. It's essential for thickening jams, jellies, and other types of preserves. Some recipes add commercial fruit pectin when more than the naturally occurring amount of pectin is needed (like when you want to thicken a fruit juice into a jelly). If your recipe does include such an ingredient, you'll see the kind of pectin (powdered or liquid) listed.

Never alter the amount of sugar your recipe calls for or use sugar substitutes. Exact amounts of sugar, fruit, and pectin are a must for a good *set* — that is, a consistency that isn't too thick to spread or too runny.

Commercial pectin basics

Commercial pectin is available in most supermarkets or where canning supplies are sold. Pectin may be in short supply in the spring and summer months because these are such popular times of year for canning. So be sure you have enough on hand before you start preparing your recipe.

Inspect the pectin container for water stains, holes, or any other sign that it's come into contact with food (like food stuck to the package). Check to make sure the package is sealed and that it's not past the use-by date.

Using pectin after the date on the package may affect your final product because the quality of the pectin may have deteriorated. Pectin wasn't always marked with a date. If your pectin container doesn't provide an expiration date, don't use it; it may be a sign that your product is extremely old.

Types of commercial fruit pectin

Pectin is available in two forms: liquid and powdered (dry). Although both products are made from fruit, they're not interchangeable. Be sure to use the correct type and amount of pectin your recipe calls for.

Using liquid fruit pectin

Liquid pectin is usually made from apples. Today, a box contains two 3-ounce pouches. The most common brand is Certo.

Liquid fruit pectin was originally sold in 6-ounce bottles. Older recipes may call for "one-half of a bottle." If you read a pouch of liquid pectin today, it states, "1 pouch equals ½ bottle."

Because you have to add your liquid pectin at the specified time and temperature, have it at the ready: Cut off the top of the pouch and stand it in a measuring cup or other container to keep it from spilling (see Figure 6-1). Then, when it's time to add the liquid pectin, add it all at the same time, squeezing the pouch with your fingers like you do to get the last bit of toothpaste out of the tube.

LIQUID PECTIN AT THE READY!

Figure 6-1: Getting a pouch of liquid pectin ready.

1. CUT OFF THE TOP OF THE POUCH...

2. STAND THE CUT POUCH IN A MEASURING CUP.

3. ADD THE LIQUID PECTIN TO THE BOWL, ALL AT ONCE!

Using powdered (dry) fruit pectin

Powdered pectin is made from citrus fruits or apples. It comes in a box similar to a gelatin- or pudding-mix box and contains 1¾ ounces (the most commonly used size) or 2 ounces. Use the size stated in your recipe ingredients, and add it before you heat the fruit mixture.

In addition to different sizes, powdered pectin comes in two varieties: fruit pectin for homemade jams and jellies, and fruit pectin for lower-sugar recipes. Use the variety your recipe calls for; they're not interchangeable.

Setting Up without Adding Pectin

Not all recipes require the addition of extra pectin. Some recipes cook the fruit mixture for a long period of time, which reduces the liquid in the mixture to achieve the desired consistency.

For this process, you need patience and the knowledge of what to look for when testing your cooked product. Basically, you need to know what the spread's gel point is. (*Gel point* is the cooking point at which jelly is considered done.)

The gel point temperature is 8 degrees above boiling at an elevation of 1,000 feet above sea level or lower (220 degrees). If you're at an altitude higher than 1,000 feet above sea level, you can determine the temperature of your gel point by bringing a pot of water to a boil. When the water boils, check the temperature on your thermometer and add 8 degrees. This is the gel point for your altitude.

Use one of the following methods for testing the gel point:

- ✔ **A candy thermometer:** This is the most accurate method for testing the gel point of your spread. Use a thermometer that's easy to read. One degree over or under the gel point makes a difference in your final product.

 It's a good idea to have two candy thermometers. They are inexpensive and critical for perfect jelly making. If one breaks, you'll have a second one for backup during canning.

- ✔ **The spoon, or sheet, test (see Figure 6-2):** Dip a cool metal spoon into your cooked fruit and hold it so the fruit runs off the spoon. When the temperature of the fruit approaches the gel point, it falls off in a couple of drops. When it slides off the spoon in one sheet, the fruit's done. Proceed with your next step.

 This test takes a bit of practice to master. Until you master it, use a candy thermometer in conjunction with this test. When the temperature of the fruit climbs toward the gel point, you'll be able to see the changes in the liquid and compare it to the sheeting from the spoon.

- ✔ **The plate test (see Figure 6-2):** Place about 1 tablespoon of cooked fruit onto a chilled plate. Put the plate in the freezer and cool the spread to room temperature. If the fruit is set and doesn't roll around on the plate, the mixture is done. Proceed to your next step.

SPOON TEST

WHEN THE JUICE HAS ALMOST REACHED THE GEL POINT, IT WILL
SLOWLY COME TOGETHER AND FALL OFF THE SPOON IN 2 DROPS.
WHEN IT SLIDES OFF THE SPOON IN A SHEET, THE JELLY IS READY!

Figure 6-2:
Gel testing
your food:
the spoon
test and the
plate test.

PLATE TEST

PLACE A SMALL AMOUNT OF SPREAD ON
A CHILLED PLATE. SET THE PLATE IN THE
FREEZER UNTIL THE MIXTURE COOLS TO ROOM
TEMPERATURE. IF THE MIXTURE IS SET,
IT IS READY TO CAN.

The Road to Sweet Canning Success

The only method for safely processing your sweet spreads, as approved by
the United States Department of Agriculture (USDA), is water-bath canning. The
harmful bacteria and microorganisms living in high-acid foods are destroyed
at the temperature of boiling water (212 degrees at 1,000 feet or lower above
sea level) by sterilizing the food and vacuum-sealing the jar. For that reason,
the recipes in the following sections all use water-bath canning. For complete
details on water-bath canning, refer to Chapter 4.

Here are a couple of other tips to help you ensure your canning success:

✔ **Stick with tested recipes.** They're always the best. Don't experiment
with different quantities of ingredients in any canning method. Quantity
adjustments to your fruit or your sugar can seriously change the acid (pH
level) in your food. And if the acidity changes, you may not use the correct
home-canning method to produce a safe product, free from microorganisms.

✔ **Always practice safe food-handling procedures.** Complete each recipe,
start to finish, without interruption. Any break between cooking your
fruit to filling the jars and processing them may produce a product of
inferior quality and one that may be unsafe for eating.

Jamming and canning

Jam is fun to make. It takes me (Karen) back to my childhood days when I
created my own daily specials from crushed leaves, flowers, dirt, rocks, and

water. I've grown up, but I still love playing with food. My husband is pleased to report that I now use real food instead of dirt and rocks!

Strawberry-Rhubarb Jam

Strawberries and rhubarb go together famously. This jam is a great way to get your family to try rhubarb, and it makes a great gift. You can make it throughout the year because frozen rhubarb works just like fresh.

Preparation time: 45 minutes

Processing time: 20 minutes

Yield: 3 pints

4 cups strawberries, crushed

2 ½ cups chopped rhubarb

¼ cup lemon juice

One 1.75-ounce package pectin powder

6 cups sugar

1 Prepare your canning jars and two-piece caps (lids and screw bands) according to the manufacturer's instructions. Keep the jars and lids hot. (For detailed instructions on preparing your jars, see Chapter 4.)

2 Hull and crush the strawberries. Clean the rhubarb; trim the ends and remove the leaves. Cut the rhubarb into ½-inch pieces.

3 Combine the strawberries, rhubarb, lemon juice, and pectin powder in a large saucepan. Bring the mixture to a boil over medium-high heat. Add the sugar, stirring to dissolve. Return the mixture to a full, rolling boil and boil hard for 1 minute. Remove the saucepan from the heat. Skim any foam from the surface with a foam skimmer, if necessary.

4 Ladle the boiling-hot jam into your hot jars, leaving ¼ inch headspace. Release any air bubbles with a nonreactive utensil (refer to Chapter 3), adding more jam as necessary to maintain the proper headspace. Wipe the jar rims; seal the jars with the two-piece caps, hand-tightening the bands.

5 Process the filled pint jars in a water-bath canner for 20 minutes from the point of boiling. (***Note:*** It doesn't matter if you have a less-than-full canner. Simply arrange the jars so that they're evenly spaced, if possible.)

6 Remove the jars from the canner with a jar lifter. Place them on a clean kitchen towel away from drafts. After the jars cool completely, test the seals. If you find jars that haven't sealed, refrigerate them and use them within two weeks.

Per 1-tablespoon serving: Calories 53 (From fat 0); Fat 0g (Saturated 0g); Cholesterol 0mg; Sodium 1mg; Carbohydrates 14g (Dietary fiber 0g); Protein 0g.

Jiggling with jelly

Jelly always has such a bright, cheerful look. It's a great last-minute appetizer that doesn't taste last-minute. Spoon a tart jelly, such as cranberry, over a block of cream cheese, allowing it to cascade over the sides. Serve it with rich, buttery crackers.

In order to achieve a bright, crystal-clear jelly, you need to properly strain your fruit. You can use a commercially manufactured stand and a jelly bag, or you can make your own by using a mesh strainer lined with several layers of cheesecloth (see Figure 6-3).

Dry fabric absorbs flavor from your fruit, weakening the flavor of your final product. Moisten your jelly bag (or cheesecloth) with cold water, wringing out any excess moisture before straining your liquid through it.

STRAINING JELLY

THROUGH CHEESECLOTH IN
A MESH OR METAL STRAINER
OR
IN A JELLY BAG WITH STAND

Figure 6-3:
Straining jelly using a jelly bag and stand or a cheese-cloth-lined strainer.

Herb Tea Jelly

Take your favorite herb teas one step further. Make them into jelly! This is a thin jelly, not thick like jam. Try your favorite herb tea blends and substitute a complimentary juice.

Preparation time: 30 minutes

Processing time: 20 minutes

Yield: 5 half-pints

2 cups water

12 tea bags of your favorite herbal tea

3 cups sugar

1 cup apple juice

One 3-ounce package of liquid pectin

1 Bring the water to a boil in a 3-quart saucepan over high heat. Remove the pan from the heat and steep the tea bags, covered, for 30 minutes.

2 While the tea is steeping, prepare your canning jars and two-piece caps (lids and screw bands) according to the manufacturer's instructions. Keep the jars and lids hot. (For detailed instructions on preparing your jars, see Chapter 4.)

3 After your tea has steeped for 30 minutes, remove the tea bags from the water and stir in the sugar and apple juice. Boil the mixture for 2 minutes; then remove the pan from the heat and stir in the pectin. Boil for 2 more minutes.

4 Fill the prepared jars with boiling liquid, leaving ¼-inch headspace. Release any air bubbles with a nonreactive utensil (refer to Chapter 3), adding more liquid as necessary to maintain the proper headspace. Wipe the jar rims; seal the jars with the two-piece caps, hand-tightening the bands.

5 Process the filled half-pint jars in a water-bath canner for 20 minutes from the point of boiling.

6 Remove the jars from the canner with a jar lifter. Place them on a clean kitchen towel away from drafts. After the jars cool completely, test the seals. If you find jars that haven't sealed, refrigerate them and use them within two weeks.

Per 1-tablespoon serving: Calories 41 (From fat 0); Fat 0g (Saturated 0g); Cholesterol 0mg; Sodium 0mg; Carbohydrates 11g (Dietary fiber 0g); Protein 0g.

Mastering marmalade, butters, and more

Introduce your family and friends to the spreads that were once more common than jams and jellies. Add variety to your canning pantry while you share the wonderful flavors and textures with those lucky enough to be around when you open a jar. After all, there's more to marmalade than oranges.

Kumquat Marmalade

Kumquats have a thin, sweet skin and a very sour flesh. Eat a kumquat by popping the whole thing into your mouth and chew (watch out for the seeds). You have to slice the fruit by hand, but it's worth the effort when you taste the fabulous flavor.

Preparation time: *30 minutes*

Cooking time: *30 minutes*

Processing time: *10 minutes*

Yield*: 7 half-pints*

2 pounds kumquats, unpeeled	*½ cup fresh lemon juice (about 2 to 3 lemons)*
1½ cups water	*5 cups granulated sugar*
⅛ teaspoon baking soda	*One 3-ounce pouch liquid fruit pectin*

1 Slice the kumquats in half lengthwise; then slice each half into fourths lengthwise. Discard the bitter seeds. Place the kumquats into a 6- to 8-quart pot. Add the water and the baking soda. Bring the mixture to a boil over medium-high heat. Reduce the heat and simmer, covered, for 20 minutes, stirring occasionally. Add the lemon juice and simmer, covered, for 10 minutes longer, stirring occasionally.

2 While the kumquats are cooking, prepare your canning jars and two-piece caps (lids and screw bands) according to the manufacturer's instructions. Keep the jars and lids hot. (For detailed instructions on preparing your jars, see Chapter 4.)

3 Stir the sugar into your cooked fruit. Bring the mixture to a full, rolling boil over high heat. Boil hard for 1 minute, stirring constantly. Remove the pan from the heat. Add the pectin, stirring to combine. Remove any foam from the surface with a foam skimmer.

4 Ladle your hot marmalade into the prepared jars, leaving ¼-inch headspace. Release any air bubbles with a nonreactive utensil (refer to Chapter 3), adding more marmalade as necessary to maintain the proper headspace. Wipe the jar rims; seal the jars with the two-piece caps, hand-tightening the bands.

5 Process the filled jars in a water-bath canner for 10 minutes from the point of boiling.

6 Remove the jars from the boiling water with a jar lifter. Place them on a clean kitchen towel away from drafts. After the jars cool completely, test the seals. If you find jars that haven't sealed, refrigerate them and use them within two months.

Per 1-tablespoon serving: Calories 40 (From fat 0); Fat 0g (Saturated 0g); Cholesterol 0mg; Sodium 2mg; Carbohydrates 10g (Dietary fiber 1g); Protein 0g.

Lime-Ginger Marmalade

This is a combination of flavors that I (Karen) was introduced to in Hawaii. It's close to the last combination I thought would become one of my many favorites.

Preparation time: 20 minutes

Cooking time: 1 hour

Processing time: 10 minutes

Yield: 4 half-pints

3 to 4 limes, cut in half lengthwise and sliced crosswise (about ⅛-inch thick), to measure 1½ cups of fruit

½ cup grated lemon zest (about 2 to 4 lemons)

5 cups water

¼ cup finely shredded fresh ginger (about a 5- to 6-inch piece)

4¼ cups granulated sugar

1 Place the lime slices, lemon zest, water, and ginger in a 5- to 6-quart saucepan. Bring the mixture to a boil over medium-high heat and boil rapidly until the fruit is tender, about 30 minutes. Remove the pan from the heat.

2 While your fruit is cooking, prepare your canning jars and two-piece caps (lids and screw bands) according to the manufacturer's instructions. Keep the jars and lids hot. (For detailed instructions on preparing your jars, see Chapter 4.)

3 Measure the hot mixture into a heatproof measuring cup and return it to the pan. For each cup of fruit, add 1 cup of sugar. Return the pan to the stove and bring the mixture to a boil over high heat, stirring often to dissolve the sugar. Cook the marmalade about 30 minutes until it sheets off of a spoon (see Figure 6-2) or registers 220 degrees on a candy thermometer. Remove the pan from the heat and cool the mixture for 5 minutes. Remove any foam from the surface with a foam skimmer.

4 Ladle your hot marmalade into the prepared jars, leaving ¼-inch headspace. Release any air bubbles with a nonreactive utensil (refer to Chapter 3), adding more marmalade as necessary to maintain the proper headspace. Wipe the jar rims; seal the jars with the two-piece caps, hand-tightening the bands.

5 Process the filled jars in a water-bath canner for 10 minutes from the point of boiling.

6 Remove the jars from the boiling water with a jar lifter. Place them on a clean kitchen towel away from drafts. After the jars cool completely, test the seals. If you find jars that haven't sealed, refrigerate them and use them within two months.

Per 1-tablespoon serving: Calories 53 (From fat 0); Fat 0g (Saturated 0g); Cholesterol 0mg; Sodium 0mg; Carbohydrates 14g (Dietary fiber 0g); Protein 0g.

Apple Butter
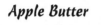

This spread is a cross between a jam and homemade applesauce. The rich flavor will almost make you feel guilty when you slather it on a toasted bagel.

Preparation time*: 20 minutes*

Cooking time: *1 hour, 10 minutes*

Processing time: *15 minutes*

Yield: *6 half-pints*

3½ cups apple cider

8 large apples (about 4 to 4½ pounds), peeled, cored, and sliced

1½ cups granulated sugar

¼ teaspoon kosher or pickling salt

¾ teaspoon ground cinnamon

One 3-inch cinnamon stick

1 Place the cider in a 5- to 6-quart pot and bring it to a boil over high heat. Add the apple slices and reduce the heat. Simmer the fruit, uncovered, for 45 minutes. Stir the fruit every 10 to 15 minutes to prevent sticking.

2 Stir in the sugar, salt, and the ground and stick cinnamon. Cook the mixture over medium-low heat, uncovered and stirring occasionally, until the mixture thickens, about 20 to 25 minutes. (The consistency should be like applesauce.) Remove and discard the cinnamon stick.

3 While the fruit cooks, prepare your canning jars and two-piece caps (lids and screw bands) according to the manufacturer's instructions. Keep the jars and lids hot. (For detailed instructions on preparing your jars, see Chapter 4.)

4 Ladle your hot fruit into the prepared jars, leaving ¼-inch headspace. Release any air bubbles with a nonreactive utensil (refer to Chapter 3), adding more fruit as necessary to maintain the proper headspace. Wipe the jar rims; seal the jars with the two-piece caps, hand-tightening the bands.

5 Process the filled jars in a water-bath canner for 15 minutes from the point of boiling.

6 Remove the jars from the boiling water with a jar lifter. Place them on a clean kitchen towel away from drafts. After the jars cool completely, test the seals. If you find jars that haven't sealed, refrigerate them and use them within two months.

Per 1-tablespoon serving: Calories 23 (From fat 0); Fat 0g (Saturated 0g); Cholesterol 0mg; Sodium 7mg; Carbohydrates 6g (Dietary fiber 0g); Protein 0g.

Any-Time-of-the-Year Strawberry Preserves

Make this recipe when you crave strawberries but their season isn't within sight. It'll lift your spirits until it's fresh berry time!

Preparation time: *10 minutes*

Cooking time: *5 minutes*

Processing time: *Half-pints, 10 minutes*

Yield: *6 half-pints*

Three 10-ounce packages of frozen, sliced strawberries, thawed

¼ cup water

1 ¾-ounce package powdered fruit pectin

6 cups granulated sugar

⅓ cup orange liqueur

3 tablespoons fresh lemon juice

1 Prepare your canning jars and two-piece caps (lids and screw bands) according to the manufacturer's instructions. Keep the jars and lids hot. (For detailed instructions on preparing your jars, see Chapter 4.)

2 Combine the strawberries with the water and pectin in a 5- to 6-quart pot. Bring the mixture to a boil over high heat, stirring occasionally to dissolve the pectin. Boil hard for 1 minute. Stir in the sugar and return the mixture to a full, rolling boil. Boil hard for 1 minute, stirring constantly. Remove the pan from the heat. Stir in the liqueur and the lemon juice. Cool for 5 minutes, stirring occasionally. Remove any foam from the surface with a foam skimmer.

3 Ladle your hot preserves into the prepared jars, leaving ¼-inch headspace. Release any air bubbles with a nonreactive utensil (refer to Chapter 3), adding more preserves as necessary to maintain the proper headspace. Wipe the jar rims; seal the jars with the two-piece caps, hand-tightening the bands.

4 Process the filled jars in a water-bath canner for 10 minutes from the point of boiling.

5 Remove the jars from the boiling water with a jar lifter. Place them on a clean kitchen towel away from drafts. After the jars cool completely, test the seals. If you find jars that haven't sealed, refrigerate them and use them within two months.

Per 1-tablespoon serving: Calories 53 (From fat 0); Fat 0g (Saturated 0g); Cholesterol 0mg; Sodium 0mg; Carbohydrates 14g (Dietary fiber 0g); Protein 0g.

Chapter 7

Condiments and Accompaniments: Chutneys, Relishes, and Sauces

Condiments and accompaniments are to food what accessories are to clothing. They're not necessary, but they enhance what's there. They cover a wide range of flavors including savory, spicy, salty, sweet, or a combination. Think of them as the bright spot on an otherwise dull winter plate.

In this chapter, we open the door to flavors and tastes from around the world. Chutneys are common in Asia and Middle Eastern countries, salsas are native to Mexico, and relish is very popular in North America. Expand your taste experience as you visit the world of fascinating and enticing flavors.

The water-bath canning principles and step-by-step instructions explained in Chapter 4 (and used in Chapters 5 through 8) apply to the recipes in this chapter. As always, use the freshest fruit and other products you need to make your recipes.

A word about herbs

Dried herbs and spices are used extensively in this chapter. The best way to guarantee the freshness and quality of your herbs is to grow your own. It's easy and doesn't take much space, because herbs grow very well in pots or small areas. To preserve this bounty, dry or freeze your herbs. For information on drying, head to Chapter 19. Chapter 15 explains how to freeze herbs. But if you can't — or don't want to — grow your own, here are some tips for purchasing the best quality dried herbs possible:

✔ **Buy small amounts.** Purchase an amount you'll use within six months to one year. Flavors deteriorate over time.

✔ **Buy the amount you need.** Stores that offer herbs and spices in containers where you can scoop out what you need are a great option. Check out the turnover rate; you don't want to buy old products.

Whether you're growing and drying your own herbs or buying them from a store, follow these storage and usage guidelines:

✔ **Store dried herbs and spices in airtight containers.** Glass or plastic jars are good choices, but make sure you screw the lid all the way back on. If you purchase cans, snap the lid in place to seal in the freshness.

✔ **Keep your dried herbs and spices in a cool, dark, dry location.** Sunlight and heat destroy flavor. Store your containers in a cabinet. (Don't freeze them. The warming and cooling that happens when you take the herbs in and out of the freezer can lead to condensation and deteriorating of the herb.)

✔ **Inventory your dried herbs and spices at least once a year.** Write the purchase date on the container. Discard any over one year old.

Complementing Your Chutney

Chutney is a condiment that contains fruit, vinegar, sugar, and spices. Chutneys range in flavor from sweet to spicy and mild to hot and have textures ranging from smooth to chunky. It usually accompanies curry dishes, but don't limit it to that. Use chutney as a bread spread or with a slice of cheddar cheese on a cracker.

The first time I (Karen) heard the word *chutney,* I cringed. I thought, "What an awful name for a food." Then I closed my eyes and took a bite. My taste buds didn't believe the flavors they were sensing — sweet and spicy, no, tart, and a toasted nut? What was going on? From this early food experience, I vowed never to prejudge any food. I gladly welcome all new taste opportunities.

Green Tomato Chutney

This recipe is a great way to use your green tomatoes. It produces a super-thick chutney that makes a great gift and looks lovely on the shelf. Although you'll be eager to try the chutney as soon as it's done, let it sit for one month before you use it, longer if you can to help develop the fine flavor. This recipe uses half-pint jars — the perfect size for a picnic basket!

Preparation time: *1 hour 15 minutes*

Processing time: *10 minutes*

Yield: *8 half-pints*

4 pounds green tomatoes, chopped

2 medium onions, chopped

1½ green apples, peeled, cored, and chopped

1 cup golden raisins

1 teaspoon salt

½ teaspoon ground red pepper

1 teaspoon allspice

1 teaspoon curry, or to taste

1 cup brown sugar

2 cups cider vinegar

1 Prepare your canning jars and two-piece caps (lids and screw bands) according to the manufacturer's instructions. Keep the jars and lids hot. (For detailed instructions on preparing your jars, see Chapter 4.)

2 Place all the ingredients in a 6-quart pot, and simmer on medium heat until the mixture is thick and rich, the consistency of very thick, chunky applesauce, about 45 minutes. Stir often to prevent scorching.

3 Ladle the mixture into the prepared jars. Leave ¼-inch headspace. Release any air bubbles with a nonreactive utensil (refer to Chapter 3), adding more mixture as necessary to maintain the proper headspace. Wipe the jar rims; seal the jars with the two-piece caps, hand-tightening the bands.

4 Process the filled half-pint jars in a water-bath canner for 10 minutes from the point of boiling.

5 Remove the jars from the canner with a jar lifter. Place them on a clean kitchen towel away from drafts. After the jars cool completely, test the seals (refer to Chapter 4 for instructions). If you find jars that haven't sealed, refrigerate them and use them within two weeks.

Per 1-tablespoon serving: *Calories 16 (From fat 0); Fat 0g (Saturated 0g); Cholesterol 0mg; Sodium 21mg; Carbohydrates 4g (Dietary fiber 0g); Protein 0g.*

Toasting nuts

Toasted nuts are delicious and simple to make. Pay close attention during the toasting process. If the nuts become over toasted (very dark), there's no going back. You have to start over. Toast more nuts than your recipe calls for and use them in salads. Store cooled nuts in an airtight container in the refrigerator.

This process takes only minutes (literally), so stay right by the oven.

1. **Spread your nuts evenly on a baking sheet and place it in a preheated 350-degree oven.**

2. **Set your timer for 3 minutes.**

   The size of the nut determines the toasting time. Three minutes will be enough for some nuts, not enough for others.

3. **After 3 minutes, check the nuts for doneness; shake or stir them.**

   If they're a color you're looking for, usually a light golden brown, remove them from the oven and cool them on the baking sheet.

4. **If the nuts aren't quite done, return them to the oven, checking them again in 2 minutes.**

   Toasting takes place quickly. Your nuts are done, or close to being done, when you can smell their wonderful aroma. If the skin is on the nut, it'll split to show you the color of the nut.

5. **Remove the finished nuts from the baking sheet to cool (if left on the sheet, they'll continue to cook).**

Reveling in Your Relish

Relish wears many hats and complements a wide variety of foods, from hamburgers and hot dogs, to meat and poultry. Relish is a cooked mixture of fruit or vegetables preserved with vinegar. Flavor can be sweet to savory and hot to mild with textures ranging from smooth to finely chopped or chunky. My family and I (Amy) like our relish to be a bit on the chunky side. That way, pieces of individual ingredients can still be seen. Either way, relish is a must-have for your pantry.

Summer Squash Relish

I (Karen) discovered this tasty relish when my best friend, Judy, planted six zucchini plants in her garden. At that time, we had no idea of the amount of squash those plants would produce! Including an overnight soak, this recipe takes two days to make.

Preparation time: *45 minutes plus 12 hours soaking time*

Processing time: *15 minutes*

Yield: *6 pints*

5 pounds (about 10 to 12) medium zucchini

6 large onions

½ cup kosher or pickling salt

Cold water to cover the vegetables (about 4 to 5 quarts)

2 cups white wine vinegar

1 cup granulated sugar

Two 4-ounce jars pimientos, undrained

2 teaspoons celery seed

1 teaspoon powdered mustard

½ teaspoon ground cinnamon

½ teaspoon ground nutmeg

½ teaspoon freshly ground black pepper

1 On the first day, finely chop the zucchini and onions. (If you're using a food processor, chop them in three batches.) Place the vegetables in a 5- to 6-quart mixing bowl and sprinkle them with the salt. Add water to cover them, place a cover on the bowl, and refrigerate overnight or at least 12 hours.

2 On the second day, drain the vegetables in a colander. Rinse well with running water; drain. Transfer the vegetables to a 5- to 6-quart pot. Add the vinegar, sugar, pimientos, celery seed, mustard, cinnamon, nutmeg, and pepper. Stir to combine.

3 Bring the vegetables to a boil over medium-high heat, stirring occasionally. Reduce the heat and simmer, uncovered, until the mixture reduces to 3 quarts, about 30 to 40 minutes. Stir the vegetables every 10 minutes to prevent sticking. The zucchini color turns a dull shade of green.

4 While your relish is cooking, prepare your canning jars and two-piece caps (lids and screw bands) according to the manufacturer's instructions. Keep the jars and lids hot. (For detailed instructions on preparing your jars, see Chapter 4.)

5 Spoon the hot relish into your prepared jars, leaving ¼-inch headspace. Compact the relish with a spoon to release any air bubbles. Add more relish as necessary to maintain the proper headspace. Wipe the jar rims; seal the jars with the two-piece caps, hand-tightening the bands.

6 Process your filled jars in a water-bath canner for 15 minutes from the point of boiling.

7 Remove the jars from the boiling water with a jar lifter. Place them on a clean kitchen towel away from drafts. After the jars cool completely, test the seals (refer to Chapter 4 for instructions). If you find jars that haven't sealed, refrigerate them and use them within 2 months.

Vary It! Use 3 pounds of zucchini and 2 pounds of patty pan or yellow crookneck squash.

Per 2-tablespoon serving: *Calories 16 (From fat 1); Fat 0g (Saturated 0g); Cholesterol 0mg; Sodium 14mg; Carbohydrates 4g (Dietary fiber 1g); Protein 0g.*

Satisfying Your Sassy Salsas and Sauces

Salsa is the Mexican word for "sauce." Traditionally, salsa was made with tomatoes, cilantro, chilies, and onions and served at room temperature. Today, it's readily available in most supermarkets in mild, hot, or fiery intensities and is used on almost any food.

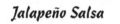

Jalapeño Salsa

This salsa isn't for those with sensitive mouths. The heat of the jalapeños grows stronger when the salsa cools and the flavors blend.

Preparation time: 30 minutes

Processing time: 15 minutes

Yield: 3 pints

2 pounds tomatoes, peeled and chopped, to measure 3 cups

7-ounce can diced jalapeño chilies or 12 fresh jalapeño chilies, finely chopped, seeds removed

1 onion, peeled and chopped

6 garlic cloves, minced

2 tablespoons finely chopped fresh cilantro

2 teaspoons ground oregano

1½ teaspoons kosher or pickling salt

½ teaspoon ground cumin

1 cup cider vinegar

1 Prepare your canning jars and two-piece caps (lids and screw bands) according to the manufacturer's instructions. Keep the jars and lids hot. (For detailed instructions on preparing your jars, see Chapter 4.)

2 Place all the ingredients in a 5- to 6- quart pot. Bring the mixture to a boil over high heat, stirring to combine. Reduce the heat to low; simmer, uncovered, for 10 minutes.

3 Ladle your hot salsa into the prepared jars; leaving ¼-inch headspace. Release any air bubbles with a nonreactive utensil (refer to Chapter 3), adding more salsa as necessary to maintain the proper headspace. Wipe the jar rims; seal the jars with the two-piece caps, hand-tightening the bands.

4 Process the filled jars in a water-bath canner for 15 minutes from the point of boiling.

5 Remove the jars from the boiling water with a jar lifter. Place them on a clean kitchen towel away from drafts. After the jars cool completely, test the seals (refer to Chapter 4 for instructions). If you find jars that haven't sealed, refrigerate them and use them within 2 months.

Per 2-tablespoon serving: Calories 6 (From fat 0); Fat 0g (Saturated 0g); Cholesterol 0mg; Sodium 99mg; Carbohydrates 2g (Dietary fiber 0g); Protein 0g.

Tomatillo Salsa

Here's a welcome change from a traditional tomato-based salsa. Use this mild salsa for a chip-dipping sauce or a topper for your tacos or cheese enchiladas. ***Note:*** Tomatillos look like small green tomatoes. Remove the parchment like husks before using them.

Preparation time*: 20 minutes*

Processing time: *15 minutes*

Yield*: 2 pints*

2 pounds tomatillos, husks removed, cored	*2 teaspoons ground cumin*
1 large onion, peeled	*½ teaspoon kosher or pickling salt*
4 large Anaheim chilies, seeds and stems removed	*½ teaspoon crushed red peppers*
4 garlic cloves, peeled	*1 cup distilled white vinegar*
2 tablespoons finely chopped fresh cilantro	*¼ cup fresh lime juice (2 or 3 limes)*

1 Prepare your canning jars and two-piece caps (lids and screw bands) according to the manufacturer's instructions. Keep the jars and lids hot. (For detailed instructions on preparing your jars, see Chapter 4.)

2 Cut the tomatillos into quarters and finely chop them in a food processor fitted with a metal blade. Transfer the tomatillos to a 5- to 6- quart pot. Finely chop the onion, chilies, and garlic cloves in two batches in the food processor. Add them to the tomatillos. Stir in the cilantro, cumin, salt, peppers, vinegar, and lime juice. Bring the mixture to a boil over high heat. Reduce the heat and simmer 10 minutes.

3 Ladle your hot salsa into the prepared jars, leaving ¼-inch headspace. Release any air bubbles with a nonreactive utensil (refer to Chapter 3), adding more salsa as necessary to maintain the proper headspace. Wipe the jar rims; seal the jars with the two-piece caps, hand-tightening the bands.

4 Process the filled jars in a water-bath canner for 15 minutes from the point of boiling.

5 Remove the jars from the boiling water with a jar lifter. Place them on a clean kitchen towel away from drafts. After the jars cool completely, test the seals (refer to Chapter 4 for instructions). If you find jars that haven't sealed, refrigerate them and use them within 2 months.

Per 2-tablespoon serving: Calories 15 (From fat 3); Fat 0g (Saturated 0g); Cholesterol 0mg; Sodium 38mg; Carbohydrates 3g (Dietary fiber 1g); Protein 1g.

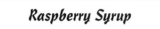

Raspberry Syrup

Even if you love pure maple syrup, you won't be able to resist this for a flavor change. This syrup is delicious on thick, grilled French toast sprinkled with ground cinnamon and powdered sugar.

Preparation time: *40 minutes*

Processing time: *10 minutes*

Yield: *6 half-pints*

5 cups fresh raspberries, hulled and cut in half	*2½ cups granulated sugar*
3 cups water	*3½ cups corn syrup*
1 tablespoon grated lemon zest	*2 tablespoons fresh lemon juice (about ½ a lemon)*

1 Place the raspberries in a 4- to 5-quart pot. Crush the berries with a potato masher. Add 1½ cups of the water and the lemon zest. Bring the mixture to a boil; reduce the heat and simmer 5 minutes. Strain the hot mixture through a jelly bag or a cheesecloth-lined mesh strainer.

2 While the berries drain, prepare your canning jars and two-piece caps (lids and screw bands) according to the manufacturer's instructions. Keep the jars and lids hot. (For detailed instructions on preparing your jars, see Chapter 4.)

3 Place the sugar and the remaining 1½ cups of water in a 4-quart saucepan. Bring the mixture to a boil over high heat, stirring to dissolve the sugar. Cook the mixture until the temperature registers 260 degrees on a candy thermometer. Add the strained berries and the corn syrup and return the mixture to a boil, boiling the syrup for 4 minutes. Remove the pan from the heat and stir in the lemon juice. Remove any foam from the surface with a foam skimmer.

4 Ladle your hot syrup into the prepared jars, leaving ¼-inch headspace. Release any air bubbles with a nonreactive utensil (refer to Chapter 3), adding more syrup as necessary to maintain the proper headspace. Wipe the jar rims; seal the jars with the two-piece caps, hand-tightening the bands.

5 Process the filled jars in a water-bath canner for 10 minutes from the point of boiling.

6 Remove the jars from the boiling water with a jar lifter. Place them on a clean kitchen towel away from drafts. After the jars cool completely, test the seals (refer to Chapter 4 for instructions). If you find jars that haven't sealed, refrigerate them and use them within 2 months.

Vary It! *Substitute other berries, or a combination of berries, for different syrup flavors.*

Per 2-tablespoon serving: *Calories 114 (From fat 1); Fat 0g (Saturated 0g); Cholesterol 0mg; Sodium 0mg; Carbohydrates 0g (Dietary fiber 1g); Protein 0g.*

Chapter 8

Pickle Me Timbers!

In This Chapter

▶ Outlining the pickling process

▶ Soaking it up in brining solutions

▶ Transforming your low-acid foods to high-acid pickled products

▶ Putting crunch in your veggies

Pickling is used for a wide range of foods, including fruits and vegetables. Although pickling isn't practiced much today, don't overlook this rewarding process. This chapter gives you an overview of pickling, describing the ingredients, the utensils, and the methods used. In no time, you'll be making easy-to-prepare pickled food and condiments to wow your taste buds.

The Art of Pickling

Pickling preserves food in a *brine solution,* a strong mixture of water, salt, vinegar, and sometimes sugar or another sweetener, like corn syrup. Brining is what gives the vegetables the pickled texture and flavor you're going for.

Some recipes (usually older ones) include a brining step before the actual canning. Other pickling recipes add the brine solution to the raw vegetable and the brining happens in the sterile canning jar as it sits on your shelf. These recipes generally have a recommendation for how many weeks to wait for best flavor.

The ingredients

The four basic ingredients for pickling are salt, vinegar, water, and herbs and spices. Use high-quality ingredients for the best results.

The perfect balance of salt, vinegar, water, and herbs and spices safely preserves your pickled food. You can achieve this balance by precisely measuring your ingredients and following each step in your recipe.

Salt

Salt is used as a preservative. It adds flavor and crispness to your food, especially pickles. Use a pure, additive-free, granulated salt. Acceptable salts are *pickling and canning salt* (a fine-grained salt containing no additives), most kosher salt, and *sea salt,* salt produced from evaporated seawater.

Additives in salt cause cloudy liquid. Always read the ingredient label on your salt container to ensure it's additive-free. Salts *not* suitable for brining and pickling solutions are

- ✔ **Table salt and iodized salt:** These contain *anti-caking agents,* additives that keep the salt from sticking together. These cloud your liquid. Iodine darkens food.

- ✔ **Rock salt:** Rock salt keeps roads free of ice and isn't made for use with food. It's okay in an ice-cream freezer because it never touches the food.

- ✔ **Salt substitutes:** These products contain little or no sodium.

Vinegar

Vinegar is a tart liquid that prevents the growth of bacteria. For pickling, you must use a vinegar with an acidity level of 5 percent. If the level of acidity isn't on the label, don't use the vinegar — the strength of the acid may not be adequate for safe food preservation.

The preferred vinegar for pickling is distilled white vinegar, which has a sharp, tart flavor, maintains the color of your food, and is relatively inexpensive. For a milder flavor, you can substitute apple cider vinegar. Keep in mind, though, that using cider vinegar will change the overall color of your finished foods, not always for the better. You may get unappetizing gray or brown results from using the wrong type of vinegar.

To avoid cloudy pickles, use a vinegar that's clear from sediment. Cider and wine vinegars often have sediment, and you may even be able to see things floating around. What causes the sediment? Vinegars that still contain the *mother,* a harmless bacterium that creates the vinegar but also causes sediment to form on the bottom of the bottle.

Never dilute or reduce the amount of vinegar in a recipe. To ensure a safe product, the brine must have the right acidity level. Never use a vinegar with less than 5 percent acidity.

If the flavor's too tart, add $1/4$ cup granulated sugar for every 4 cups of vinegar. Treating flavors in this manner won't upset the balance of your vinegar. If you don't like the flavor when you make the recipe, try another recipe. Don't forget to jot down your changes on your recipe card!

Water

Soft water is the best water for your brine solution. Too much iron in your water can cause discoloration of the finished product. *Distilled water,* water with all minerals and other impurities removed, is also a good choice. If you use tap water, make sure it's of drinking quality; if it doesn't taste good to you, it won't taste better in your food. Also, avoid using sparkling water.

Herbs and spices

Use the exact amount of herbs or spices called for in your recipe. If your recipe calls for a fresh herb, use the fresh herb. If your recipe calls for a dried spice, use one with a strong aroma. (For more information on drying herbs and spices, check out Chapter 19.)

Pickling spices are blends of many spices including allspice, bay leaves, cardamom, cinnamon, cloves, coriander, ginger, mustard seed, and peppercorns. They're mixed by the manufacturer and vary in flavor. Although these spices are generally whole and therefore good keepers, it is best to buy fresh, new spices each year, before you start canning.

Brining education

The brining process is a key part of the pickling process because it does these important things:

- Chemically, it draws out the natural juices and replaces them with salty/vinegar solution, giving your veggies that familiar pickled flavor and texture.

- It extracts juice and sugar from your food, forming *lactic acid,* a bitter-tasting tart acid. This lactic acid serves as the preservative in your pickled food.

- Because the brining solution typically includes vinegar (an acid), it safely converts your low-acid foods (those with a pH level over 4.6) to high-acid foods (with a pH level of 4.6 or less), making it safe for water-bath canning. (This is why you must prepare your recipe as it's written and *not* modify the amounts.).

As mentioned previously, sometimes you brine your vegetables before canning; other times, you add the brine solution to the raw vegetables and let the brining occur in the canning jar. The following sections explain how to prepare your veggies for each.

Fresh (or raw) packing: Adding brine to the raw veggies

In this method, you place fresh raw vegetables in prepared jars and then cover them with hot flavored liquid, usually a spicy vinegar, and process the filled jars in your water-bath canner. To ensure the pickling process can occur uniformly, make sure your vegetables are completely submerged in the brining solution. Most of the recipes in this chapter require raw packing.

Complete precooking

In this method, you cook your food completely before filling your jars. The following relish recipe is precooked before canning. The taste of the relish is present before you add it to the jars, and it's ready to eat once it is cooked.

Brining before canning

When brining your vegetables beforehand, how long you let your vegetables soak can vary anywhere from a few hours to several weeks. Your recipe provides the details. Here's what you need to know about these long or short brines:

- ✔ **Long brine:** This process is primarily used for making pickles from cucumbers. The veggies stay in the brine anywhere from 5 days to 6 weeks. The brine solution is quite heavy with salt and may contain some vinegar and spices. None of the recipes in this chapter require a long brine.

- ✔ **Short brine:** The soaking period for this method is 24 hours or less. Follow your recipe for the correct proportions in your brine solution. You use a short brine for the Sweet Pickle Relish and Zucchini Bread and Butter Pickles.

In both cases, you submerge the food in the brine solution, where it *ferments* (stays in the solution) for the recommended period of time. (Your recipe gives you the details.) After fermenting, follow your recipe and make a fresh brine solution for filling your jars.

Be sure to keep your food completely submerged in the brine solution, whether it's for a few hours or longer. To do this, place a sealed, water-filled glass jar on top of your food. The jar applies pressure to keep the foods submerged when you cover your brining container.

Stoneware crocks are excellent choices for brining food. You can find them at specialty cookware stores or where canning supplies are sold. But there's an important caveat: Don't use a crock that you've gotten from a thrift store or other secondhand store. Without the original packaging, you have no way of knowing whether it's lead-free and suitable for brining.

Old-time canning recipes may instruct you to "soak your pickles in salt brine strong enough to float an egg." This equates to a 10-percent brine mixture of 1 pound (about $1^1/_2$ cups) of salt dissolved in 1 gallon of water.

Adding crunch to your food

The best method for maintaining crispness, crunch, and firmness in your vegetables during the soaking period is to add ice, preferably crushed ice, to your soaking solution. This works best for short brine soaking.

After the soaking period, drain your vegetables in a colander, following your recipe instructions for any rinsing. Some recipes instruct you to roll the drained food in clean kitchen towels to dry it. This works well for larger pieces of food (it isn't for finely chopped relishes).

Note: In older pickling recipes, you may see the addition of alum or pickling (slaked) lime. The recipes in this chapter don't add either of these products because they aren't necessary when you're using modern canning methods.

For the best tasting pickles, follow these four tips:

- ✔ Pick produce that is blemish free and pickle your produce within 24 hours of harvesting. Never use vegetables that you have to trim off spoiled or moldy parts.

- ✔ To ensure that every piece is pickled at the same time, always pack your jars with uniformly sized vegetables.

- ✔ Scrub the vegetables well to get rid of any dirt, which contains bacteria, and trim ⅛ inch from the blossom and stem ends of cucumbers. These ends may have enzymes that will spoil or soften your pickles.

- ✔ Pack your jars tightly. Because pickling causes vegetables to shrink slightly, having them tightly filled helps prevent them from floating.

Pickling Equipment and Utensils

In addition to the basic equipment for water-bath canning (refer to Chapter 4), you need nonreactive utensils and equipment for handling, cooking, and brining your food. *Nonreactive* items are made of stainless steel, nonstick-surfaced items (without a damaged nonstick surface), enamelware, or glass.

Don't use enamelware with chips or cracks or equipment or utensils made from or containing copper, iron, or brass. These items react with the acids and salt during the pickling process, altering the color of your food and giving the finished product a bad taste. *Definitely* don't use galvanized products, which contain zinc. These produce a poison when the acid and the salt touch the zinc, which is transferred to your food causing serious illness (or worse).

Pickled Toppers

Relish is a staple in many kitchens. Use this pickled treat anytime you'd use a relish, on a hamburger or hot dog, in tuna salad, or anytime you want to add flavor to a sandwich.

Sweet Pickle Relish

One advantage of homemade relish is mixing flavors you don't find in commercially produced relishes. Make more than you believe your family will consume in a year because this relish has a way of disappearing. Try it in homemade Thousand Island dressing.

Preparation time: *55 minutes plus 2 hours soaking time*

Processing time: *Halp-pints and pints, 10 minutes*

Yield: *7 half-pints or 3 pints*

5 to 6 medium cucumbers	3 cups granulated sugar
3 to 4 green and/or red bell peppers	2 cups cider vinegar
3 to 4 medium onions	2 ½ teaspoons celery seeds
¼ cup kosher or pickling salt	2 ½ teaspoons mustard seed
Cold water, about 4 to 6 quarts	½ teaspoon turmeric

1 Peel the cucumbers, cut them in half lengthwise, and remove the seeds (see Figure 8-1). Finely chop the cucumbers in a food processor fitted with a metal blade, to measure 6 cups. Remove the stems and seeds from the bell peppers. Finely chop them in a food processor fitted with a metal blade, to measure 3 cups. Remove the skin of the onions. Finely chop them in a food processor fitted with a metal blade, to measure 3 cups.

2 Combine the vegetables in a 5- to 6-quart bowl. Sprinkle them with salt and add cold water to cover them. Cover the bowl; let the veggies stand at room temperature for 2 hours. Rinse the vegetables with running water in batches in a colander. Drain well.

3 Combine the sugar, vinegar, celery seeds, mustard seeds, and turmeric in a 5- to 6-quart pot. Bring the liquid to a boil over high heat, stirring occasionally to dissolve the sugar. Add the drained vegetables and return the mixture to a boil. Reduce the heat to medium-high and simmer, uncovered, stirring occasionally, for 20 to 30 minutes or until most of the excess liquid has evaporated.

4 While your relish is cooking, prepare your canning jars and two-piece caps (lids and screw bands) according to the manufacturer's instructions. Keep the jars and lids hot. (For information on preparing your jars, see Chapter 4.)

5 Spoon and lightly compact the hot relish into the prepared jars. Release any air bubbles with a nonreactive utensil (refer to Chapter 3), adding more relish and liquid as necessary to maintain the proper headspace. Wipe the jar rims; seal the jars with the two-piece caps, hand-tightening the bands.

6 Process your filled jars in a water-bath canner for 10 minutes from the point of boiling.

7 Remove the jars from the boiling water with a jar lifter. Place them on a clean kitchen towel away from drafts. After the jars cool completely, test the seals (see Chapter 4). If you find jars that haven't sealed, refrigerate them and use them within two months.

Tip: *This recipe is ready to eat as soon as you're done precooking it. So save one jar to cool for dinner the night you make it.*

Per 2-tablespoon serving: *Calories 51 (From fat 1); Fat 0g (Saturated 0g); Cholesterol 0mg; Sodium 499mg; Carbohydrates 13g (Dietary fiber 0g); Protein 0g.*

How to Seed a Cucumber

Figure 8-1:
Seeding a
cucumber
with ease.

Remove the
peel with a
knife or peeler.

Cut in half,
lengthwise...

and scoop out
the seeds with
a small spoon.

Pickled Cucumbers Are Just Pickles

So what's so important about what kind of cucumber you use for pickles? After all, a cucumber is a cucumber, right? This is definitely not the case. The common salad cucumber has a thick, dark-green, waxy skin. Don't use this cucumber for making pickles because the brine solution won't penetrate the waxy coating. Use this cucumber when your recipe doesn't specify "pickling cucumbers."

A pickling cucumber is the only cucumber to use for making pickles. The skin of a pickling cucumber is thin, not waxy, and is left on the cucumber. Pickling cucumbers are about 4 inches in length, smaller than salad cucumbers. Don't eat pickling cucumbers raw; their flavor can be extremely bitter. Some varieties are now sold for both pickling and slicing. These are fine to use. For pickling, use the smaller size of this variety; for slicing, use the larger size. Always look for cucumbers that are recommended for pickling, such as Kirby or Boston Pickling.

Speedy Dill Pickles

This recipe makes an old-fashioned dill pickle in almost the blink of an eye. It's an excellent confidence-builder for the beginning canner. Try it!

Preparation time: *35 minutes*

Processing time: *Pints, 10 minutes; quarts, 15 minutes*

Yield: *6 pints or 3 quarts*

4 pounds pickling cucumbers	*1 tablespoon whole mixed pickling spices*
6 tablespoons kosher or pickling salt	*18 black peppercorns*
3 cups distilled white vinegar	*3 tablespoons dill seed*
3 cups water	*Fresh dill springs (optional)*

1 Wash your cucumbers. Leave them whole if they're smaller than 4 inches in diameter. For larger cucumbers, cut them into slices or lengthwise, in halves or quarters.

2 Prepare your canning jars and two-piece caps (lids and screw bands) according to the manufacturer's instructions. Keep the jars and lids hot. (For information on preparing your jars, see Chapter 4.)

3 Combine the salt, water, and vinegar in a 3- to 4-quart saucepan. Bring the liquid to a boil over high heat, stirring occasionally to dissolve the sugar. Keep the liquid hot over medium heat.

4 Snuggly pack the cucumbers into your prepared jars. To each pint jar, add ½ teaspoon of pickling spices, 3 peppercorns, and 1½ teaspoons of dill seed. To each quart jar, add 1 teaspoon of pickling spices, 6 peppercorns, and 1 tablespoon of dill seed. If you're using fresh dill, add a sprig or two to each pint or quart jar in between the inside edge of the jar and the cucumbers.

5 Ladle the hot liquid into your filled jars, leaving ¼-inch headspace in the pint jars and ¹/₂-inch headspace in the quart jars. Completely submerge the cucumbers in the liquid. If they protrude from the jar, adjust them until you have the proper headspace, because the lids may not properly seal from the internal pressure. Release any air bubbles with a nonreactive tool (refer to Chapter 3), adding more liquid as necessary to maintain the proper headspace. Wipe the jar rims; seal the jars with the two-piece caps, hand-tightening the bands.

6 Process your filled jars in a water-bath canner for 10 minutes (pints) or 15 minutes (quarts) from the point of boiling.

7 Remove the jars with a jar lifter. Place them on a clean kitchen towel away from drafts. After the jars cool completely, test the seals (see Chapter 4). If you find jars that haven't sealed, refrigerate and use them within two months.

8 Keep the pickles on the pantry shelf for at least two weeks for the taste to develop.

Vary It! For kosher-style dill pickles, add 2 cloves of peeled, halved garlic to each jar of pickles.

Per 2-ounce serving: Calories 11 (From fat 1); Fat 0g (Saturated 0g); Cholesterol 0mg; Sodium 1,308mg; Carbohydrates 2g (Dietary fiber 1g); Protein 1g.

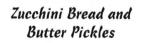

Zucchini Bread and Butter Pickles

Wait until you try these tartly sweet pickles. These are the perfect solution to being overrun with zucchini. Pick your vegetables when they are cucumber sized, and use that day for the best texture. *Note:* These pickles are ready to eat as soon as they cool.

Preparation time: 40 minutes plus 3 hours soaking time

Processing time: 10 minutes

Yield: 12 pints

6 pounds thinly sliced zucchini	*2 quarts distilled white vinegar*
2 cups thinly sliced onions	*¼ cup whole mustard seed*
½ cup kosher or pickling salt	*¼ cup celery seed*
2 cups sugar	*1 teaspoon turmeric*
2 quarts ice water	

1 Slice the zucchini into ¼-inch thick rounds. Peel the onions and cut them in half lengthwise from the tip to the bottom core. Lay them on a cutting board, cut side down; then slice them, starting at the top of the onion, to a thickness of ¼ inch.

2 Place the zucchini and onion slices in a 12-quart nonreactive stock pot. Sprinkle them with salt. Add ice water to cover the vegetables. Stir them once; then cover the bowl and let the veggies stand at room temperature for 3 hours. Transfer the veggies to a colander and rinse them thoroughly with running water (you may need to do this in more than one batch). Drain well. Roll the pieces in a clean, dry kitchen towel to partially dry them.

3 Prepare your canning jars and two-piece caps (lids and screw bands) according to the manufacturer's instructions. Keep the jars and lids hot. (For information on preparing your jars, see Chapter 4.)

4 In the nonreactive pot, combine the sugar, vinegar, mustard, celery seed, and turmeric. Bring the liquid to a boil over high heat, stirring occasionally to dissolve the sugar and mix the spices. Add the vegetables and return the mixture to a boil.

5 Pack the boiling hot pickles into the prepared jars and add the hot liquid, leaving ½-inch headspace. Release any air bubbles with a nonreactive tool (refer to Chapter 3), adding more pickles and liquid as necessary to maintain the proper headspace. Wipe the jar rims; seal the jars with the two-piece caps, hand-tightening the bands.

6 Process your filled jars in a water-bath canner for 10 minutes from the point of boiling.

7 Remove the jars with a jar lifter. Place them on a clean kitchen towel away from drafts. After the jars cool completely, test the seals (see Chapter 4). If you find jars that haven't sealed, refrigerate and use them within two months.

Per 2-ounce serving: *Calories 22 (From fat 0); Fat 0g (Saturated 0g); Cholesterol 0mg; Sodium 116mg; Carbohydrates 6g (Dietary fiber 1g); Protein 0g.*

Pickled Vegetables

Pickled vegetables are delicious additions to green salads or a relish plate. Enjoy these treats for a change of pace from plain, raw vegetables. They still retain their crisp texture, but with an extra added bite from the brine.

Avoid long boiling periods for your vinegar solution. Lengthy boiling reduces the acetic-acid level in vinegar, changing the pH level of the food. This change may compromise the safety of your pickled food.

Dilly Beans

Serve these beans in a Bloody Mary in place of a piece of celery. For a variation, use a combination of green and yellow string beans.

Preparation time: *16 minutes*

Processing time: *10 minutes*

Yield: *4 to 5 pints*

2 ½ cups distilled white vinegar

2 ½ cups water

¼ cup coarse kosher or pickling salt

2 ½ pounds fresh green beans, washed, with the ends and strings removed

4 stalks fresh dill, washed and drained

4 cloves garlic, peeled

4 dried whole red chile peppers

1 teaspoon cayenne pepper

1 teaspoon dill seed

1 Prepare your canning jars and two-piece caps (lids and screw bands) according to the manufacturer's instructions. Keep the jars and lids hot. (For information on preparing your jars, see Chapter 4.)

2 Combine the vinegar, water, and salt in a 6- to 8-quart pot. Bring the liquid to a boil over high heat; boil for 1 minute, stirring to dissolve the salt. Reduce the heat to low and keep the mixture hot.

3 Pack the beans into the prepared jars (see Figure 8-2), leaving ¼-inch headspace (trim the tops of the beans, if necessary). Add the following to each jar: a sprig of dill, 1 garlic clove, 1 dried red chile pepper, ¼ teaspoon cayenne pepper, and ¼ teaspoon dill seed.

4 Ladle the hot liquid over the beans, leaving ¼-inch headspace, covering the tops of the beans. Release any air bubbles with a nonreactive tool (refer to Chapter 3), adding more liquid as necessary to maintain the proper headspace. Wipe the jar rims; seal the jars with the two-piece caps, hand-tightening the bands.

5 Process your filled jars in a water-bath canner for 10 minutes from the point of boiling.

6 Remove the jars from the boiling water with a jar lifter. Place them on a clean kitchen towel away from drafts. After the jars cool completely, test the seals (see Chapter 4). If you find jars that haven't sealed, refrigerate them and use them within two months.

7 Let the beans sit for two weeks on your pantry shelf for the flavors to fully develop.

Per ½-cup serving: Calories 40 (From fat 2); Fat 0g (Saturated 0g); Cholesterol 0mg; Sodium 167mg; Carbohydrates 10g (Dietary fiber 2g); Protein 1g.

Figure 8-2:
Packing raw
beans into
a jar.

PACK RAW BEANS INTO A JAR
BY HOLDING THE JAR AT AN
ANGLE ON ITS SIDE.

Pickled Asparagus

Asparagus is one of those foods that you either wish for or have too much of. Pickling the young asparagus spears provides a great way to add a new dimension to this early spring vegetable. Put these up in pints, as part of their charm is the look of the straight spears packed like soldiers inside.

Preparation time: *10 minutes*

Processing time: *10 minutes*

Yield: *8 pints*

12 pounds young asparagus spears	*8 cloves garlic*
8 small dried peppers (optional)	*5 cups distilled vinegar*
4 tablespoons dill seed	*5 cups water*
4 teaspoons whole mustard seed	*½ cup canning salt*

1 Prepare your canning jars and two-piece caps (lids and screw bands) according to the manufacturer's instructions. Keep the jars and lids hot. (For information on preparing your jars, see Chapter 4.)

2 Wash the asparagus thoroughly and cut it into lengths to fit your pint jars.

3 Place 1 hot pepper, ½ teaspoon dill, ½ teaspoon mustard seed, and 1 clove of garlic in each jar.

4 Firmly pack the asparagus spears vertically into the jars, but don't force them. If necessary, trim the spears to leave ½-inch headspace.

5 In a 8-quart nonreactive pot, combine the vinegar, water, and salt and heat to boiling. Pour the boiling hot solution over the asparagus spears, leaving ½-inch headspace. Release any air bubbles with a nonreactive utensil (refer to Chapter 3), adding more liquid as necessary to maintain the proper headspace. Wipe the jar rims; seal the jars with the two-piece caps, hand-tightening the bands.

6 Process the filled jars in a water-bath canner for 10 minutes from the point of boiling.

7 Remove the jars from the boiling water with a jar lifter. Place them on a clean kitchen towel away from drafts. After the jars cool completely, test the seals (see Chapter 4). If you find jars that haven't sealed, refrigerate them and use them within two weeks.

8 Let these beautiful spears sit for two weeks on the pantry shelf for the flavors to develop.

Per ¼-cup serving: Calories 26 (From fat 5); Fat 1g (Saturated 0g); Cholesterol 0mg; Sodium 358mg; Carbohydrates 4g (Dietary fiber 2g); Protein 2g.

Spiced Pickled Beets

Use beets that are small and tender, not larger than 2 inches in diameter. Purchase beets with the top leaves attached. If the leaves are wilted and quite dark, the beets aren't fresh; continue your search for fresher beets. *Note:* Once canned, these beets are ready for eating.

Preparation time*: 1 hour and 35 minutes*

Processing time: *30 minutes*

Yield: *4 to 5 pints*

4 pounds beets

3 cups thinly sliced white or yellow onions (about 3 medium)

2 ½ cups cider vinegar

1 ½ cups water

2 cups granulated sugar

1 teaspoon kosher or pickling salt

1 tablespoon mustard seed

1 teaspoon whole allspice

1 teaspoon whole cloves

3 cinnamon sticks, broken into pieces

1 Trim your beets, leaving the taproots and 2 inches of the stems. Wash and drain the beets, using a stiff brush to remove any clinging soil. Cover the beets with water in a 5- to 6-quart pot. Bring the water to a boil over high heat and cook the beets until they pierce easily with a fork, about 20 to 30 minutes. Drain the beets. Run cold water over them and remove the skin. Remove the stem and taproot. Slice the beets into ¼-inch-thick slices. Place the beets in a bowl; set them aside.

2 Prepare your canning jars and two-piece caps (lids and screw bands) according to the manufacturer's instructions. Keep the jars and lids hot. (For information on preparing your jars, see Chapter 4.)

3 Place the onions, vinegar, water, sugar, salt, mustard seed, allspice, cloves, and cinnamon sticks in the pot. Bring the mixture to a boil over high heat; reduce the heat and simmer for 5 minutes. Add your beet slices and simmer the mixture to heat the beets, about 3 to 5 minutes. Remove the cinnamon stick pieces.

4 Pack the hot beets and onions into the hot jars and ladle the hot liquid over the beets, leaving ¼-inch headspace. Release any air bubbles (refer to Chapter 3), adding more beets and liquid as necessary to maintain the proper headspace. Wipe the jar rims; seal the jars with the two-piece caps, hand-tightening the bands.

5 Process your jars in a water-bath canner for 30 minutes from the point of boiling.

6 Remove the jars with a jar lifter. Place them on a clean kitchen towel away from drafts. After the jars cool completely, test the seals (see Chapter 4). If you find jars that haven't sealed, refrigerate them and use them within two months.

*****Per ¼-cup serving:*** *Calories 71 (From fat 2); Fat 0g (Saturated 0g); Cholesterol 0mg; Sodium 107mg; Carbohydrates 17g (Dietary fiber 1g); Protein 1g.*

Pickled Brussels Sprouts

Brussels sprouts are an unusual treat when pickled and canned. In fact, you can eat them as a condiment.

Preparation time: 15 minutes

Processing time: 10 minutes

Yield: 6 pints

12 to 14 cups young Brussels sprouts	2 cups distilled vinegar
½ cup canning salt	3 tablespoons dill weed

1 Prepare your canning jars and two-piece caps (lids and screw bands) according to the manufacturer's instructions. Keep the jars and lids hot. (For information on preparing your jars, see Chapter 4.)

2 Wash the Brussels sprouts and remove any outer leaves that have insect damage or brown edges. Cook the sprouts for 5 minutes in boiling water and then dip them immediately into cold water. Drain.

3 Pack the sprouts into your hot pint jars, leaving ½-inch headspace. To each jar, add 1½ teaspoons dill weed. Combine the vinegar and salt and pour this solution over the sprouts, leaving ½-inch headspace. Release any air bubbles with a nonreactive utensil (refer to Chapter 3), adding more liquid as necessary to maintain the proper headspace. Wipe the jar rims; seal the jars with the two-piece caps, hand-tightening the bands.

4 Process the filled jars in a water-bath canner for 10 minutes from the point of boiling.

5 Remove the jars from the boiling water with a jar lifter. Place them on a clean kitchen towel away from drafts. After the jars cool completely, test the seals (see Chapter 4). If you find jars that haven't sealed, refrigerate them and use them within two weeks.

6 Let your pickled Brussels sprouts sit for two weeks so that the flavors can develop.

Per ¼-cup serving: Calories 26 (From fat 2); Fat 0g (Saturated 0g); Cholesterol 0mg; Sodium 475mg; Carbohydrates 6g (Dietary fiber 1g); Protein 1g.

Part III
Pressure Canning

The 5th Wave   By Rich Tennant

"Oh, that gave me such a start! When you're pressure canning game birds, dear, remember to remove the heads."

In this part . . .

The chapters in this part explore the world of pressure canning, the canning method you use to preserve vegetables, meat, poultry, seafood, and other low-acid foods. Preserving low-acid foods requires more care than processing high-acid foods (discussed in Part II), but the rewards are well worth the additional effort. With this part, you'll safely be preserving your favorite low-acid foods in no time.

Chapter 9

Don't Blow Your Top: Pressure Canning

*P*ressure canning is a process for preserving food with a low-acid content by exposing the food to a high temperature (240 degrees) under a specific pressure for a specific period of time in a specific type of pot: the pressure canner.

People who hear someone talking about pressure canning often ask, "Is it safe?" or "Won't the pressure canner explode?" These concerns are certainly valid ones, but rest assured, when you know the right way to use a pressure canner, you can safely process a variety of low-acid foods. While pressure cookers and canners of the past may have once exploded if not closed properly, the new generation of canners and cookers are much lighter in weight and have built-in safety features that release steam if the pressure gets too high. None of your grandparents' pressure cooking equipment had this.

This chapter leads you step by step through the pressure-canning process, including an explanation of pressure canning, what to look for when purchasing a pressure canner, and how to fill your canner and safely process your filled jars.

Only one form of canning — pressure canning — is approved for safely processing low-acid foods. And only one piece of equipment — a pressure canner — is approved for safely processing low-acid foods. Don't allow yourself to think you can use a substitute process or piece of equipment.

Understanding the Fuss about Low-Acid Foods

Low-acid foods contain little natural acid and require more care during the canning process than other types of foods. (If you're a techie, note that low-acid foods are foods with a *pH factor* — that's a measure of acidity in food — higher than 4.6.) Foods in this category include vegetables, meats, poultry, seafood, and combination foods (like soups, meat sauces, and salsas) that contain low-acid and high-acid ingredients. Exceptions to these low-acid foods sometimes include tomatoes, which are really a fruit and can be water-bath canned (although for safety's sake, you still add acid to tomatoes) and vegetables converted to high-acid foods such as sauerkraut, pickles, or pickled vegetables (discussed in Chapter 8).

Low-acid foods require pressure canning to kill microorganisms that are harmful if not destroyed before ingesting the food. Pressure canning at 240 degrees kills the botulism bacteria. If this temperature isn't achieved and the bacteria isn't destroyed, one taste of this spoiled food can kill you. And to make matters worse, these botulism-causing bacteria are odorless, have no taste, and actually thrive in low-acid foods that are in a moist environment and not in contact with air — the exact condition provided in a jar of canned food. Simply boiling food on the stovetop will not kill any botulism and should not be considered a safety step.

In a water-bath canner, the temperature of boiling water never increases above 212 degrees (the boiling point for water). While 212 degrees is fine for water-bath canning high-acid foods, it's *not* sufficient to safely can low-acid foods. For that, you need to superheat your filled jars to a temperature of 240 degrees, which only a pressure canner can achieve. Be sure to use a pressure canner that's approved for pressure canning by the United States Department of Agriculture (USDA).

Choosing Your Pressure Canner

A *pressure canner,* shown in Figure 9-1, is a heavy kettle made for processing home-canned food. It includes a locking, tight-fitting cover that makes the kettle airtight. The purpose of pressure canning is to sterilize the food by destroying hard-to-kill microorganisms, especially the bacteria that cause botulism (see Chapter 3).

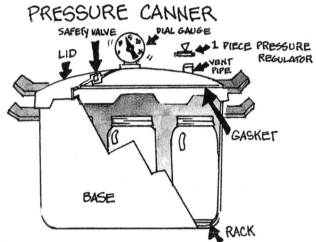

Figure 9-1:
A pressure
canner.

Don't confuse pressure canners with pressure cookers. A pressure canner is used to process and sterilize home-canned, low-acid foods. The purpose of a pressure cooker is to cook food fast. Check out *Pressure Cookers For Dummies*, by Tom Lacalamita (Wiley Publishing, Inc.), for the low down on pressure cooking. Pressure canners and pressure cookers are *not* interchangeable. Pressure cookers are not large enough to hold the jars and the amount of water necessary to can properly. They also do not have pressure gauges that allow you to maintain the constant pressure required.

When shopping for a pressure canner, keep these things in mind:

- **Size:** Pressure canners come in many sizes, holding from 4- to 19(!)-quart jars. For the home canner, however, a pressure canner with a capacity of 16 to 22 quarts is fine. This size holds seven 1-quart jars and permits good air circulation during processing.

- **Price:** The cost of a pressure canner may vary from $100 on the low end to upward of $600. Some reasons for the variance are size, features, and reputation of the manufacturer.

When making your purchasing decision, study your options and estimate how frequently (or infrequently) you plan to pressure-can. You may even consider co-owning a pressure canner with a friend. If you're buying a pressure canner secondhand, take it to your local county extension office to have it checked for proper seal and be sure it's still safe to use.

✔ **Features:** All pressure canners — regardless of features — safely process your filled jars of low-acid food in the same manner because a pressure canner operates in only one way. Each pressure canner has a locking cover, a pressure gauge, and an overpressure plug. Manufacturers of pressure canners, however, slightly vary the same features and add accessories in much the same way car manufacturers add extras to a basic car model.

The following sections explain the different features various pressure canners offer so that you can determine which features you prefer. The type of pressure canner you choose doesn't matter as long as the model is made and approved for processing home-canned foods.

No matter which type or size of pressure canner you choose, the goal is always the same: to superheat and process low-acid food at a high temperature (240 degrees) that destroys microorganisms.

Cover: With a gasket or without

You can find two types of covers for pressure canners: a lock-on cover and a metal-to-metal cover that's attached with wing nuts. The difference is that one has a rubber gasket to ensure an airtight seal; the other one doesn't. For a beginner, a lock-on cover is the easiest and most fail-proof to use.

Lock-on cover

A lock-on cover (see Figure 9-2) usually has a rubber gasket between the cover and the base unit to ensure to the airtight seal. To securely fasten the cover to the pressure canner, rotate the cover on the base to the locked position (matching up the handles or matching arrows or other markings on the unit) or with a type of clamping handle. To ensure that the pressure canner is properly closed, refer to your owner's manual for precise instructions.

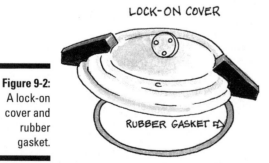

LOCK-ON COVER

RUBBER GASKET

Figure 9-2:
A lock-on cover and rubber gasket.

Over time, the rubber gasket may stretch out of shape or begin to rot and deteriorate (indicated by cracking or splitting). If your gasket is in this condition, don't use your pressure canner until you've replaced the gasket. A gasket in poor condition may prevent the canner from reaching the pressure required to superheat the food and kill microorganisms.

After each use, carefully remove the gasket from the cover. Thoroughly wash the gasket in hot, soapy water and dry it well. After the gasket is completely dry, put it back on the cover so that your pressure canner is always ready for use. Some manufacturers suggest lightly coating the gasket with cooking oil, but check your owner's manual before doing this.

Metal-to-metal cover with wing nuts

A metal-to-metal cover (see Figure 9-3) doesn't require a gasket to create a tight seal; instead, this pressure canner uses wing nuts. To secure a cover with wing nuts, tighten two wing nuts on opposite sides of the canner at the same time by hand (don't use a tool and don't tighten one side at a time). Repeat this process for the remaining wing nuts.

Never tighten one nut at a time because uneven results will occur. If your wing nuts aren't tightened properly, as soon as the pressure starts to rise, water leaks out. You then have to carefully remove the canner from the heat and wait for the pressure to subside before untightening and retightening all over again.

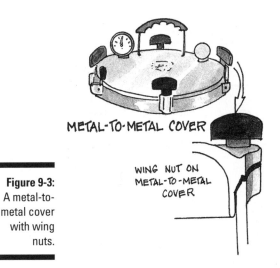

METAL-TO-METAL COVER

WING NUT ON METAL-TO-METAL COVER

Figure 9-3:
A metal-to-metal cover with wing nuts.

Every year, check for nicks and dents in the rim of both the lid and the canner itself. These imperfections will prevent the canner from making a seal.

Gauges

Gauges are located on the top of the pressure canner cover and regulate pressure within the canner. Two types of gauges are available: a weighted gauge and a dial gauge (see Figure 9-4). A dial gauge indicates the pressure of the canner, while a weighted gauge indicates and regulates the pressure of the contents. If you're a beginner, go with the weighted gauge.

Figure 9-4:
The two types of gauges available on pressure canners: A dial gauge and a weighted gauge.

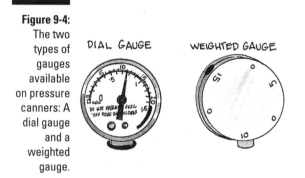

Weighted gauge

A *weighted gauge* is simple and accurate. It's sometimes referred to as an *automatic pressure control* or a *pressure regulator weight.* This gauge allows you to cook without looking: The weighted gauge automatically controls the pressure by jiggling as the canner reaches the correct pressure. When the pressure in the canner is too high, the weighted gauge jiggles faster, and may hiss, as it releases excess steam from the canner.

A weighted gauge has a preset control that needs no service or testing to ensure an accurate pressure measurement. The pressure settings are indicated by three numbers marked on the gauge (refer to Figure 9-4): 5, 10, and 15. The numbers represent the pounds per square inch (psi) of pressure created by the trapped steam from the boiling water in the pressure canner.

The most common pressure used in pressure canning is 10 pounds, but never guess — always refer to your recipe.

Dial or steam pressure gauge

A *dial* or *steam pressure gauge* (refer to Figure 9-4) is a numbered instrument that indicates the pressure in the canner. You have to watch dial gauges carefully to be sure they don't rise too high, and you have to turn the heat up or down to keep the pressure in the right area.

Unlike the weighted gauge that requires no service, you must check this control for accuracy each season or at least once every year of use. To obtain service, refer to your owner's manual for service locations, check with the store where you purchased the canner, or contact your local cooperative extension services (see Chapter 22).

If your annual service shows that your dial gauge is off by 5 or more pounds, replace the gauge. An inaccurate reading may not produce the temperature required to kill all microorganisms. You can have your canner checked for a nominal fee, if not free, at your local hardware store or county extension office.

Vent tube, pipe vent, or petcock

Whatever the name of this feature — *vent tube, pipe vent,* or *petcock* — the function is the same (see Figure 9-5). These terms refer to an opening in the pressure-canner cover for emitting steam. Sometimes the weighted gauge sits on the vent tube.

VENT OR VENT TUBE

BEING CLEANED
WITH A PIPE CLEANER

Figure 9-5:
A vent tube.

To work properly, the vent tube opening cannot be obstructed with food or other matter. Obstructions restrict the optimum pressure and temperature required for your recipe. To check the vent for obstructions, hold it up to the light. If the vent appears to be clogged, insert a piece of wire (or other item suggested in your owner's manual) into the tube. Rinse the vent with hot water. Repeat the procedure if you still see an obstruction.

Overpressure plug

An *overpressure plug* (see Figure 9-6) releases (pops up) if too much pressure exists in your pressure canner due to a blocked vent tube. The overpressure plug is a safety feature that's solely for your protection. If you follow the instruction manual for your pressure-canner operation, chances are this plug will never be used.

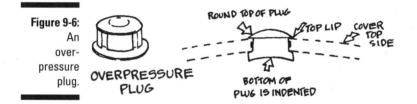

Figure 9-6: An over-pressure plug.

Rack

Your pressure canner should come with a rack. (If the rack is missing, contact the store where you made your purchase.) The perfect rack lies flat in the bottom of your canner and has lots of holes and openings that allow steam to circulate around your filled jars. Figure 9-7 is an example of a canner rack.

Figure 9-7: A rack for holding jars in the bottom of your pressure canner.

Make sure your rack is stable when you place it in the bottom of the canner. A stable rack holds jars in place, thus preventing the jars from tipping, touching other jars, or touching the sides of the canner.

A-Canning You Will Go: Instructions for Successful Pressure Canning

In order to ensure a processed product of high quality, free from microorganisms, be sure to follow each step in this section. Don't omit or modify any part. You may spend a bit more time canning low-acid foods with a pressure canner than you would canning high-acid foods in a water-bath canner, but the end result is worth the extra effort.

In this section, you begin your journey of pressure-canning low-acid foods. Avoid any temptation to omit any step or portion of any step in the process. Each step is important to produce safe, home-canned foods.

If you've never used a pressure canner before, do a trial run with no jars: Heat up the canner and go through the steps of pressurizing and depressurizing to familiarize yourself with the sounds the pressure canner makes as it builds and then releases pressure. You'll hear the steam escaping, the weight gauge shaking, and the ticking of the canner as it heats and cools; if you don't know what to expect, you could misinterpret these noises as scary or wrong.

Step 1: Gearing up

At least a couple of weeks before you want to use it, check your pressure canner and replace any gasket or missing part, have a dial gauge checked professionally, and replace a missing manual. Also count your jars and two-piece caps and examine the jars for nicks or chips, the screw bands for proper fit and corrosion, and the new lids for imperfections and scratches. It's also a good idea to select your recipe, and inventory your pantry for any nonperishable ingredients, adding any needed items to your shopping list. Your goal is to have all the supplies you need and your pressure canner in good working order on the day you're ready to can.

Preparing your pressure canner before the actual canning season means you will not find the store out of supplies and the extension agent too busy to check your gauge in time to begin canning when the produce is ripe.

On the actual canning day, get your tools ready by following these steps:

1. **Assemble your prechecked equipment and utensils.**

   In addition to your pressure canner and the standard canning supplies (jars with two-piece lids), other items can make your canning easier: things like a food scale, extra pans for cooking your veggies and keeping a water reserve on hand, a wide-mouth funnel, and so on. Head to Chapter 2 for a list of canning supplies.

2. **Wash your jars and screw bands in warm, soapy water, rinsing well to remove any soap residue.**

   Double-check for nicks and dents and discard any damaged items.

3. **Place your clean jars and lids in a kettle of hot — not boiling — water until you're ready to fill them.**

   Never boil the lids because the sealant material may be damaged and won't produce a safe vacuum seal.

4. **Ready your canner by filling it with 2 to 3 inches of water and heating the water.**

Always read the manufacturer's instructions for your pressure canner and follow them to the letter.

Also, assemble the other canning items you need. You can find a complete list in Chapter 2.

Step 2: Preparing your food

Always start with food of the highest, freshest quality. Food that's spoiled or bruised doesn't improve in quality during the pressure-canning process! To prepare your food for pressure canning, follow these steps:

1. **Wash all food prior to packing it in the jars or precooking it.**

   For detailed instructions on washing your food, refer to Chapter 3.

2. **Thoroughly cut away all evidence of spoilage or discard any inferior products.**

3. **Prepare the food by precisely following your recipe.**

   Some recipes call for you to fill your jars with raw food; others may want you to precook the food. If you're precooking your low-acid food before filling your jars, don't discard the cooking liquid; use this liquid for filling your jars.

Work in manageable batches. To determine just what a "manageable batch" is, consider how much food fills one canner load at a time. Most recipes are geared for manageable batches, but if you're in doubt, check the yield for the recipe.

Step 3: Filling your jars

Always place your product into hot jars (you keep them hot by leaving them in a kettle of hot water, as explained in the earlier section "Step 1: Gearing up.") To fill your jars, follow these steps:

1. **Remove a jar from the kettle and pack the food into the jar so that the food is snug, yet loose enough for liquid to circulate into the open spaces.**

2. **Ladle boiling water (or the liquid from precooking the vegetables) into the jars, leaving the amount of headspace stated in your recipe.**

   If you're adding cooking liquid, divide the cooking liquid evenly among the jars and finish filling the jars with boiling water, if necessary. That way, if you run short of the cooking liquid, you won't have one jar filled with only boiling water.

3. **Release any air bubbles with a nonmetallic spatula or a tool to free bubbles.**

   If the headspace drops, add additional food and liquid to the jar.

4. **Wipe the jar rims with a clean, damp cloth.**

   Have a few rags handy to be sure you're using a clean one every time.

5. **Place a lid on the jar (seal side down) and secure the lid in place with a screw band.**

   Hand-tighten the band without overtightening it.

Always work quickly, stopping for nothing. Time is of the essence! Your hot foods need to remain hot, your lids seal best if placed on the jars while hot, and your food needs to be processed as quickly as possible to preserve the most flavor and quality.

Step 4: Placing the jars in the canner

Place your filled and closed jars carefully on the rack in the pressure canner, making sure you have the recommended amount of simmering water in the bottom of the canner. Don't crowd the jars or place more jars in the canner than is recommended for your size of pressure canner. Place them so that they're stable, won't tip, and don't touch each other or the side of the canner.

If your recipe makes more jars than your canner can hold, only fill enough jars for one canner load and do the rest in the next batch. Do not fill all the jars and leave a few waiting for the next canner load.

Unlike water-bath canning (see Chapter 4), you can process a second layer of pint or half-pint jars at the same time as long as your canner accommodates the height of the two layers. To build the second layer, place a second rack on top of the first layer of jars. Stagger the second layer of jars so they aren't directly above the bottom layer. This permits proper air circulation for achieving the proper pressure and temperature. After you have a few simple canning sessions successfully under your belt, try this technique to save a little time.

Step 5: Closing and locking the canner

For optimum performance, steam must be allowed to steadily escape from the canner for a specified period. This process is called *exhaustion*. Properly closing and locking your pressure canner ensure that exhaustion can take place. Closely follow your owner's manual when closing and locking the pressure canner. (If not sealed properly, the canner won't build pressure and/or hot water will spit out.)

Step 6: Processing your filled jars

Once your canner lid is locked on, you're ready to beginning processing your filled jars. Follow these steps:

1. **Allow a steady stream of steam to escape from the pressure canner for 10 minutes or the time recommended in your manual.**

2. **Close the vent, bringing the pressure to the amount specified in your recipe.**

   If you live in higher altitudes, see the section "Pressure Canning at Higher Altitudes" for information on how to adjust the pounds of pressure used during processing.

   Processing time starts when your canner reaches the required pressure. The pressure must remain constant for the entire processing time. If your pressure drops at any time during processing, so will your temperature. To remedy this problem, return the pressure to the specified amount by increasing the heat. After your pressure has been regained, start your processing time from the beginning.

3. **After the processing time has passed, turn the heat off and allow the pressure to return to 0.**

   Allowing the pressure to return to 0 may take as long as 30 minutes. Don't disturb the canner; jars that are upset may not seal properly.

Step 7: Releasing the pressure after processing

Approximately 10 minutes after the pressure returns to 0, or at the time stated in the manual, remove the lid, opening the cover away from you and allowing the steam to flow away from you.

We can't emphasize enough the importance of following the instructions in your owner's manual, step by step, for releasing the pressure in the canner after your processing time is concluded. There's no quick-release method for a pressure canner as there is for a pressure cooker. Don't confuse the two!

Running water over your pressure canner to reduce the pressure is a definite no-no. The sudden change in temperature can cause the jars to burst.

Step 8: Removing and cooling the jars

Ten minutes after you release the pressure (Step 7), remove the jars from the pressure canner with a jar lifter. Place them on a clean towel, away from drafts with 1 to 2 inches of space around the jars.

The jars may take as long as 24 hours to completely cool. Don't be tempted to play with the lids or adjust the bands.

As your jars cool, you'll hear a popping noise coming from them, indicating a vacuum seal. You will soon learn to look forward to these tiny pings and dings. My children (Amy's) often give a shout each time they hear one. This canning music means you have successfully saved your summer bounty.

Step 9: Testing the seal and storing your bounty

The final pressure-canning step is to test the seals on your completely cooled jars: Push on the center of the lid. If the lid feels solid and doesn't indent, you've produced a successful seal. If the lid depresses when applying pressure, this jar isn't sealed. Refrigerate any unsealed jars immediately, using the contents within two weeks or the period stated in your recipe.

To store jars, do the following:

1. **Remove the screw bands of the sealed jars.**

2. **Remove any residue by washing the jars, lids, and bands in hot, soapy water; then dry them.**

3. **Label your jars with the content and date of processing.**

4. **Store the jars without the screw bands, in a cool, dark, dry place.**

Disposing of Spoiled Products

Although you may follow all the steps and procedures for pressure canning low-acid foods (see the preceding section), you still have a chance for spoilage. Knowing the signs to look for is part of the food-preservation process.

Here are some visual signs that may indicate a spoiled product:

- A bulging lid or a broken seal
- A lid that shows signs of corrosion
- Food that has oozed or seeped under the lid
- Gassiness, indicated by tiny bubbles moving upward in the jar
- Food that looks mushy, moldy, or cloudy
- Food that gives off an unpleasant or disagreeable odor when the jar is opened
- Spurting liquid from the jar when the seal is broken

Storing your sealed jars without the bands allows you to see any signs of food seepage that indicates a potentially spoiled product.

As discussed in Chapter 3, botulism poisoning can be fatal. Because botulism spores have no odor and can't be seen, you can't always tell which jars are tainted. *If you suspect that a jar of food is spoiled, never, never, never taste it.* Instead, dispose of the food responsibly.

When you need to dispose of spoiled low-acid foods, use one of the two disposal methods described in the following sections. The first method is for sealed jars and second is for jars with broken seals.

If your jar is still sealed

If the jar has the seal intact, you can simply place your container in a garbage bag, tie it tightly, and discard it in the trash. This keeps the product from coming in contact with any human or animal and eliminates the transfer of bacteria. Be sure to thoroughly wash your hands and any surface that may have come in contact with spoiled food or its juices.

If your jar has a broken seal

If you see signs that the seal is broken or not tight, place the jar, the lid, the screw band, and the contents of the jar in a deep cooking pot. Cover the items with 1 to 2 inches of water, taking care not to splash any of the contents outside of the pot (this can cause cross-contamination with other foods in your household).

Cover the pot with a tight-fitting cover. Bring the contents to a boil. Keep the contents boiling for 30 minutes. Turn off the heat and allow the contents to cool while remaining covered. Discard the contents in a sealed container in the trash or bury them deeply in the soil.

Never pour the contents into a water source, a sink or garbage disposal, or down the toilet, because the contents may come into contact with humans or animals through a water-reclamation process.

Using a solution made up of one part household chlorine bleach to four parts *tepid* (lukewarm) water, thoroughly wash all equipment, working surfaces, clothing, and body parts that may have come in contact with the jar or spoiled food. You may also add dishwashing soap. Dispose of the jar, the lid and screw band, and any sponges or dishcloths used in any phase of this process by wrapping the items in a trash bag, sealing the bag, and placing it in the trash.

Pressure Canning at Higher Altitudes

If you're canning at an elevation higher than 1,000 feet above sea level, adjust the pounds of pressure used during processing, according to Table 9-1. Your pressure-canner processing time will remain the same.

Table 9-1 **High-Altitude Processing Times for Pressure Canning**

Altitude	Process at This Pressure
2,000–3,000	11½ pounds
3,000–4,000	12 pounds
4,000–5,000	12½ pounds
5,000–6,000	13 pounds
6,000–7,000	13½ pounds
7,000–8,000	14 pounds
8,000–9,000	14½ pounds
9,000–10,000	15 pounds

If you don't know your altitude level, you can get this information by contacting your public library, a local college, or the cooperative extension service in your county or state. Or go to `http://national4-hheadquarters.gov/Extension/index.html`. Click on your state on the map and follow the instructions on your state's Web site.

Chapter 10

Preserving the Harvest:
Just Vegetables

- -

In This Chapter

▶ Organizing your vegetables

▶ Filling your jars: raw packing versus hot packing

▶ Processing vegetables perfectly

▶ Preparing nutritious meals from your canned vegetables

- -

Don't you just love the time of year when you're starting your garden — preparing the soil, sowing seeds, pulling weeds, looking for pests, and asking the gardening gods for perfect weather and an abundant harvest? Then, after months of hard work and dirty fingernails, you're rewarded with fresh vegetables. At first, your garden produces enough each day for one or two meals, and then the explosion starts. Tomatoes, zucchini, and beans, to name a few, abound. You wonder, "How can just a few plants produce so many vegetables?" You're proud to share your bounty with friends, neighbors, and coworkers, but there's a limit to how much you can give away!

Now, reality sets in. You have to do something with this harvest or it will go to waste! It's time to get out your pressure canner, check your equipment, and get busy pressure canning. You must act quickly if you plan to preserve these vegetables for use in the winter and spring.

This chapter gives you basic information on selecting and preparing your vegetables, understanding which packing method (raw or hot) works best, knowing the correct pressure and processing times, and using the proper jar sizes for your vegetables.

Selecting Your Vegetables

When choosing your vegetables, be picky. The quality of your final product is affected by the quality of the food you start with. You can find specific guidelines of what to look for for each particular vegetable in the "Pressure Canning Vegetables" section of this chapter.

Picking the perfect produce

Whether harvesting your vegetables from the garden or shopping at a farmer's market or your local supermarket, select vegetables that are free of bruises and imperfections. These marks could encourage the growth of bacteria in your food. Follow this basic rule for evaluating damage on vegetables for canning: If you won't eat that portion of the vegetable, don't buy it and can it.

The key to keeping all this wonderful, perfect freshness? Process the vegetables the day of harvesting or purchasing — the sooner the better. If you need to wait a day, store the items in your refrigerator to preserve the quality and prevent deterioration of your food. Don't make your vegetables wait longer than one day! For more information on how to successfully process your canned vegetables, head to the section "Processing Tips for Successful Results."

Even if you don't have a garden (or access to one), you can find vegetables of high quality at your local farmer's market or supermarket. Purchasing vegetables in season (when they're abundant) is usually the best time to find the best pricing. Look for vegetables that are locally grown — they'll taste fresher and won't be covered with wax that prolongs the life of veggies.

Vegetables not recommended for pressure canning

Some vegetables shouldn't be preserved by pressure canning because the food may discolor, produce a stronger flavor when canned, or just lose its look (meaning it disintegrates or falls apart when placed under high heat and high pressure). Other methods, such as pickling (see Chapter 8) or freezing (see Chapter 13), may be better preserving choices for these foods. Table 10-1 lists some vegetables you may be tempted to pressure-can but that will preserve better in other ways.

Table 10-1	Vegetables Not Recommended for Pressure Canning
Vegetable	*Suggested Preservation Method*
Broccoli	Freezing
Brussels sprouts	Freezing
Cabbage	Pickling (to make sauerkraut)
Cauliflower	Pickling
Cucumbers	Pickling
Eggplant	Pickling
Mushrooms (For safety, use ones that are commercially grown; don't go out and pick some yourself.)	Pickling
Parsnips	Pickling
Rutabagas	Pickling
Turnips	Pickling

Prepping Your Veggies

You can prepare your clean vegetables for filling your jars in two ways: raw pack or hot pack. Not all vegetables are suited for both methods. Follow your recipe instructions or check out the "Pressure Canning Vegetables" section in this chapter.

Cleaning your vegetables

Properly cleaning your vegetables is important to your finished product (refer to Chapter 3 for more on cleaning vegetables). The method and amount of cleaning required is determined by where the vegetables were grown: above the ground (like beans or squash) or in the ground (like carrots or beets).

- **Vegetables growing above the ground:** These vegetables usually have a thinner, more tender skin than vegetables grown in the ground. Remove any stems and leaves. Run water over them, gently rub the skin with your fingers and remove any dirt. Shake off the excess water and place your food on clean kitchen or paper towels.

✓ **Vegetables growing in the ground:** Root vegetables, such as carrots and beets, may require soaking to loosen any clinging soil. After first rinsing the vegetables, immerse them in a basin of cool water. Using a stiff brush (a new toothbrush works well), scrub the surface of the vegetables, removing any clinging soil. Rinse thoroughly with running water, placing the vegetables on clean kitchen or paper towels to drain.

Raw packing versus hot packing

Raw packing and hot packing foods refers to the way the food is treated before it is placed in the jars. In raw packing, you don't cook the food prior to processing. In hot packing, you do. The following sections go into more details on which method is preferable when you're canning vegetables.

Packing food raw or hot doesn't change your processing time. Reaching the required pressure in your canner, usually 10 pounds, takes the same amount of time, regardless of the temperature of your raw- or hot-packed jars.

Raw (cold packing)

The *raw packing* (also called cold packing) method uses raw, unheated vegetables for filling your prepared jars. Filling the jars with raw vegetables keeps them firm without being crushed during processing. Refer to your recipe instructions to decide whether to remove the skin or cut the vegetables into pieces.

Disadvantages of using raw vegetables include the following:

✓ **Floating food:** During the pressure-canning process, air is removed from the vegetable fiber, causing the food to shrink. With more room in the jars, the vegetables have room to float toward the top of the jar (this is called *floating food*). Floating food doesn't affect the quality of your final product, but it may be unattractive.

✓ **Discoloring:** *Discoloring* occurs when the food comes in contact with air in the jar, causing a color change in your food after two or three months of storage. The flavor of your product is not affected, but the change in color in a portion of the food may appear odd.

To fill your jars using a raw packing method, follow these instructions:

1. **Wash your vegetables.**

2. **Prepare the hot liquid (refer to your recipe) for filling your jars.**

3. **Fill the hot, prepared jars with your raw vegetables.**

4. **Add the hot liquid and canning salt, if required.**

5. **Release any air bubbles with a nonreactive tool (refer to Chapter 3).**

   If the headspace in your jar drops, add additional food and liquid to maintain the headspace stated in your recipe.

6. **Wipe the jar rims; add the two-piece caps, and process the filled jars in a pressure canner (see Chapter 5).**

Hot packing

When you hot pack, you precook or heat your vegetables prior to placing them in your prepared canning jars. It's the preferred method for the majority of vegetables, particularly firm ones, such as carrots and beets. Using precooked vegetables improves the shelf life of the processed food by increasing the vacuum created in the jar during the pressure-canning period.

Precooking your vegetables in a boiling liquid, usually water, preshrinks the food and makes it more pliable, which allows you to pack more food into your jars. This results in using fewer jars. The method is a simple one:

1. **Wash your vegetables.**

2. **Heat your liquid to a boil in a large pot and add the vegetables, precooking them as directed in your recipe.**

3. **Immediately fill your prepared jars with the hot vegetables, followed with the hot cooking liquid.**

4. **Release any air bubbles with a nonreactive tool.**

   If the headspace in your jar drops, add additional food and liquid to maintain the headspace stated in your recipe.

5. **Wipe the jar rims, add the two-piece caps, and process the filled jars in a pressure canner (see Chapter 9).**

Processing Tips for Successful Results

Because vegetables are low-acid foods, you must use the pressure-canning method outlined in Chapter 9. In addition to the pressure-canner-processing steps there, use these tips for producing a product of high quality that's safe for eating.

- ✔ **Get your supplies ready ahead of time.** About one week before you begin pressure canning, assemble and check your equipment (see Chapter 9). Locate your recipe and review the ingredients you need to have on hand. Stopping at any stage of food preparing or processing adversely affects the quality of your final product.

  During the canning season (summer), canning supplies may be in short supply and challenging to find. Inventorying your products early and purchasing missing items keeps you ready to can on a moment's notice. Jars, lids, and screw bands don't have a shelf life or expiration date.

- ✔ **If you add salt, use pickling or canning salt, which doesn't have preservatives, to eliminate cloudiness in the liquid.**

  Using or not using salt in your vegetables is a personal preference. Add ½ teaspoon to each pint jar and 1 teaspoon to each quart jar before adding the hot liquid.

- ✔ **Cover the vegetables with liquid, allowing the proper headspace.** This prevents discoloration and spoilage. Head to Chapter 3 for detailed information on why headspace is important.

- ✔ **Release air bubbles.** Releasing all trapped air bubbles between the food pieces prevents a decrease in the liquid level of your final product, keeping the correct air space in the jar. After releasing air bubbles, you may need to add additional food or liquid to the jar. Go to Chapter 3 for more information how to release air bubbles.

- ✔ **Be ready to process your jars immediately after filling them and process them exactly as the recipe indicates.** This decreases the opportunity for microorganisms to reenter the jars.

- ✔ **Cool your jars.** Let your jars cool naturally. This may take as long as 24 hours.

Pressure Canning Vegetables

This section offers instructions and guidelines for pressure canning some of the more common fresh vegetables. Included are tips for selecting your vegetables, determining the approximate amounts of fresh vegetables for yielding 1 quart of a finished product, and which method is preferred.

Before you begin, take a few minutes to acquaint yourself with the steps for pressure-canner processing in Chapter 9. Always check your recipe to ensure you're processing your food for the correct time, pressure, and jar size. Also keep in mind the following:

- ✔ When canning at altitudes over 1,000 feet above sea level, refer to the altitude chart in Chapter 9 for pressure adjustments.

- ✔ If it's safe to use either quart jars or pint jars for your vegetables, the correct processing time for each size is listed. Quarts typically take longer to process than pints because there's a larger amount of food to heat to properly destroy all microorganisms. If only one size jar is listed, that food may not be suitable for canning in the alternative-size jar due to the thickness of the finished product.

- ✔ Use only one size jar (pints or quarts) for each batch of food. This allows you to complete the correct processing time required to evenly heat the jars and destroy microorganisms.

- ✔ When using low-acid, pressure-canned vegetables, always boil your food for 15 minutes *before you taste the food.* For altitudes over 1,000 feet above sea level, extend the boiling period 1 minute for each increase of 1,000 feet.

Asparagus

Select firm, bright-green stalks with tightly closed tips. Stalks with small diameters indicate a young, tender vegetable. Cut stalks into 1-inch pieces or can them whole, placing the tips of the stalks toward the top of the jar (be sure to trim them from the bottom to maintain the headspace indicated in the recipe).

Canned Asparagus

Canning asparagus is a great way to preserve this delicate vegetable. With only one short season, it is usually a special treat or pricy delicacy during the rest of the year. Keeping plenty on hand will ensure that your family can enjoy this treat any time it wants. In Chapter 8, you can find a recipe for Pickled Asparagus.

***Preparation time**: 15 minutes*

***Processing time:** Pints, 30 minutes; quarts, 40 minutes*

***Pressure level:** 10 pounds*

***Yield:** 14 pints or 7 quarts*

24 pounds fresh, young asparagus　　　　　　　*Canning salt*
Boiling water

1 Prepare your canning jars and two-piece caps (lids and screw bands) according to the manufacturer's instructions. Keep the jars and lids hot. (For detailed instructions on preparing your jars, see Chapter 4.)

2 Wash the asparagus spears. Cut them into 1-inch pieces. In a 12-quart pot, bring water to a boil. Heat the asparagus pieces in the boiling water for 2 to 3 minutes, until the spears are bright green but still firm inside. Do not drain.

3 Loosely pack the cut spears into jars (don't press them down). Pour the boiling cooking liquid over the pieces, leaving 1-inch headspace. Add ½ teaspoon salt to each pint jar or 1 teaspoon salt to each quart jar. Release any air bubbles with a nonreactive utensil, adding more liquid as necessary to maintain the proper headspace (refer to Chapter 3). Wipe the jar rims; seal the jars with the two-piece caps, hand-tightening the bands.

4 Process the filled jars in a pressure canner at 10 pounds pressure for 30 minutes (pints) or 40 minutes (quarts). When the processing time is done, allow the pressure to return to 0, wait an additional 10 minutes, and then carefully open the canner lid. (Head to Chapter 9 for detailed processing instructions for pressure canning.)

5 Remove the jars from the canner with a jar lifter. Place them on a clean kitchen towel away from drafts. After the jars cool completely, test the seals (refer to Chapter 4). If you find jars that haven't sealed, refrigerate them and use them within two weeks. Prior to eating or tasting, boil the food for 15 minutes.

*Per ½-**cup serving:** Calories 23 (From fat 3); Fat 0g (Saturated0); Cholesterol 0mg; Sodium 301mg; Carbohydrates 4g (Dietary fiber 2g); Protein 3g.*

Beans

You can put up either fresh or dried beans. Regardless which type of beans you use, be sure to thoroughly examine them:

- ✔ **Fresh beans:** Select only those that are free from bruising, rust, or mushiness; discard any beans fitting this description.

- ✔ **Dried beans:** Examine dried beans for any nonbean material, such as stems or stones.

Green (pole or bush), string, Italian, or wax

When you can green, string, Italian, or wax beans, select ones that are tender and small. Remove the ends and strings from the beans, as shown in Figure 10-1. Can them whole or cut them into 1- to 2-inch pieces.

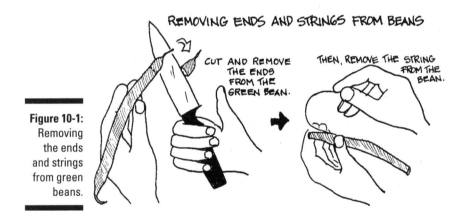

REMOVING ENDS AND STRINGS FROM BEANS

CUT AND REMOVE THE ENDS FROM THE GREEN BEAN.

THEN, REMOVE THE STRING FROM THE BEAN.

Figure 10-1:
Removing the ends and strings from green beans.

Canned Fresh Green Beans

Garden fresh green beans are a staple for any pantry. This is a great first recipe for the beginning pressure canner. Although this recipe specifically uses green beans, all colors of beans — green, yellow or purple — work equally well.

Preparation time: *15 minutes*

Processing time: *Pints, 20 minutes; quarts, 25 minutes*

Pressure level: *10 pounds*

Yield*: 16 pints or 8 quarts*

4 pounds fresh green beans

Boiling water

Canning salt

1 Prepare your canning jars and two-piece caps (lids and screw bands) according to the manufacturer's instructions. Keep the jars and lids hot. (For information on preparing your jars, see Chapter 4.)

2 In an 8-quart pot, bring 2 quarts of water to a boil. While water is boiling, trim off the ends of the beans and cut them into 2-inch pieces.

3 Tightly pack the cut beans into the prepared jars. Pour the boiling water over the beans, leaving 1-inch headspace. Add ½ teaspoon salt to each pint jar or 1 teaspoon salt to each quart jar. Release any air bubbles with a nonreactive utensil, adding more water as necessary to maintain the proper headspace (refer to Chapter 3). Wipe the jar rims; seal the jars with the two-piece caps, hand-tightening the bands.

4 Process the filled jars in a pressure canner at 10 pounds pressure for 20 minutes (pints) or 25 minutes (quarts). Allow the pressure to return to 0, wait an additional 10 minutes, and then carefully open the canner lid. (Head to Chapter 9 for detailed processing instructions for pressure canning.)

5 Remove the jars from the canner with a jar lifter. Place them on a clean kitchen towel away from drafts. After the jars cool completely, test the seals (refer to Chapter 4). If you find jars that haven't sealed, refrigerate them and use them within two weeks. Prior to eating or tasting, boil the food for 15 minutes.

*Per ½-**cup serving**: Calories 10 (From fat 1); Fat 0g (Saturated 0g); Cholesterol 0mg; Sodium 292mg; Carbohydrates 2g (Dietary fiber 1g); Protein 1g.*

Dried beans (kidney, navy, pinto, split peas, and so on)

Rinse the dried beans before you soak them to remove any dust or dirt particles: Do this by placing the beans in a colander and running cold water over them while stirring them with your hands or a spoon.

Canned Dried Beans

Dried beans are a great way to add protein and richness to many dishes. Beans are inexpensive and work well blended as a thickener, a recipe-extender, and a plain stick-to-your-ribs addition to any meal. Add rice to beans and you have complete protein. Delicious! Dried beans suitable for canning include peas, soy, lima, and so on.

Preparation time: *15 minutes plus 12 hours soaking time*

Processing time: *Pints, 40 minutes; quarts, 50 minutes*

Pressure level: *10 pounds*

Yield: *14 pints or 7 quarts*

3 pounds dried beans (or dried peas)   Canning salt

1 Rinse the beans in a colander and remove any stones or broken bean pieces. Place them in a 12-quart pot and cover them with cold water. Let the beans soak at least 12 hours (set them to soaking overnight).

2 Prepare your canning jars and two-piece caps (lids and screw bands) according to the manufacturer's instructions. Keep the jars and lids hot. (For information on preparing your jars, see Chapter 4.)

3 Pour out the soaking water and add more cold water to cover the beans. Bring the covered beans to a boil and allow them to boil for 30 minutes, or until they're tender. Do not drain.

4 Using a slotted spoon, loosely pack the hot beans into your canning jars, leaving 1-inch headspace. Pour the cooking liquid over the beans, maintaining the proper headspace. Add ½ teaspoon salt to each pint jar or 1 teaspoon salt to each quart jar. Release any air bubbles with a nonreactive utensil, adding more liquid as necessary to maintain the proper headspace (refer to Chapter 3). Wipe the jar rims; seal the jars with the two-piece caps, hand-tightening the bands.

5 Process the filled jars in a pressure canner at 10 pounds pressure for 40 minutes (pints) or 50 minutes (quarts). Allow the pressure to return to 0, wait an additional 10 minutes, and then carefully open the canner lid. (Head to Chapter 9 for detailed processing instructions for pressure canning.)

6 Remove the jars from the canner with a jar lifter. Place them on a clean kitchen towel away from drafts. After the jars cool completely, test the seals (refer to Chapter 4). If you find jars that haven't sealed, refrigerate them and use them within two weeks. Prior to eating or tasting, boil the food for 15 minutes.

Per ½-cup serving: Calories 71 (From fat 2); Fat 0g (Saturated 0g); Cholesterol 0mg; Sodium 292mg; Carbohydrates 13g (Dietary fiber 4g); Protein 5g.

Beets

Select beets with a deep red color. A beet with a diameter of 1 to 2 inches is the most desirable size for pressure canning. Larger-size beets are best pickled (head to Chapter 8 for information on pickling and a Spiced Pickled Beets recipe).

Canned Beets

To preserve the bright, red color of the beet, add 1 tablespoon of vinegar (with an acidity of 5 percent) to each quart of liquid before sealing the jars.

Preparation time: *15 minutes*

Processing time: *Pints, 30 minutes; quarts, 35 minutes*

Pressure level: *10 pounds*

Yield: 14 pints or 7 quarts

21 pounds beets without tops   *Canning salt*

1 Prepare your canning jars and two-piece caps (lids and screw bands) according to the manufacturer's instructions. Keep the jars and lids hot. (For information on preparing your jars, see Chapter 4.)

2 Scrub your beets clean of dirt and remove the tap roots (see Figure 10-2). Place the cleaned beets in a 12-quart pot and cover them with water. Boil the beets for 15 to 20 minutes. When beets are cool enough to handle, the skins will peel off easily. Remove them from the water and peel. Trim the remaining root and stem. Leave small beets whole, and cut larger beets in half for a better fit in the jar. Reserve the cooking liquid.

3 Pack the beets into your prepared jars. Pour the cooking liquid over the beets, leaving 1-inch headspace. Add ½ teaspoon salt to each pint jar or 1 teaspoon salt to each quart jar. Release any air bubbles with a nonreactive utensil, adding more liquid as necessary to maintain the proper headspace (see Chapter 3). Wipe the jar rims; seal the jars with the two-piece caps, hand-tightening the bands.

4 Process the filled jars in a pressure canner at 10 pounds pressure for 30 minutes (pints) or 35 minutes (quarts). Allow the pressure to return to 0, wait an additional 10 minutes, and then carefully open the canner lid. (Head to Chapter 9 for detailed processing instructions for pressure canning.)

5 Remove the jars from the canner with a jar lifter. Place them on a clean kitchen towel away from drafts. After the jars cool completely, test the seals (refer to Chapter 4). If you find jars that haven't sealed, refrigerate them and use them within two weeks. Prior to eating or tasting, boil the food for 15 minutes.

Per ½-cup serving: Calories 72 (From fat 3); Fat 0g (Saturated 0g); Cholesterol 0mg; Sodium 416mg; Carbohydrates 0g (Dietary fiber 0g); Protein 0g.

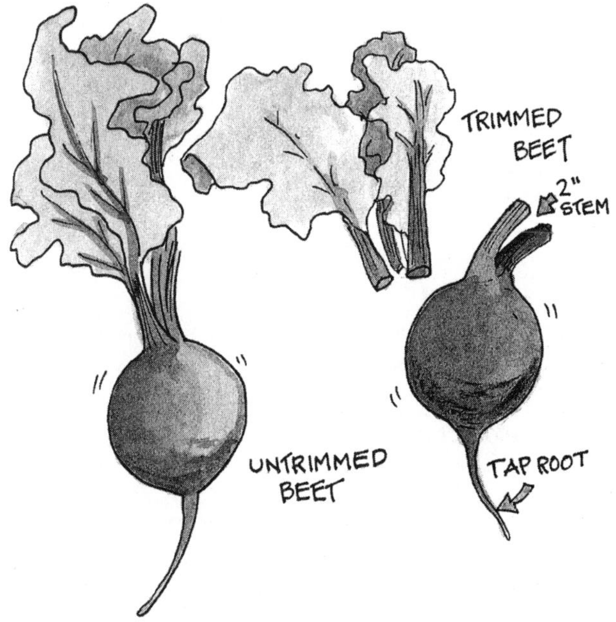

TRIMMED
BEET

2"
STEM

UNTRIMMED
BEET

TAP ROOT

Figure 10-2:
A trimmed
beet
ready for
precooking.

Bell peppers (green, red, orange, yellow)

Sweet, firm bell peppers produce the best results. With so many beautiful colored peppers available, a jar of canned bell peppers could turn into a lovely gift.

Because of the extremely low acid level in this vegetable, you must adjust the acidity level of the bell peppers by adding bottled lemon juice. Use only pint or half-pint jars for this extremely low-acid vegetable.

To peel peppers easily, heat them in a 400-degree oven for 6 to 8 minutes, or until the skin blisters. Then cover them with a damp cloth and let them cool. Voilá! You can now easily remove skins with a knife or simply by rubbing them with your hands as you run cool water over the pepper.

Canned Bell Peppers

Canned peppers come out tender and full of flavor. Heat them up with sautéed onions and hot sausage.

Preparation time: *15 minutes*

Processing time: *Half-pints, 35 minutes; pints, 40 minutes*

Pressure level: *10 pounds*

Yield: *10 half-pints or 5 pints*

5 pounds sweet peppers	*Canning salt*
Boiling water	*Lemon juice*

1 Prepare your canning jars and two-piece caps (lids and screw bands) according to the manufacturer's instructions. Keep the jars and lids hot. (For information on preparing your jars, see Chapter 4.)

2 Wash the peppers and cut them into quarters and remove the stem and seeds. Meanwhile bring 2 quarts of water to a boil.

3 Pack flattened peppers firmly into jars. Pour the boiling water over the peppers, leaving 1-inch headspace. Add ½ tablespoon lemon juice and ¼ teaspoon salt to each half-pint jar or 1 tablespoon lemon juice and ½ teaspoon salt to each pint jar. Release any air bubbles with a nonreactive utensil, adding more water as necessary to maintain the proper headspace (see Chapter 3). Wipe the jar rims; seal the jars with the two-piece caps, hand-tightening the bands.

4 Process the filled jars in a pressure canner at 10 pounds pressure for 35 minutes (half-pints) or 40 minutes (pints). Allow the pressure to return to 0, wait an additional 10 minutes, and then carefully open the canner lid. (Head to Chapter 9 for detailed processing instructions for pressure canning.)

5 Remove the jars from the canner with a jar lifter. Place them on a clean kitchen towel away from drafts. After the jars cool completely, test the seals (refer to Chapter 4). If you find jars that haven't sealed, refrigerate them and use them within two weeks. Prior to eating or tasting, boil the food for 15 minutes.

Per ½-cup serving: Calories 32 (From fat 2); Fat 0g (Saturated 0g); Cholesterol 0mg; Sodium 584mg; Carbohydrates 8g (Dietary fiber 2g); Protein 1g.

Carrots

For canning, choose carrots with a diameter of 1 to 1½ inches. Canned carrots make a favorite side dish even faster. Once reheated, add brown sugar and butter for a sweet treat.

Canned Carrots

Carrots are an inexpensive vegetable at farmer's markets during their season, and canning is an excellent way to preserve them. They keep all of their sweet flavor and the texture remains very nice.

Preparation time: 15 minutes

Processing time: Pints, 25 minutes; quarts, 35 minutes

Pressure level: 10 pounds

Yield: 6 pints or 3 quarts

12 pounds of carrots, peeled and without tops   *Canning salt*

1 Prepare your canning jars and two-piece caps (lids and screw bands) according to the manufacturer's instructions. Keep the jars and lids hot. (For information on preparing your jars, see Chapter 4.)

2 Rinse and scrub the carrots with a brush to remove any dirt. Alternatively, remove the skin with a vegetable peeler. Remove the carrot tops. Cut the carrots into ¼-inch slices or dice the carrots, being sure that all the diced pieces are approximately the same size.

3 Place the sliced or diced carrots in a 12-quart pot and cover them with water. Bring them to a boil. Reduce heat to medium and allow the carrots to simmer for 5 minutes, or until they're still slightly firm in the center but tender on the outside. Do not drain.

4 Pack the hot carrots into your prepared jars. Pour the cooking liquid over them, leaving 1-inch headspace. Add ½ teaspoon salt to each pint jar or 1 teaspoon salt to each quart jar. Release any air bubbles with a nonreactive utensil, adding more liquid as necessary to maintain the proper headspace (see Chapter 3). Wipe the jar rims; seal the jars with the two-piece caps, hand-tightening the bands.

5 Process the filled jars in a pressure canner at 10 pounds pressure for 25 minutes (pints) or 35 minutes (quarts). Allow the pressure to return to 0, wait an additional 10 minutes, and then carefully open the canner lid. (Head to Chapter 9 for detailed processing instructions for pressure canning.)

6 Remove the jars from the canner with a jar lifter. Place them on a clean kitchen towel away from drafts. After the jars cool completely, test the seals (refer to Chapter 4). If you find jars that haven't sealed, refrigerate them and use them within two weeks. Prior to eating or tasting, boil the food for 10 minutes.

Per ½-cup serving: Calories 94 (From fat 3); Fat 0g (Saturated 0g); Cholesterol 0mg; Sodium 424mg; Carbohydrates 22g (Dietary fiber 7g); Protein 2g.

Corn

Starting with corn that has the husks on and the silk attached allows you to assess the freshness of the corn. Choose ears with brightly colored husks that are free of spots and moisture; silks should be golden, not matted or brown.

Here's a surefire way to select corn that is sure to be juicy and tender (see Figure 10-3): Slightly peel back the husk to check for any pests. If all is clear (no bugs or mold), use your thumbnail to depress a kernel about an inch below the top of the corn. If the ear has adequate moisture, liquid will squirt out. Buy this ear! If no spitting occurs, select another ear and repeat the test.

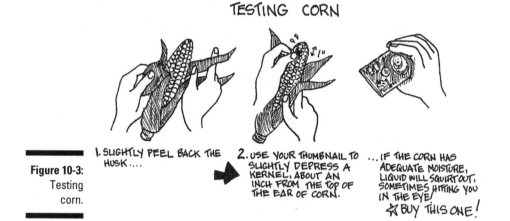

TESTING CORN

1. SLIGHTLY PEEL BACK THE HUSK....

2. USE YOUR THUMBNAIL TO SLIGHTLY DEPRESS A KERNEL, ABOUT AN INCH FROM THE TOP OF THE EAR OF CORN.

...IF THE CORN HAS ADEQUATE MOISTURE, LIQUID WILL SQUIRT OUT, SOMETIMES HITTING YOU IN THE EYE! ☆ BUY THIS ONE!

Figure 10-3: Testing corn.

Canned Corn

Canned corn is a staple in most people's homes. Many don't realize how easy it is to store this tasty vegetable.

Preparation time: *15 minutes*

Processing time: *Pints, 55 minutes; quarts, 1 hour 25 minutes*

Pressure level: *10 pounds*

Yield*: 12 pints or 6 quarts*

24 pounds fresh corn on the cob　　　　　　　　*Canning salt*

Boiling water

1 Prepare your canning jars and two-piece caps (lids and screw bands) according to the manufacturer's instructions. Keep the jars and lids hot. (For information on preparing your jars, see Chapter 4.)

2 Remove the husk and silk from the corn. Using a sharp knife, slice the corn from the cob, measuring the corn as you go so that you know how many total pints or quarts of corn kernels you have. Meanwhile, bring 1 gallon of water to a boil in an 8-quart pot (you'll use this as a reserve).

3 Place the corn in a 12-quart pot. For each pint of corn, add 1 cup of boiling water; for each quart of corn, add 2 cups of boiling water. Place the pot over medium-high heat and bring to a simmer. Then reduce heat to medium and allow the corn to simmer for 5 minutes.

4 Ladle the corn into your prepared jars and pour additional boiling water over it if necessary, leaving 1-inch headspace. Add 1 teaspoon salt to each quart jar or ½ teaspoon salt to each pint jar. Release any air bubbles with a nonreactive utensil, adding more water as necessary to maintainthe proper headspace (see Chapter 3). Wipe the jar rims; seal the jars with the two-piece caps, hand-tightening the bands.

5 Process the filled jars in a pressure canner at 10 pounds pressure for 55 minutes (pints) or 1 hour 25 minutes (quarts). Allow the pressure to return to 0, wait an additional 10 minutes, and then carefully open the canner lid. (Head to Chapter 9 for detailed processing instructions for pressure canning.)

6 Remove the jars from the canner with a jar lifter. Place them on a clean kitchen towel away from drafts. After the jars cool completely, test the seals (refer to Chapter 4). If you find jars that haven't sealed, refrigerate them and use them within two weeks. Prior to eating or tasting, boil the food for 15 minutes.

Per ½-up serving: Calories 136 (From fat 15); Fat 2g (Saturated 0g); Cholesterol 0mg; Sodium 312mg; Carbohydrates 32g (Dietary fiber 3g); Protein 4g.

Canned Creamed Corn

Creamed corn doesn't actually contain cream. Its creaminess comes from the naturally sweet juice, or *milk,* of the kernel. To obtain the creaminess, simply cut off the kernels and run your knife against the cob a second time, even closer to release the milk. Creamed corn is a great base for soups and makes a classic comfort food. This recipe uses pints (quarts aren't recommended).

***Preparation time**: 20 minutes*

***Processing time:** Pints, 1 hour 35 minutes*

***Pressure level:** 10 pounds*

***Yield:** 9 pints*

20 pounds corn

Boiling water

Canning salt

1 Prepare your canning jars and two-piece caps (lids and screw bands) according to the manufacturer's instructions. Keep the jars and lids hot. (For information on preparing your jars, see Chapter 4.)

2 In a 12-quart pot, bring 2 gallons of water to a boil. Remove the husk and silk from the corn. Blanch the corn on the cob for 4 minutes in the boiling water. Allow the corn to cool enough to handle. Slice the corn kernels from cob with a sharp knife. Then run the knife blade along the ear again to remove the extra juice or milk. Measure the corn as you go so that you know how many pints of corn and corn milk you have.

3 Place the corn and corn milk in a 12-quart pot. For each pint of corn and corn milk, add 2 cups of water. Heat the corn to boiling.

4 Using a canning funnel, pour the corn and corn milk mixture into your prepared jars, leaving 1-inch headspace. Add ½ teaspoon salt to each jar. If necessary to attain the required headspace, add boiling water to the jars. Release any air bubbles with a nonreactive utensil, adding more water as necessary to maintain the proper headspace (see Chapter 3). Wipe the jar rims; seal the jars with the two-piece caps, hand-tightening the bands.

5 Process the filled pint jars in a pressure canner at 10 pounds pressure for 1 hour 35 minutes. Allow the pressure to return to 0, wait an additional 10 minutes, and then carefully open the canner lid. (Head to Chapter 9 for detailed processing instructions for pressure canning.)

6 Remove the jars from the canner with a jar lifter. Place them on a clean kitchen towel or paper towels away from drafts. After the jars cool completely, test the seals (refer to Chapter 4). If you find jars that haven't sealed, refrigerate them and use them within 2 weeks. Prior to eating or tasting, boil the food for 10 minutes.

Per ½-cup serving: Calories 151 (From fat 16); Fat 2g (Saturated 0g); Cholesterol 0mg; Sodium 605mg; Carbohydrates 35g (Dietary fiber 4g); Protein 5g.

Greens

Greens is a catchall term that refers to the green, leafy portions of a variety of plants that, when cooked (traditionally simmered in water with some type of pork fat), creates a delicious addition to many meals. You can use any combination: beets, collard, kale, mustard, spinach, Swiss chard, and turnip.

Select tender stems and leaves to produce a superior product after cooking and pressure canning. Large, older stems and leaves tend to produce a strong-tasting or stringy product.

Corn, glorious corn!

Corn is a wonderful vegetable to get to know. It has a traceable history of nearly 7,000 years! From the Aztecs to Native Americans to the modern world of today, corn has a multi-faceted place in our society.

In addition to eating corn one the cob or off, here are a variety of other traditional dishes made from corn:

- **Spoon bread:** A pudding-like bread made of corn mush mixed with eggs, butter, and milk that you eat with a spoon or fork.

- **Hoecakes:** Thin cornmeal batter fried in a griddle

- **Corn pone:** An eggless corn bread batter cooked in a skillet

- **Hushpuppies:** Deep-fried cornmeal bread.

- **Hominy:** Corn without the germ that is traditionally boiled and served with butter or syrup

- **Grits:** A maize-based porridge

- **Succotash:** A dish consisting primarily of corn mixed with a variety of other beans

Corn isn't just for human consumption, however. Corn and all its parts are used for everything from animal feed to making nylon, plastics, and lubricating oils. In fact, about 60 percent of the corn grown in the United States is grown for animal feed. Although edible, animal feed corn is nothing like the super sweet corn we all know and love.

Canned Greens

Canned greens are a fast way to add nutrients to any meal. Add these to soups and stews during the last 15 minutes of cooking time.

Preparation time*: 15 minutes*

Processing time: *Pints, 1 hour 10 minutes; quarts, 1 hour 30 minutes*

Pressure level: *10 pounds*

Yield: *14 pints or 7 quarts*

28 pounds fresh, young greens

1 Prepare your canning jars and two-piece caps (lids and screw bands) according to the manufacturer's instructions. Keep the jars and lids hot. (For information on preparing your jars, see Chapter 4.)

2 Thoroughly wash the greens, changing the water in the sink once or twice to be sure all the grit is removed. Place the greens in a 12-quart pot and add enough water to cover. Heat the greens on medium-high until they're wilted, about 5 to 7 minutes. Using a slotted spoon, remove the greens from the water and cut them into small pieces (about 1 inch). Reserve the cooking liquid.

3 Loosely pack the greens into jars (don't press down) and pour the boiling hot cooking liquid over them, leaving 1-inch headspace. Release any air bubbles with a nonreactive utensil, adding more liquid as necessary to maintain the proper headspace (refer to Chapter 3). Wipe the jar rims; seal the jars with the two-piece caps, hand-tightening the bands.

4 Process the filled jars in a pressure canner at 10 pounds pressure for 1 hour 10 minutes (pints) or 1 hour 30 minutes (quarts). Allow the pressure to return to 0, wait an additional 10 minutes, and then carefully open the canner lid. (Head to Chapter 9 for detailed processing instructions for pressure canning.)

5 Remove the jars from the canner with a jar lifter. Place them on a clean kitchen towel away from drafts. After the jars cool completely, test the seals (refer to Chapter 4). If you find jars that haven't sealed, refrigerate them and use them within two weeks. Prior to eating or tasting, boil the food for 15 minutes.

Per ½-cup serving: *Calories 55 (From fat 4); Fat 0g (Saturated 0g); Cholesterol 0mg; Sodium 53mg; Carbohydrates 10g (Dietary fiber 7g); Protein 6g.*

Onions

Onions are a staple ingredient in many recipes. Their savory flavor often is the finishing touch to your favorite meal. Canning onions leave them soft but flavorful. Keep these onions in your pantry as an important ingredient for your favorite recipe.

Canned Onions

Canned onions are useful for any quick meal. They are great if eaten on a burger, heated and added to gravy, or just eaten as a condiment.

Preparation time: *20 minutes*

Processing time: *Pints and quarts, 40 minutes*

Pressure level: *10 pounds*

Yield: *20 pints or 10 quarts*

20 pounds fresh onions   *Canning salt*

1 Prepare your canning jars and two-piece caps (lids and screw bands) according to the manufacturer's instructions. Keep the jars and lids hot. (For information on preparing your jars, see Chapter 4.)

2 Peel and wash the onions. If you're using large onions, chop them or slice them into ½-inch pieces.

3 Place the onions in a 12-quart pot, cover them with water, and bring them to a boil over medium high heat. Boil them for 5 minutes, or until they're translucent.

4 Using a slotted spoon, remove the onions from cooking liquid (reserve the liquid for filling the jars) and firmly pack them into the prepared jars. Add ½ teaspoon salt to each pint jar or 1 teaspoon salt to each quart jar. Pour the hot cooking liquid over the onions, leaving 1-inch headspace. Release any air bubbles with a nonreactive utensil, adding liquid as necessary to maintain the proper headspace (refer to Chapter 3). Wipe the jar rims; seal the jars with the two-piece caps, hand-tightening the bands.

5 Process the filled jars in a pressure canner at 10 pounds pressure for 40 minutes (pints or quarts). Allow the pressure to return to 0, wait an additional 10 minutes, and then carefully open the canner lid away. (Head to Chapter 9 for detailed processing instructions for pressure canning.)

6 Remove the jars from the canner with a jar lifter. Place them on a clean kitchen towel away from drafts. After the jars cool completely, test the seals (refer to Chapter 4). If you find jars that haven't sealed, refrigerate them and use them within two weeks. Prior to eating or tasting, boil the food for 15 minutes.

Per ½-cup serving: *Calories 42 (From fat 2); Fat 0g (Saturated 0g); Cholesterol 0mg; Sodium 294mg; Carbohydrates 10g (Dietary fiber 1g); Protein 1g.*

Peas

There is nothing like the taste of garden fresh peas. If your kids have decided they don't like cooked peas, convince them that your own canned peas are worth a try.

Canned Peas

You can pack a lot of peas in a jar. Try canned peas mixed with rice and tamari sauce.

Preparation time: 15 minutes

Processing time: Pints and quarts, 40 minutes

Pressure level: 10 pounds

Yield: 14 pints or 7 quarts

28 to 30 pounds fresh, young peas in the pod   *Canning salt*

1 Prepare your canning jars and two-piece caps (lids and screw bands) according to the manufacturer's instructions. Keep the jars and lids hot. (For information on preparing your jars, see Chapter 4.)

2 Wash and remove the pods. Place the peas in a 8-quart pot, cover them with water, and bring to a boil over **high heat. Allow the peas** to boil for 3 to 5 minutes, or until they're bright green but not fully cooked.

3 Remove the peas from the cooking liquid (reserve the liquid for filling jars) and loosely pack the peas into the prepared jars. Pour hot cooking water over them, leaving 1-inch headspace Add ½ teaspoon salt to each pint jar or 1 teaspoon salt to each quart jar. Release any air bubbles with a nonreactive utensil, adding liquid as necessary to maintain the proper headspace (refer to Chapter 3). Wipe the jar rims; seal the jars with the two-piece caps, hand-tightening the bands.

4 Process the filled jars in a pressure canner at 10 pounds pressure for 40 minutes (pints or quarts). Allow the pressure to return to 0, wait an additional 10 minutes, and then carefully open the canner lid. (Head to Chapter 9 for detailed processing instructions for pressure canning.)

5 Remove the jars from the canner with a jar lifter. Place them on a clean kitchen towel away from drafts. After the jars cool completely, test the seals (refer to Chapter 4). If you find jars that haven't sealed, refrigerate them and use them within two weeks. Prior to eating or tasting, boil the food for 15 minutes.

Per ½-cup serving: Calories 70 (From fat 3); Fat 0g (Saturated 0g); Cholesterol 0mg; Sodium 295mg; Carbohydrates 13g (Dietary fiber 4g); Protein 5g.

Potatoes

The only potatoes recommended for pressure canning are sweet potatoes, yams, and white, or Irish, potatoes. Using any other potatoes yields inferior results because of their chemical makeup (texture and composition).

- **White or Irish:** These potatoes are round and white with a thin skin. Peel the potatoes prior to precooking. Small potatoes (2 to 3 inches in diameter) may be left whole; cut larger potatoes into quarters before precooking.

- **Sweet potatoes and yams:** Sweet potatoes are roots and yams are tubers — so they're actually from two different plant species. Even though sweet potatoes and yams are unrelated, they're suitable for the same uses. Sweet potatoes have skin colors ranging from light yellow to dark orange and flesh colors ranging from pale yellow to medium orange and are sweeter than yams. Yams contain more natural sugar and have a higher moisture content than sweet potatoes; they're white to deep red in flesh color with skin colors ranging from creamy white to deep red. Small potatoes may be left whole; cut larger ones into quarters before removing the skins.

Canned White Potatoes

I (Amy) drain my canned potatoes and use them in homemade hash in the winter. They are hearty breakfast fare after a cold morning at the farm.

Preparation time: 15 minutes

Processing time: Pints, 35 minutes; quarts, 40 minutes

Pressure level: 10 pounds

Yield: 14 pints or 7 quarts

7 pounds fresh, young potatoes   Canning salt

1 Prepare your canning jars and two-piece caps (lids and screw bands) according to the manufacturer's instructions. Keep the jars and lids hot. (For information on preparing your jars, see Chapter 4.)

2 In a 12-quart pot, bring 2 gallons of water to boil. Wash and peel your potatoes. Cube the potatoes into ½-inch pieces. Carefully place the potatoes in the boiling water and cook for 2 minutes or until potatoes are partially cooked but still firm.

3 Pack the hot potatoes into the prepared jars (reserve the liquid you cooked them in). Add ½ teaspoon salt to each pint jar or 1 teaspoon salt to each quart jar. Pour the cooking liquid over the potatoes, leaving 1-inch headspace. Release any air bubbles with a nonreactive utensil, adding liquid as necessary to maintain the proper headspace (refer to Chapter 3). Wipe the jar rims; seal the jars with the two-piece caps, hand-tightening the bands.

4 Process the filled jars in a pressure canner at 10 pounds pressure for 35 minutes (pints) or 40 minutes (quarts). Allow the pressure to return to 0, wait an additional 10 minutes, and then carefully open the canner lid. (Head to Chapter 9 for detailed processing instructions for pressure canning.)

5 Remove the jars from the canner with a jar lifter. Place them on a clean kitchen towel away from drafts. After the jars cool completely, test the seals (refer to Chapter 4). If you find jars that haven't sealed, refrigerate them and use them within two weeks. Prior to eating or tasting, boil the food for 15 minutes.

Per ½-cup serving: Calories 36 (From fat 1); Fat 0g (Saturated 0g); Cholesterol 0mg; Sodium 292mg; Carbohydrates 7g (Dietary fiber 1g); Protein 1g.

Canned Sweet Potatoes

Sweet potatoes can compliment a meal, with their rich, naturally sweet flavor. The bright orange color makes a dish pop, and many who think they don't like any veggies are pleasantly surprised at the delicious taste of the sweet potato. This recipe produces a firmer finished product with much more flavor — a definite improvement over store-bought sweet potatoes from a can.

Preparation time*: 15 minutes*

Processing time: *Pints, 1 hour 5 minutes; quarts, 1 hour 30 minutes*

Pressure level: *10 pounds*

Yield: *14 pints or 7 quarts*

21 pounds sweet potatoes   *Canning salt*

1 Prepare your canning jars and two-piece caps (lids and screw bands) according to the manufacturer's instructions. Keep the jars and lids hot. (For information on preparing your jars, see Chapter 4.)

2 In a 12-quart pot, bring 2 gallons of water to boil. Wash and peel the sweet potatoes. Cube them into ½-inch pieces. Carefully place the sweet potatoes into the boiling water and cook for 10 minutes, or until the potatoes are partially cooked but still firm. Reserve the cooking liquid.

3 Pack the hot sweet potatoes into the prepared jars. Add ½ teaspoon salt to each pint jar or 1 teaspoon salt to each quart jar. Pour the cooking liquid over the sweet potatoes, leaving 1-inch headspace. Release any air bubbles with a nonreactive utensil, adding liquid as necessary to maintain the proper headspace (refer to Chapter 3). Wipe the jar rims; seal the jars with the two-piece caps, hand-tightening the bands.

4 Process the filled jars in a pressure canner at 10 pounds pressure for 1 hour 5 minutes (pints) or 1 hour 30 minutes (quarts). Allow the pressure to return to 0, wait an additional 10 minutes, and then carefully open the canner lid. (Head to Chapter 9 for detailed processing instructions for pressure canning.)

5 Remove the jars from the canner with a jar lifter. Place them on a clean kitchen towel away from drafts. After the jars cool completely, test the seals (refer to Chapter 4). If you find jars that haven't sealed, refrigerate them and use them within two weeks. Prior to eating or tasting, boil the food for 15 minutes.

Per ½-cup serving: Calories 139 (From fat 4); Fat 0g (Saturated 0g); Cholesterol 0mg; Sodium 308mg; Carbohydrates 32g (Dietary fiber 2g); Protein 2g.

Sauerkraut

Sauerkraut is a tangy, fermented food that sometimes has to grow on you. Once you enjoy the taste, you find different ways to bring this delicious treat into your diet. Sauerkraut in fits simplest form is nothing more than cabbage and salt. There are many variations, however. Some recipes add dill or caraway seed. I (Amy) have had much luck adding onion and garlic to mine. Once you have made plain sauerkraut a few times, try adding your own spices and create your favorite version.

Here's an easy sauerkraut you can use in the Canned Sauerkraut recipe:

1. **Finely shred the cabbage and layer it with salt, in a glass or stoneware crock until full.**

   Use 1 tablespoon salt for every 5 pounds of cabbage.

2. **Make an airtight seal by using a food-safe plastic bag of water to seal the top.**

   Just fill a plastic bag with water and place it over the top of the container. It doesn't have to overlap; it just sits on top like a plug.

3. **Allow the cabbage to ferment at room temperature (68 to 72 degrees) for five to six weeks.**

Cabbage's health benefits

Cabbage is an ancient vegetable and has had a long history in European and Asian diets. Even the Greeks and Romans appreciated it for what they considered its medicinal qualities. But somewhere along the line, cabbage got a bad wrap. It became the food that stunk up the house when cooked and, let's be honest, stunk up other things after being eaten.

The reputation of cabbage and the other vegetables in the Brassica genus (including bok choi, cauliflower, broccoli, turnips, Brussels sprouts, and more) has finally been redeemed. Among the good things eating these veggies can do for you: increase your dietary fiber, provide you with necessary vitamins and minerals (especially Vitamin C), lower your cholesterol, and prevent certain types of cancer.

Canned Sauerkraut

If you love the tang of a crisp pickle, then you will surely love the taste of homemade sauerkraut on your plate. Canning it only ensures you will have enough to last the entire winter season. Sauerkraut is simply cabbage and salt, covered and allowed to ferment for a few weeks. There are many recipes available for creating your own.

Preparation time: *15 minutes*

Processing time: *Pints and quarts: 20 minutes*

Pressure level: *10 pounds*

Yield: *14 pints or 7 quarts*

7 quarts sauerkraut   *Boiling water*

1 Prepare your canning jars and two-piece caps (lids and screw bands) according to the manufacturer's instructions. Keep the jars and lids hot. (For information on preparing your jars, see Chapter 4.)

2 Place your sauerkraut in a 8-quart pot and bring it to a simmer over medium heat, stirring often to prevent sticking. In a separate pan, bring additional water to boil to use as a reserve for filling the jars to the recommended level.

3 Ladle the boiling hot sauerkraut and juice into the prepared jars. Add additional water from your reserve to cover the tightly packed sauerkraut, leaving 1-inch headspace. Release any air bubbles with a nonreactive utensil, adding water as necessary to maintain the proper headspace (refer to Chapter 3). Wipe the jar rims; seal the jars with the two-piece caps, hand-tightening the bands.

4 Process the filled jars in a pressure canner at 10 pounds pressure for 20 minutes (pints or quarts). Allow the pressure to return to 0, wait an additional 10 minutes, and then carefully open the canner lid. (Head to Chapter 9 for detailed processing instructions for pressure canning.)

5 Remove the jars from the canner with a jar lifter. Place them on a clean kitchen towel away from drafts. After the jars cool completely, test the seals (refer to Chapter 4). If you find jars that haven't sealed, refrigerate them and use them within two weeks. Prior to eating or tasting, boil the food for 15 minutes.

Per ½-cup serving: Calories 13 (From fat 2); Fat 0g (Saturated 0g); Cholesterol 0mg; Sodium 429mg; Carbohydrates 3g (Dietary fiber 2g); Protein 0g.

Summer squash

Summer squash include crookneck, zucchini, and patty pan, to name a few. The skins are thin and edible, eliminating the need to peel them.

Canned Summer Squash

Summer squash is one of those vegetables that seems to grow faster than anyone can use it. Here is an easy way to keep that sunny flavor for the winter months and add some brightness to soups and stews.

Preparation time: *15 minutes*

Processing time: *Pints, 30 minutes; quarts, 40 minutes*

Pressure level: *10 pounds*

Yield: *14 pints or 7 quarts*

18 to 20 pounds summer squash   *Canning salt*

1 Prepare your canning jars and two-piece caps (lids and screw bands) according to the manufacturer's instructions. Keep the jars and lids hot. (For information on preparing your jars, see Chapter 4.)

2 In a 12-quart pot, bring 2 gallons of water to boil. Wash and cut the summer squash into ¼-inch slices or 1-inch cubes. Carefully place the cubed or sliced squash into your boiling water and return to a boil for 5 minutes, or until slightly softened. Reserve the cooking liquid.

3 Using a canning funnel, loosely pack the squash into the prepared jars. Pour the hot cooking liquid over the squash, leaving ½-inch headspace. Add ½ teaspoon salt to each pint jar or 1 teaspoon salt to each quart jar. Release any air bubbles with a nonreactive utensil, adding liquid as necessary to maintain the proper headspace (refer to Chapter 3). Wipe the jar rims; seal the jars with the two-piece caps, hand-tightening the bands.

4 Process the filled jars in a pressure canner at 10 pounds pressure for 30 minutes (pints) or 40 minutes (quarts). Allow the pressure to return to 0, wait an additional 10 minutes, and then carefully open the canner lid. (Head to Chapter 9 for detailed processing instructions for pressure canning.)

5 Remove the jars from the canner with a jar lifter. Place them on a clean kitchen towel away from drafts. After the jars cool completely, test the seals (refer to Chapter 4). If you find jars that haven't sealed, refrigerate them and use them within two weeks. Prior to eating or tasting, boil the food for 10 minutes.

Per ½-cup serving: Calories 28 (From Fat 3); Fat 0g (Saturated 0g); Cholesterol 0mg; Sodium 294mg; Carbohydrate 6g (Dietary Fiber 3g); Protein 2g.

Winter squash and pumpkins

Winter squash is also good for canning. Winter squash varieties include banana, butternut, Hubbard, spaghetti, and turban squash. Because pumpkins are similar in texture to winter squash, you can use these instructions to can pumpkin also. Canning winter squash and pumpkins is a bit labor-intensive — some of these winter vegetables can be difficult to peel and clean — but the rewards are oh, so good!

Squash blossoms

If you've ever seen a field of squash grow, you know that the vine produces lovely, orange-to-yellow trumpet-shaped flowers. These flowers, when pollinated, produce the squash you're so fond of eating. What you may not know is that the flowers themselves are edible.

Blossoms from summer and winter varieties of squash are considered a delicacy by many. Simply pick them when they're wide open and use them within two days—the sooner the better.

You can eat them off the vine, chop them up and add them to dishes, or sauté them, but the most popular way to serve squash blossoms is to deep fry them.

To prepare the blossoms for consumption, follow these steps:

1. **Remove the stamen and *sepals* (the small, sharp leaves attached to the buds).**

2. **Fill the blossom with your choice of cheesy filling and twist the petal tops to seal.**

   I (Amy) use my homemade goat cheese.

3. **Coat the filled blossoms with a light batter.**

4. **Deep fry them until the batter is golden brown.**

These treats are truly a fantastic and an utterly unique way to add a fresh food to your diet. Plus they really impress your guests!

Canned Winter Squash

So naturally sweet and rich tasting, you will find yourself turning to this vegetable many times during the dreary winter months. Add winter squash to stews, mash and sweeten them with brown sugar and butter for a great side dish, or simply heat and serve. ***Note:*** Although this recipe is for winter squash, you follow exactly the same steps and amounts to make canned pumpkin.

Preparation time*: 15 minutes*

Processing time: *Pints, 55 minutes; quarts, 1 hour 25 minutes*

Pressure level: *10 pounds*

Yield: *14 pints or 7 quarts*

21 pounds winter squash (or pumpkin)   *Canning salt*

1 Prepare your canning jars and two-piece caps (lids and screw bands) according to the manufacturer's instructions. Keep the jars and lids hot. (For information on preparing your jars, see Chapter 4.)

2 Cut the winter squash into 3-by-5-inch pieces. Scrape out the fiber and seeds. Place the squash in a 12-quart pot and cover it with water. Bring the squash to a simmer on medium-high heat, and allow it to simmer until soft, approximately 10 to 30 minutes, depending on the variety.

3 Carefully remove the squash from the cooking liquid and discard the liquid. Scrape the pulp from the softened skin and place it in a sturdy mixing bowl. Using a potato masher, mash the pulp until smooth. Return the mashed pulp to the empty pot and bring it to a boil over medium-high heat. Boil for 10 minutes, stirring often to prevent sticking.

4 Pack the boiling hot pulp into the prepared jars, leaving 1-inch headspace. Add ½ teaspoon salt to each pint jar or 1 teaspoon salt to each quart jar. Release any air bubbles with a nonreactive utensil (refer to Chapter 3), making sure that no air is trapped inside the thick pulp. Add pulp as necessary to maintain the proper headspace.

5 Process the filled jars in a pressure canner at 10 pounds pressure for 55 minutes (pints) or 1 hour 25 minutes (quarts). Allow the pressure to return to 0, wait an additional 10 minutes, and then carefully open the canner lid. (Head to Chapter 9 for detailed processing instructions for pressure canning.)

6 Remove the jars from the canner with a jar lifter. Place them on a clean kitchen towel away from drafts. After the jars cool completely, test the seals (refer to Chapter 4). If you find jars that haven't sealed, refrigerate them and use them within two weeks. Prior to eating or tasting, boil the food for 15 minutes.

Per ½-cup serving: Calories 65 (From fat 2); Fat 0g (Saturated 0g); Cholesterol 0mg; Sodium 295mg; Carbohydrates 17g (Dietary fiber 5g); Protein 1g.

Using Canned Vegetables

Seeing a shelf lined with pressure-canned vegetables is quite rewarding, knowing all the care and effort applied to the process. Are you wondering, though, what you can do with all this nutritious food? Try the following:

✔ **Serve a canned vegetable as a side dish:** Use vegetables that have a firm texture such as corn or carrots for a side dish. Softer vegetables like squash and onions are better used as a flavor ingredient in a recipe.

✔ **Combine your canned vegetables with meats and other ingredients to create easy, nutritious meals.** The following recipes offer a few suggestions.

When using low-acid, pressure-canned vegetables, always boil your food for 15 minutes *before you taste the food.* For altitudes over 1,000 feet above sea level, extend the boiling period 1 minute for each increase of 1,000 feet.

Easy Vegetable Soup

Don't have time to make vegetable soup from scratch? No problem! You can whip up a delicious vegetable soup in no time just by using the canned veggies you have in your pantry. This recipe uses canned corn, carrots, peas, and bell peppers, but you can use any combination that strikes your fancy — or that you have on hand. Serve this hearty soup in large bowls with Parmesan cheese shavings and sourdough bread.

Preparation time*: 30 minutes*

Yield: *4 servings*

1 pint jar each of corn, carrots, peas, and bell peppers (or any combination you prefer)

1 cup dried pasta, any kind

1 teaspoon Italian seasoning (optional)

¼ cup Parmesan cheese, grated

1 Combine one jar each of corn, carrots, peas, and bell peppers (or your favorite vegetable mix) along with their canning liquids into a large soup pot. Add enough additional water to cover the ingredients by an inch. Bring the vegetables to a boil over medium-high heat and boil for 15 minutes.

2 Add the dried pasta and Italian seasoning to the boiling vegetables. Continue boiling the soup until the pasta is tender, about 15 minutes longer.

3 Ladle the soup into four large serving bowls and sprinkle each with 1 tablespoon Parmesan cheese.

Per serving: *Calories 435 (From fat 40); Fat 4g (Saturated 1g); Cholesterol 4mg; Sodium 1,713mg; Carbohydrates 90g (Dietary fiber 18g); Protein 17g.*

Beans with Beef

Served over noodles with warm dinner rolls as a side, this hearty meal is great for a warm fall night. Add canned peaches for an easy and delicious dessert. (You can find instructions for Canned Peaches in Chapter 5.)

Preparation time*: 30 minutes*

Yield: *4 servings*

1 quart Canned Ground Beef (Chapter 11), or any ground meat	½ teaspoon Italian or Mexican Herb Mix (Chapter 19), or to taste
1 quart canned beans, any variety	Salt and pepper, to taste
4 ounces dried elbow noodles	

1 In a 10-inch frying pan, bring the ground meat to a simmer and heat for 15 minutes. Season with salt, pepper, and your favorite herbs or spice blend. (***Note:*** If you're not using canned ground beef, brown your meat over medium heat until done.)

2 While the meat is reheating, bring the canned dried beans to a boil in a large pot. Boil the beans for 15 minutes.

3 Carefully add the heated meat to the beans. Simmer over medium heat for 10 minutes to combine the flavors. While the meat and beans are simmering, prepare the noodles according to the package instructions, keeping them warm until ready to use.

4 To serve, divide the noodles evenly onto four plates and ladle the beans and beef mixture over the hot noodles.

Per serving: *Calories 600 (From fat 215); Fat 24g (Saturated 9g); Cholesterol 116mg; Sodium 655mg; Carbohydrates 47g (Dietary fiber 9g); Protein 49g.*

Baked Chicken with Peppers

Here is a fast-and-easy dinner that can impress unexpected guests. With the ingredients at your fingertips, dinner is ready in a flash. Serve the chicken with the bell pepper pieces over your favorite rice, with a salad on the side.

Preparation time: 15 minutes

Yield: 4 servings

4 to 6 boneless, skinless chicken breasts

1 pint of canned bell peppers

1 teaspoon Italian or Mexican Herb Mix (Chapter 19) or any other seasoning mix

4 cups cooked rice

1 Preheat your oven to 350 degrees.

2 Boil 1 pint of canned bell peppers and the canning liquid in a 6-quart saucepan for 15 minutes. While the peppers boil, arrange the chicken breasts in an ovenproof pan. Pour the bell peppers and their liquid over the chicken breasts. Season as desired.

3 Tightly cover the pan with aluminum foil to seal in the moisture and bake the chicken at 350 degrees for 30 to 45 minutes, or until the chicken is done.

4 Serve over rice.

Per serving: Calories 380 (From fat 34); Fat 4g (Saturated 1g); Cholesterol 73mg; Sodium 649mg; Carbohydrates 52g (Dietary fiber 4g); Protein 32g.

Chapter 11

Don't Forget the Meats!

Canning meats is an often forgotten area of home canning, which is a shame. Canning a variety of meats is a great way to add a protein component to your pantry and build up a quantity of the most expensive part of your grocery bill as you can afford to. In this chapter, you discover how to safely can meat, game, poultry, and fish and seafood. These items will add variety to your pantry and give you delicious dinner foods that your whole family will want to eat.

The Lowdown on Canning Meats

Canning meat results in a tender product. Since canning meat draws out, but keeps, the natural juices, the meat is succulent and delicious naturally. Often, no additional seasoning is necessary, meaning you can rest assured that your family is eating only healthy food and not flavor-enhancing additives and preservatives.

Without fail, canning meat, as well as poultry and seafood, means using the pressure canner. These foods are low-acid foods and are unsafe to can using the water-bath canning method. Meats cannot be successfully canned using any method other than pressure canning, regardless of stories you may have heard to the contrary.

Canning meat and poultry can be done either *hot pack,* lightly cooked and then put into the jars while still hot, or *cold packed,* placed into jars raw so the canning pressure cooks the meat thoroughly (refer to Chapter 5 for more on these techniques) As a rule, cold pack recipes are generally for delicate meats and seafood that may fall apart from too much handling. Hot pack is usually used for partially cooked meats that are a bit firmer and won't fall apart so readily. You can, however, find both hot and cold pack recipes for any type of meat. Each results in a different end product. You may find that your family likes the results from one method over another.

Be sure to follow the directions of the recipe carefully. Making changes can result in serious illness.

Tips for safety and efficiency

Meats need to be cut and canned as quickly as possible. Because bacteria can grow quickly in meat and poultry, your goal is to can the meat before it reaches room temperature, and not to allow your cut-up meat to sit out for any length of time between cutting and canning.

If you find that you have more meat cut than you can possibly process in one day, keep the extra in a refrigerator at 32 – 38 degrees Fahrenheit, and can that meat first the next day, before cutting more. Keep canning all the meat until finished, even if it means working for more than one day. (Although you can freeze meat as soon as you purchase it for canning later, you risk canning an inferior product. Better to buy it the day you plan to can it.)

Usually when canning meats, you will be processing a large portion at a time. To can meat in the safest and quickest way possible, follow the advice in the next sections.

Practice first

Every time you can — and no matter how many times you've canned in the past — set up all the necessary equipment and supplies and do a dry run to be sure you have everything ready and in the right place.

Be sure that you know how to close the canner properly and quickly; do it a few times if you need to. Once it's filled with steaming hot water and filled jars, closing it is a bit harder. If your canner doesn't get closed properly, you may not know it until after it's been filled and is coming to a rolling boil, at which point the canner may leak steam, hiss, and spit hot water. Then you'll be forced to wait until the canner cools and the pressure gauge returns to normal before you can reopen and reclose it. This is wasting valuable time that your raw meat is not being processed.

Stick to the plan

Canning meat is not the time to experiment with a recipe. Follow the recipe to the letter, making notes on your experience, so you can then see how to change your technique, if desired, the next time.

Check everything twice

Make sure your pressure canner is in excellent condition (refer to Chapter 9 for what constitutes "excellent condition"). Before using the pressure canner, be sure to check its safety valve. You can do this with a string or fine wire. A sure way to know that the safety valve is clean is to hold the lid up to the light. When clean, you will be able to see light through the hole. Check the safety valve every time you can. Check it between loads of jars during a single canning session as well. It only takes a couple of seconds and can eliminate any major accidents.

Also make sure to check all your jars for nicked rims before and after sanitizing (glass jars with lids and bands are recommended). Sometimes a jar will be perfect when coming out of storage but will get a small nick or crack in the cleaning process. A nicked rim won't keep a jar sealed.

Be as clean as a whistle

Wash all your work surfaces with hot soapy water and rinse well. You may want to add bleach to the rinse water and let the surfaces dry on their own. This ensures you have a sanitary work surface to sit your jars and utensils on. *Note:* You don't have to sanitize the entire kitchen, just the area that you will be working at (doing a trial run lets you know exactly where your work surfaces are). You also need to ensure that your jars, rims, and lids are sanitized (go to Chapter 4 for details).

Selecting and preparing the meat

When canning meat, use only the best meat you can buy. This means the freshest meat that has been raised and handled properly. Here are some ways to ensure that you are starting out with the best meat.

- Raise your own food animals
- Buy from a local small farmer
- Buy from a local butcher

You can certainly use meat from the local big-chain grocery store, but note that they won't have the freshest meat available, and the meat itself may be raised in a way that you may not want to support.

When preparing meats to can, you remove as much bruising, gristle, and fat that you can. You remove the first two because they're blemishes that don't can well. You remove the fat because fatty meat shouldn't be canned; it increases the chance of spoilage and can lend an off flavor to the finished product. You won't be able to remove every trace of fat, but cut off as much as possible during preparation.

How you cut the meat — into cubes, strips, and so forth — depends on the type of meat you're canning. You can find specific guidance for the various types of meats in the upcoming sections.

Only prepare enough meat for one canner full of jars at a time. You do not want meat to sit out at room temperature for any longer than necessary. Meat is more susceptible to bacterial growth than other foods and must remain as cold as possible until used.

Meat canning, step by step

Your equipment and supplies are checked and assembled, and you're ready to begin. The following steps provide a general overview of the process for canning meat; for detailed instructions on canning low-acid foods, refer to Chapter 9.

1. **Place the wire jar rack into the canner and add the water to the canner following your canner's manufacturer's instructions.**

2. **Fill the jars following the recipe's instructions and close them hand tight.**

   For info on preparing your meat, refer to the earlier section "Selecting and preparing the meat."

   Don't overtighten the jars. By hand-tightening them, you leave a miniscule amount of room between the rim and the lid, enabling the pressure of the canner to force air out of each jar as it becomes pressurized during the canning process. As the pressurized cans then cool, the lids will be sucked tightly onto the jars, providing an airtight seal.

3. **Place the hand-tightened jars in the canner and then place the lid on the canner and fasten, following the manufacturer's instructions. Begin processing.**

   When the water comes to a boil, vent the steam for at least 10 minutes to ensure that the pressure gauge has an accurate reading.

4. **After the 10 minutes venting time, close the vent and watch the pressure build; then maintain the pressure specified in the recipe for the recommended period of time.**

Stay nearby because you need to adjust the heat source so that the pressure builds high enough but not too high. Read your particular pressure canner's instructions to be sure of the technique the manufacturer recommends for your unit. If at any time your pressure falls below the recommended level during the canning process, you must bring it back up to the correct pressure and start timing all over again.

5. **After the specified cooking time has elapsed, allow the pressure to return to 0. Then remove the jars from the canner, allow them to cool completely, and then store.**

6. **Before tasting or eating, boil the contents of each jar for 15 minutes.**

The following sections provide specific instructions for various types of meats.

Canning Beef and Pork: Cubed Meat

Cubed meats, such as beef, pork, goat, and sheep, are easy to can and can be the main ingredient of many delicious dishes. You can use strips, cubes, and ground meats (covered in the next section) in any recipe that calls for that type of meat.

Canning is an excellent way to use the less expensive cuts of meat and still end up with a delicious dish. When you preserve meat this way, your family will never know that you started with a tougher cut of meat, and children often prefer canned meat to the noncanned version.

Preparing the meat

Before placing the meat into the jars, cut it into bite-sized pieces, about 1-inch square, and cook it in a frying pan on high heat until it's about halfway done and lightly browned on each side. Meats that have a strong flavor can be soaked in salted water for an hour before cooking. You can also use a tomato-based liquid in these strong-flavored meats (as the Wild Game in Gravy recipe does later in this chapter).

You can also cut strips of your desired meats from roasts and steaks. If you do so, make sure you cut with the grain of the meat so that it will fit the length of the jar. Cutting in this way results in a more tender and aesthetic-looking piece of meat. Cutting across the grain can cause the meat to fall apart and result in a stringy texture.

Filling the jars

Pack the cubed meat while still hot into hot jars. (When canning chunky meats, use wide-mouthed jars; this makes it easier to fill the jars when you're canning and easier to remove the foods later on.) Leave 1-inch headspace.

Fill the jars until they're full but not overly packed. By leaving a bit of room, you allow all the air to be driven out of the meat. If packed too tightly, some air may become trapped, and your resulting meat won't be safe to use.

Pour your hot liquid of choice (tomato juice, boiling water, or stock) over the meat. This additional liquid fills in any air spaces that remain. (*Don't* use thickened gravy because it becomes gooey or too thick during the canning process and you'll end up with an unsatisfactory product.)

Using a plastic or nonreactive utensil (not metal), release any air bubbles and add liquid as necessary to maintain the proper headspace. Then hand-tighten lids and process according to the recipe's instructions.

Chopped or Cubed Meat

Cubed meat is tender and delicious and is guaranteed to be one of the first things you reach for when you need a fast meal maker. Whenever a recipe calls for cubed or chopped meat, use this and cut out a major portion of the work. Serve this meat over biscuits in wintertime for a stick-to-your-ribs meal that really tastes great.

Preparation time: 1 hour

Processing time: Pints, 1 hour 15 minutes; quarts, 1 hour 30 minutes

Pressure level: 10 pounds

Yield: About 8 pints or 4 quarts

6 pounds lean meat

Water, tomato juice, or broth

Canning salt or beef bouillon (optional)

1 Cut meat into cubes and brown lightly in dry skillet until the meat is about halfway done (the canning process finishes the cooking). While the meat is browning, heat up your choice of liquid until boiling.

2 Prepare the canning jars and two-piece caps (lids and screw bands) according to the manufacturer's instructions. Keep the jars and lids hot. (For detailed instructions on preparing your jars, see Chapter 4.)

3 Ladle the cooked meat and your choice of boiling liquid into hot jars, leaving 1-inch headspace. Add a bouillon cube or ¼ teaspoon salt to each pint jar or ½ teaspoon salt to each quart jar, if desired. Release any air bubbles with a nonreactive utensil (refer to Chapter 3). Wipe the jar rims; seal the jars with the two-piece caps, hand-tightening the bands.

4 Process your filled jars in pressure canner at 10 pounds pressure for 1 hour 15 minutes (pints) or 1 hour 30 minutes (quarts). When the processing time is done, allow the pressure to return to 0, wait an additional 10 minutes, and then carefully open canner lid. (Head to Chapter 9 for detailed processing instructions for pressure canning.)

5 Remove the hot jars with a jar lifter. Place the jars on a clean kitchen towel in a draft-free area. After the jars cool completely, test the seals (refer to Chapter 4). (If you find jars that haven't sealed, immediately refrigerate them and use them within one week.) Boil the contents of each jar for 15 minutes before tasting or eating.

Per 4-ounce serving: Calories 266 (From fat 115); Fat 13g (Saturated 5g); Cholesterol 115mg; Sodium 76mg; Carbohydrates 0g (Dietary fiber 0g); Protein 35g.

Wild Game in Gravy

Wild game is inexpensive, and the unique taste is often a welcome change. You can use this recipe for venison and rabbit, as well as any goat that might have a stronger-than-normal flavor. Although this recipe works well with strong flavored meats, it is still imperative to start with fresh, clean meat.

Preparation time: 1 hour, 30 minutes

Processing time: Pints, 1 hour 15 minutes; quarts, 1 hour 30 minutes

Pressure level: 10 pounds

Yield: About 4 pints or 2 quarts

3 pounds game

Canning salt

Beef broth or tomato juice

Water

1 Cut your meat into 1-inch chunks. In a large nonreactive bowl, cover the meat with a brine solution made up of 1 tablespoon of salt per quart of water. Leave the meat in the brine for 1 hour. Then rinse thoroughly. In a 8-quart pot, brown the game over medium or medium-high heat until it is about two-thirds done. While meat is browning, bring your choice of liquid to a boil.

2 Prepare the canning jars and two-piece caps (lids and screw bands) according to the manufacturer's instructions. Keep the jars and lids hot. (For detailed instructions on preparing your jars, see Chapter 4.)

3 Fill the prepared jars with pieces of game and boiling hot liquid (broth or tomato juice), leaving 1-inch headspace. Release any air bubbles with a nonreactive utensil, adding liquid as necessary to maintain the proper headspace (refer to Chapter 3). Wipe the jar rims; seal the jars with the two-piece caps, hand-tightening the bands.

4 Process your filled jars in a pressure canner at 10 pounds pressure for 1 hour 15 minutes (pints) or 1 hour 30 minutes (quarts). When the processing time is done, allow the pressure to return to 0, wait an additional 10 minutes, and then carefully open the canner lid. (Head to Chapter 9 for detailed processing instructions for pressure canning.)

5 Remove the hot jars with a jar lifter. Place the jars on a clean kitchen towel in a draft-free area. After the jars cool completely, test the seals (refer to Chapter 4). (If you find jars that haven't sealed, immediately refrigerate them and use them within one week.) Boil the contents of each jar for 15 minutes before tasting or eating.

Per 4-ounce serving of venison: Calories 126 (From fat 51); Fat 6g (Saturated 2g); Cholesterol 63mg; Sodium 251mg; Carbohydrates 0g (Dietary fiber 0g); Protein 18g.

Per 4-ounce serving of rabbit: Calories 126 (From fat 46); Fat 5g (Saturated 2g); Cholesterol 50mg; Sodium 341mg; Carbohydrates 0g (Dietary fiber 0g); Protein 19g.

Canning Ground Meat

Ground meat is a family favorite. Canning it makes this handy staple even faster and easier to use. When canning ground meat, use any that your family enjoys. From poultry to red meat, all of it tastes wonderful when preserved this way. Use canned ground meat in the same way as you normally would — in any recipe that calls for already-cooked ground meat. You may find that your family prefers ground meat cooked this way, as it is far more flavorful than cooking in a frying pan.

When canning ground meat, keep these points in mind:

- **Preparing the ground meat:** Brown the meat just until it loses its pink color.

- **Filling the jars:** Using a wide mouth canning funnel, carefully fill the jars with ground meat, leaving 1-inch headspace. It is not necessary to add any additional liquid because the canning process forces out the meat's natural juices. This juice is rich in natural meat flavor.

Canned Ground Beef

This basic canning recipe makes the most of a common food: burger! Use this tasty food in any recipe that calls for ground beef. You may find the texture to be a little finer, but the flavor is outstanding. Remember, you may have to use a spoon to remove the ground meat from jars. No worries — once it's heated, it'll again be the crumbly texture you know.

Preparation time: *1 hour*

Processing time*: Pints, 1 hour 15 minutes; quarts, 1 hour 30 minutes*

Pressure level*: 10 pounds*

Yield*: 8 pints or 4 quarts*

8 pounds lean ground beef	*Canning salt (optional)*
Water, tomato juice, or beef broth	

1 Lightly brown ground beef in a dry skillet. While the beef is browning, bring your water, tomato juice, or beef broth to a boil.

2 While the meat is cooking and your liquid is coming to a boil, prepare the canning jars and two-piece caps (lids and screw bands) according to the manufacturer's instructions. Keep the jars and lids hot. (For detailed instructions on preparing your jars, see Chapter 4.)

3 Ladle the ground beef into each prepared jar and cover with boiling liquid, leaving 1-inch headspace. Add ¼ teaspoon salt to each pint jar or ½ teaspoon salt to each quart jar, if desired. Release any air bubbles with a nonreactive utensil (refer to Chapter 3). Wipe the jar rims; seal the jars with the two-piece caps, hand-tightening the bands.

4 Process your filled jars in the pressure canner at 10 pounds pressure for 1 hour 15 minutes (pints) and 1 hour 30 minutes (quarts). When the processing time is done, allow the pressure to return to 0, wait an additional 10 minutes, and then carefully open the canner lid. (Head to Chapter 9 for detailed processing instructions for pressure canning.)

5 Remove the hot jars with a jar lifter. Place the jars on a clean kitchen towel in a draft-free area. After the jars cool completely, test the seals (refer to Chapter 4). (If you find jars that haven't sealed, immediately refrigerate them and use them within one week.) Boil the contents of each jar for 15 minutes before tasting or eating.

Vary It!: *Add a single bouillon cube per quart in place of the salt for a slightly different flavor.*

Per 4-ounce serving: Calories 261 (From fat 123); Fat 14g (Saturated 10g); Cholesterol 101mg; Sodium 99mg; Carbohydrates 0g (Dietary fiber 0g); Protein 32g.

Poultry

Poultry is chicken, turkey, and other birds. To can fresh chickens (those that haven't been frozen), you use the cold pack method. To can chickens that have been previously frozen, you use the hot pack method.

Canning is the perfect way to use roosters and older hens. (An older hen, known as a *stewing hen,* is one that is older than 1½ years.) These traditionally tougher birds are made tender and succulent through the canning process. The younger chickens tend to become too soft and are better if frozen.

Canning fresh chicken: Cold packing

Cold packing is recommended for poultry that has never been frozen and makes a fast and efficient way to preserve poultry for your pantry.

- ✔ **Preparing the chicken:** If you have whole chickens, remove the breasts to freeze separately and can the remaining parts of the bird. Separate the leg pieces at the joint, so you have a thigh and drumstick for each leg. Place the pieces of cold chicken in a large bowl, only preparing enough chickens for a full canner load.

  Make sure that the drumstick bone is not too tall for a lid to sit flush on the rim of the jar. If so, chop off the excess bone with a cleaver, or refit.

- ✔ **Filling the jars:** When canning chicken, fit one chicken per quart. Cold-pack chicken pieces into each quart jar. Place the pieces close together, but not jammed in, fitting them like a puzzle, working around the jar until no more room is left (see Figure 11-1). Add one bouillon cube into each jar before hand-tightening the lid. Don't add any additional liquid to cold pack chicken because the canning process yields a surprising amount of liquid.

The natural gelatin in the chicken bones gives the cooled liquid a jellylike consistency. Once heated, this jelly will liquefy and be full of flavor.

FITTING A WHOLE CHICKEN INTO A JAR

Figure 11-1:
Fit in the chicken pieces like a puzzle — but not too tightly.

Canning prefrozen chicken: Hot packing

You may also can prefrozen chickens. Say you have a freezer full of chicken and your freezer suddenly breaks down. Now you need to process a large amount of poultry, and fast. You can successfully can prefrozen poultry as long as it's not freezer damaged and you thaw it slowly in a refrigerator. (This is not a technique to use on old, forgotten chicken that you suddenly found at the bottom of your freezer.) A good rule of thumb: Can chicken that's been frozen for 4 months or less.

✓ **Preparing the chicken:** To can prefrozen chicken, you use the hot pack method: Cut up the chicken and separate the pieces at all the joints so that you end up with thighs and drumsticks. Save the more desirable breast pieces for a separate meal. Remove the skin if you like (doing so reduces the amount of fat in the jar). Then cook the pieces about two-thirds of the way through. The meat finishes cooking in the canner.

✓ **Filling the jars:** Fill hot jars with hot chicken pieces, fitting them together like puzzle pieces, until the jar is full, leaving 1-inch headspace.

Never Fail Canned Chicken

Canned fresh chicken is probably the most superbly flavored way to cook poultry. It's canned in the simplest manner as well: cold packed into hot jars. This chicken is perfect for any recipe calling for cooked or shredded chicken. Once canned, the chicken falls off the bone, making cleaning it a snap.

Preparation time: *30 minutes*

Processing time: *1 hour 15 minutes*

Pressure level: *10 pounds*

Yield: *7 quarts (each containing one 3-pound chicken)*

Seven 3-pound chickens   Canning salt or bouillon cubes (optional)

1 Cut each chicken into parts, separating legs into thigh and drumstick pieces. Place the pieces in a large bowl, keeping them cold as you continue to cut. Remove the skin, if desired. Remove the breasts and use or freeze them separately.

2 Prepare the canning jars and two-piece caps (lids and screw bands) according to the manufacturer's instructions. Keep the jars and lids hot. (For detailed instructions on preparing your jars, see Chapter 4.)

3 Fill the prepared jars with the chicken pieces until full, leaving 1-inch headspace. Add 1 bouillon cube or ½ teaspoon canning salt to each quart jar, if desired. Release any air bubbles with a nonreactive utensil (refer to Chapter 3). Wipe the jar rims; seal the jars with the two-piece caps, hand-tightening the bands. (***Note:*** Due to the each chicken being a little different, you may find that you fit different numbers of pieces into each jar.)

4 Process your filled jars in a pressure canner at 10 pounds pressure for 1 hour 15 minutes. When the processing time is done, allow the pressure to return to 0, wait an additional 10 minutes, and then carefully open the canner lid. (Head to Chapter 9 for detailed processing instructions for pressure canning.)

5 Remove the hot jars with a jar lifter. Place the jars on a clean kitchen towel in a draft-free area. After the jars cool completely, test the seals. (If you find jars that haven't sealed, immediately refrigerate them and use them within one week.) Boil the contents of each jar for 5 minutes before tasting or eating.

Vary It! *If you are canning chicken that has been previously frozen and then thawed, cook it two-thirds of the way through before filling the canning jars.*

Per 4-ounce serving: *Calories 214 (From fat 88); Fat 10g (Saturated 3g); Cholesterol 97mg; Sodium 85mg; Carbohydrates 0g (Dietary fiber 0g); Protein 29g.*

Fish and Seafood

Many people are surprised to know that both fish and seafood can be canned successfully. Doing so is great if you're a sportsman or sportswoman and often end up with bags of frozen fillets you don't know what to do with. You can add seasoned broth or tomato juice to the jars, and the resulting food is delicious as well as a unique addition to your pantry.

Both fish and seafood fall into the delicate category. Both should be cold packed, and you must follow the recipe closely and handle the food with care throughout the process. But because they make wonderful additions to savory pies and soups or stews, they're worth the extra effort and care it takes to make a healthy and delicious product.

Fish and seafood differ from other meats because they are extremely low in acidity, which means that there is an even greater chance of error if you don't follow the recipe carefully. Because of the increased chance of error, canning fish is not the best project for a beginner. Try canning some other foods first. When you feel proficient with canning easier items (like fruits and vegetables), move up to meats, and then to fish and seafood.

Picking your fish

When canning fish, use a mild-flavored fish from clean waters. With fishing being a sport that requires an inexpensive license and a worm on a pole, you may find that fishing can fill a pantry for little to no cost.

Check with your local health department for official warnings and recommendations about eating freshly caught fish in your area.

Preparing fish and seafood

To prepare fish, you clean and scale it, but you don't remove the skin. You don't have to remove the tiny bones, either (they'll become soft and edible when canned). Then you cut it into pieces long enough to fill the jar and leave 1-inch headspace. If cutting chunks is desired, simply cut into pieces roughly the same size, again leaving 1-inch headspace.

To measure how long to cut your fish pieces, place the size jar you are using alongside a fillet of fish.

Filling the jar

Place the fish pieces into pint jars, skin side facing out (for a prettier finished jar), and leave 1-inch headspace, as shown in Figure 11-2. (Fish is not suitable for quart canning.)

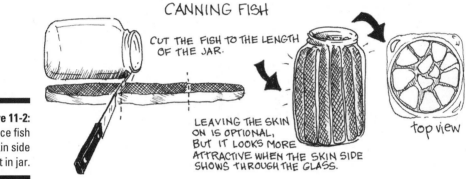

CANNING FISH

CUT THE FISH TO THE LENGTH OF THE JAR.

LEAVING THE SKIN ON IS OPTIONAL, BUT IT LOOKS MORE ATTRACTIVE WHEN THE SKIN SIDE SHOWS THROUGH THE GLASS.

top view

Figure 11-2:
Place fish
skin side
out in jar.

Fish and seafood need to be canned as quickly as possible — preferably the day it's caught. If you want to can either of these foods, make a plan that includes the actual trip out to catch them. That way, your supplies are organized and ready to use when you return to the kitchen. When you have a basket of fish waiting to be canned, that is no time to be looking for your canning tongs.

Canned Freshwater Fish

This recipe is one that my family loves. I (Amy) use it primarily as the base for a quick fish chowder. On a cold night, it tastes wonderful with crusty bread and a canned fruit on the side.

Preparation time: *1 hour*

Processing time: *1 hour 40 minutes*

Pressure level: *10 pounds*

Yield: *12 pints*

25 pounds fresh fish   *Canning salt*

1 Prepare the canning jars and two-piece caps (lids and screw bands) according to the manufacturer's instructions. Keep the jars and lids hot. (For detailed instructions on preparing your jars, see Chapter 4.)

2 Clean the fish, removing the entrails, scales, head, tail, and fins. Leave the skin intact. Cut the pieces of cleaned fish to fit the jars minus 1 inch for the required headspace; see Figure 11-2.

3 Fill the hot jars with fish, skin side out (refer to Figure 11-2) and add 1 teaspoon salt to each jar. Wipe the jar rims; seal the jars with the two-piece caps, hand-tightening the bands.

4 Process the filled jars in a pressure canner at 10 pounds pressure for 1 hour 40 minutes. When the processing time is done, allow the pressure to return to 0, wait an additional 10 minutes, and then carefully open the canner lid. (Head to Chapter 9 for detailed processing instructions for pressure canning.)

5 Remove the hot jars with a jar lifter. Place the jars on a clean kitchen towel in a draft-free area. After the jars cool completely, test the seals (refer to Chapter 4). (If you find jars that haven't sealed, immediately refrigerate them and use them within one week.) Boil the contents of each jar for 15 minutes before tasting or eating.

Per 4-ounce serving: *Calories 212 (From fat 85); Fat 9g (Saturated 2g); Cholesterol 83mg; Sodium 788mg; Carbohydrates 0g (Dietary fiber 0g); Protein 30g.*

Including Meats in Other Canned Mixes

When thinking about your pantry contents, don't forget to add a few canned dishes that contain both vegetables and meats. These complete meals in a jar not only taste better than convenience food you can buy in a store, but they're also fresher and definitely more healthy.

Canning a soup or stew gives you a little more breathing room for experimentation. Because you are canning based on the meat — the item that needs to be pressurized the longest — any other vegetable will be safely canned right along with it. When you are designing these soups and stews for your family, you can easily substitute vegetables or add more of another veggie that your family especially enjoys.

Following are some pointers:

  ✔ **When using strongly flavored vegetables, remember a little goes a long way.** Strongly flavored veggies, like those in the Brassica family (cabbage, Brussels sprouts, broccoli, and cauliflower, for example) tend to have an even more pronounced flavor after canning. If you are adding any of these vegetables, use a light touch. You can add cabbage to any soup you make, for example, but add only about half the amount you add of the other vegetables.

  ✔ **Leave out the noodles or rice when canning.** Otherwise, your noodles end up overcooked and too soft. Rice seems to do fairly well; brown holds up better than white rice, but again it may become too soft for your family to enjoy.

Since you are going to bring the canned product to a boil for at least 15 minutes before eating, that's the perfect time to add your noodles or rice. The noodles can cook as the canned ingredients heat.

When you open a can of homemade soup or stew, you may find that it's thicker (in the case of the stew) or that the vegetables have gathered together at the bottom of the jar. This is harmless. After warming, it will thin and combine into the soup or stew you started out with. For recipes that combine meats and other ingredients, go to Chapter 12.

Chapter 12

Combining the Harvest: Soups, Sauces, and Beans

In This Chapter

▶ Discovering the benefits of mixing your vegetables

▶ Choosing a safe processing method

▶ Loading your meals with flavor

▶ Getting along with tomatoes

▶ Mixing it up with beans

*N*ot all canned foods are simply one ingredient. Canning combinations of foods gives you meals that are as fast and easy as store-bought heat-and-eat varieties. With a little bit of advanced planning during the growing season, you'll keep your shelves stocked with a variety of meals for people on the go. In this chapter, you get tips for combining high- and low-acid foods into savory soups, delectable sauces, or hearty one-pot meals. After your family gets a whiff of the aroma coming out of the kitchen, they'll think you've been slaving over the stove all day!

Whenever you combine low- and high-acid foods, as the recipes in this chapter do, always use pressure canning. For complete details on pressure canning, refer to Chapter 9.

The Lowdown on Canning Combined Foods

Pressure canning soups, sauces, and one-pot meals is the answer for healthy, quick meals without filling up your freezer. Pressure canning is a major timesaver in the long run: If you spend one day (or even a weekend) preparing soups, sauces, and other hearty meals, you can get a hot meal on the table in a flash and keep your freezer for ice cream and other treats!

But you have to think about more than which food combos go well together: You also have to know which processing method to use to safely preserve combined foods, which may contain both high- and low-acid foods.

Choosing a processing method

As we've mentioned elsewhere in this book, the only processing methods approved by the United States Department of Agriculture (USDA) for safely home-canning food are

- ✔ **Water-bath canning:** For canning high-acid foods (like fruit and tomatoes)
- ✔ **Pressure canning:** For canning low-acid foods (including vegetables and meat) and for canning high- and low-acid foods combined.

Mixing low-acid foods and high-acid foods

Knowing that a pot of chili or spaghetti sauce contains both high-acid and low-acid foods (the chili contains tomatoes and vegetables, and the spaghetti sauce contains meat, tomatoes, and vegetables), how do you determine which method is right while still ensuring a safe product? Follow this rule:

Whenever you combine low- and high-acid foods, process the food as though it were low-acid: Use the pressure-canning method. For the same reason, whenever you include meat, fish, poultry, or seafood in your canned product, use pressure canning. Pressure canning, explained in detail in Chapter 9, is the *only* safe processing method to use when combining low-acid and high-acid foods. (For detailed instructions for pressure canning meat, fish, poultry, or seafood, refer to Chapter 11.)

Quite simply, adding low-acid foods to high-acids foods raises the acidity level of the food being processed above 4.6 pH (see Chapter 3), and the higher the acidity number, the less acidic a food is.

Mixing like foods with like

When you mix like foods with like (high-acid foods with other high-acid foods, for example, or low-acid foods with other low-acid foods), you process them in the manner suggested for their acidity level. Two high-acid fruits can be processed in a water-bath canner, and two low-acid foods can be pressure canned together. Always follow a recipe and make no changes.

Tips for a successful meal

Obviously, the most important thing to know about processing combined products is to use the right processing method (as explained in the preceding section). Beyond that, there are other things you can do to ensure a successful product and a delicious (and easy) meal, explained in the following sections.

Cut all ingredients uniformly to ensure even heating

Make sure all your fruits, vegetables, and meat pieces are as even as possible, the same as you would for regular stove cooking.

Use the longest processing time given when combining foods

For example, the processing time for corn alone in a 1-quart jar is 1 hour 25 minutes. The processing time for lima beans alone in a 1-quart jar is 50 minutes. Therefore, the correct processing time for combining corn and lima beans in a 1-quart jar is 1 hour 25 minutes.

Follow the recipe exactly

Don't be tempted to add or adjust the ingredients in your recipe. Any variation changes the acidity level as well as the processing time (and sometimes the processing method) needed to destroy the microorganisms that cause botulism, the most serious form of food poisoning (refer to Chapter 3).

And always use the jar size recommended in your recipe. Some combination foods may be canned in either pints or quarts; other foods may be suited only for pints.

Don't add uncooked pasta or rice to your food before canning your jars

While these are wonderful additions to soups, the intense heat of pressure canning disintegrates your pasta or rice. For example, if your pasta cooking time in boiling water is 8 to 10 minutes and you extended the period to 30 minutes or longer at a temperature higher than boiling water (as occurs in the pressure canner), you end up with something that doesn't resemble pasta or rice. For best results when adding uncooked pasta or rice to your soup, do the following:

  1. **Complete the 15-minute boiling period for your canned food.**

2. **Add the pasta (or rice) to the boiling soup, cooking it for the time recommended on the package.**

3. **Test the pasta (or rice) for doneness.**

Getting your meal on the table

After selecting a jar from your pantry, follow these simple steps for quick, timesaving meals:

1. **Bring your canned food to a boil in a large pot, boiling the food for 15 minutes.**

   Don't be tempted to taste your food until after the boiling period has elapsed.

2. **Add your seasonings, such as salt, pepper, and fresh herbs.**

3. **Serve and enjoy!**

Whenever you pressure-can, you *must* boil the contents of the jar for 15 minutes before tasting or eating. Refer to Chapter 3 for safety information.

Stocking Up on Soup

Soup is the ultimate comfort food. The road to great soup starts with a flavorful *stock,* which is water infused with the flavors of vegetables and/or the bones from beef, poultry, or fish. A *reduced stock* is boiled rapidly, thus reducing the amount of liquid by evaporation and producing an intense flavor.

Chicken Stock

You can either purchase chicken and reserve the meat for another use or use the parts you may not normally eat, such as the neck, the back, the wings, or the less-often used heart, liver, and gizzards. These pieces are packed with flavor, but using or not using them is up to you.

Preparation time: *2 hours*

Processing time: *Pints, 20 minutes; quarts, 25 minutes*

Pressure level: *10 pounds*

Yield: *About 8 pints or 4 quarts*

3 to 4 pounds chicken pieces	*2 medium onions, quartered*
4 quarts water	*15 peppercorns*
2 stalks celery, leaves attached, cut into 1-inch pieces	*3 bay leaves*
	Salt, to taste

1 Combine the chicken and water in a 6- to 8-quart pot; bring the mixture to a boil over high heat. Add the celery, onions, peppercorns, bay leaves, and salt. Reduce the heat; simmer, covered, about 2 hours or until the chicken is tender. Remove from the heat; skim off any foam. Remove the chicken pieces, reserving the chicken for another use.

2 While the stock is simmering, prepare your canning jars and two-piece caps (lids and screw bands) according to the manufacturer's instructions. Keep the jars and lids hot. (For information on preparing your jars, see Chapter 4.)

3 Strain the stock through a mesh strainer or several layers of cheesecloth into a large bowl. Once the stock has cooled enough to place it in the refrigerator, chill the stock until you can easily remove the fat.

4 Once the fat is removed, return the stock to the pot and bring it to a boil.

5 Ladle the boiling hot stock into your prepared jars, leaving 1-inch headspace. Wipe the jar rims; seal the jars with the two-piece caps, hand-tightening the bands.

6 Process your filled jars in a pressure canner at 10 pounds pressure for 20 minutes (pints) or 25 minutes (quarts). After the pressure in the canner has returned to 0, wait an additional 10 minutes, and then carefully open the canner lid. (Head to Chapter 9 for detailed processing instructions for pressure canning.)

7 Remove the hot jars with a jar lifter. Place them on a clean kitchen towel away from drafts. After the jars cool completely, test the seals (refer to Chapter 4). (If you find jars that haven't sealed, immediately refrigerate them and use them within one week.) Boil the contents of each jar for 15 minutes before tasting or eating.

Per 1-cup serving: *Calories 6 (From fat 2); Fat 0g (Saturated 0g); Cholesterol 3mg; Sodium 39mg; Carbohydrates 0g (Dietary fiber 0g); Protein 1g.*

Turkey Stock with Vegetables

This is a great recipe to make after a holiday meal when you have a turkey left over that is mostly picked clean of meat. There is still plenty of delicious flavor in the carcass, and this soup is a family favorite.

Preparation time: *4 hours 30 minutes*

Processing time: *Pints, 1 hour; quarts, 1 hour 25 minutes*

Pressure level: *10 pounds*

Yield: *About 14 pints or 7 quarts*

Carcass from a 12- to 15-pound turkey	*4 cups sweet corn*
3 quarts water	*2 cups chopped cabbage*
1 quart Beans with Salt Pork (later in this chapter)	*2 cups chopped onions*
	2 cups sliced carrots
2 quarts Canned Tomatoes (Chapter 6)	*2 cups sliced celery*

1 Combine the water and turkey carcass in a 10- to 12-quart pot. Bring the mixture to a boil over high heat. Reduce the heat; simmer, covered, for 2 hours. Remove the lid and continue cooking for 2 hours more.

2 Strain and remove the bones from the stock. Check the broth for seasoning, taking note that there may be salt and seasoning in the broth from the previous roasting of the turkey. Add additional seasonings to taste.

3 Add the beans, tomatoes, corn, cabbage, onions, carrots, and celery to the strained stock and return it to a boil. Boil for 5 minutes. (Your goal is simply to heat the soup to a boil so that it's as hot as possible for canning. Your goal is *not* to completely cook your vegetables.)

4 While the stock is simmering, prepare the canning jars and two-piece caps (lids and screw bands) according to the manufacturer's instructions. Keep the jars and lids hot. (For information on preparing your jars, see Chapter 4.)

5 Ladle the hot soup into your prepared jars, leaving 1-inch headspace. Release any air bubbles with a nonreactive utensil (refer to Chapter 3), adding more stock as necessary to maintain the proper headspace. Wipe the rims; seal the jars with the two-piece caps, hand-tightening the bands.

6 Process your filled jars in a pressure canner at 10 pounds pressure for 1 hour (pints) and 1 hour 25 minutes (quarts). After the pressure in the canner has returned to 0, wait an additional 10 minutes, and then carefully open the canner lid. (Head to Chapter 9 for detailed instructions for pressure canning.)

7 Remove the jars from the canner with a jar lifter. Place them on a clean kitchen towel away from drafts. After the jars cool completely, test the seals (refer to Chapter 4). (If you find jars that haven't sealed, immediately refrigerate them and use them within one week.) Boil the contents of each jar for 15 minutes before tasting or eating.

Per 1-cup serving: Calories 120 (From fat 34); Fat 4g (Saturated 1g); Cholesterol 10mg; Sodium 62mg; Carbohydrates 17g (Dietary fiber 4g); Protein 7g.

Teaming Up with Tomatoes

Although tomatoes alone can be water-bath canned (see Chapter 5), if you combine them with low-acid vegetables, it changes the pH (acidity level). These combined foods must be treated and processed as low-acid foods — that means with a pressure canner.

Heirloom tomatoes and a bit of tomato trivia

If you have only ever eaten the round, red variety of tomato from the supermarket, you must go out and find a local market or roadside stand and feast on some heirloom varieties.

Unlike commercial tomatoes, which have been bred to enhance characteristics other than taste (like disease resistance or tougher skins), heirloom tomatoes haven't been scientifically engineered in any way. They have the same characteristics as their ancestors, whose seeds have been passed down from generation to generation. In addition, heirloom tomatoes are an "open-pollinated" tomato plant, meaning that they're pollinated naturally rather than artificially.

Heirloom tomatoes come in a surprising variety of colors: striped, pink, red, yellow, orange, black, and even white. Some heirloom tomatoes are perfectly ripe and yet remain perfectly green!

Once you bite into the rich, juicy taste of one of these homegrown beauties, you'll scoff at the perfectly shaped but tasteless varieties that seem to be available all the time in the produce aisle of big grocery stores.

Here's a bit of trivia: You may have learned in elementary school that earlier American settlers avoided tomatoes because they thought they were poisonous. Know why? Some people speculate their hesitation was the result of two things: the tomato plants rank smell and the fact that tomatoes are related to "deadly nightshade" (also called henbane), a poisonous herb.

Stewed Tomatoes with Celery

Homemade stewed tomatoes are perfect in soups or sauces, as a condiment on scrambled eggs, or spooned over steamed summer squash with a grating of cheddar cheese.

Preparation time: *20 minutes*

Cooking time: *15 minutes*

Processing time: *Pints, 15 minutes; quarts, 20 minutes*

Yield: *About 6 pints or 3 quarts*

5 to 6 pounds of peeled tomatoes to measure 4 quarts, chopped and seeded, reserving all liquid

1 large stalk celery, chopped

½ medium onion, chopped

¼ green bell pepper, chopped

1 tablespoon granulated sugar

2 teaspoons salt

1 Prepare your canning jars and two-piece caps (lids and screw bands) according to the manufacturer's instructions. Keep the jars and lids hot. (For instructions on preparing your jars, see Chapter 4.)

2 Combine the tomatoes, celery, onions, bell pepper, sugar, and salt in a 5- to 6-quart pot. Bring the mixture to a boil over high heat. Reduce the heat to medium, cover, and simmer for 10 minutes, stirring to prevent sticking.

3 Ladle the hot tomatoes into the prepared jars, leaving 1-inch headspace. Release any air bubbles with a nonreactive utensil (refer to Chapter 3), adding more tomatoes as necessary to maintain the proper headspace. Wipe the jar rims; seal the jars with the two-piece caps, hand-tightening the bands.

4 Process your filled jars in a pressure canner at 10 pounds pressure for 15 minutes (pints) or 20 minutes (quarts). After the pressure in the canner has returned to 0, wait an additional 10 minutes, and then carefully open the canner lid. (Head to Chapter 9 for detailed instructions on pressure canning.)

5 Remove the hot jars with a jar lifter. Place them on a clean kitchen towel away from drafts. After the jars cool completely, test the seals (refer to Chapter 4). (If you find jars that haven't sealed, immediately refrigerate them and use them within one week.) Boil the contents of each jar for 15 minutes before tasting or eating.

Per 1-cup serving: *Calories 40 (From fat 0); Fat 0g (Saturated 0g); Cholesterol 0mg; Sodium 535mg; Carbohydrates 8g (Dietary fiber 2g); Protein 3g.*

Italian Style Tomatoes

These seasoned tomatoes are the perfect addition to any Italian meal. Cook them down even further and you have an amazing Marinara sauce. These tomatoes are a staple ingredient in any well-stocked pantry.

Preparation time: *10 minutes*

Processing time: *Pints, 15 minutes; quarts, 20 minutes*

Pressure level: *10 pounds*

Yield: *6 pints or 3 quarts*

4 quarts chopped tomatoes	*1 tablespoon sugar*
¾ cup chopped celery	*2 teaspoons dried marjoram*
¾ cup chopped onion	*4 cups sugar*
½ cup green pepper	

1 Prepare your canning jars and two-piece caps (lids and screw bands) according to the manufacturer's instructions. Keep the jars and lids hot. (For detailed instructions on preparing your jars, see Chapter 4.)

2 Combine all ingredients in a heavy pot; then cover and cook them for 10 minutes.

3 Ladle the hot mixture into the prepared jars, leaving 1-inch headspace. Release any air bubbles with a nonreactive utensil (refer to Chapter 3), adding more of the mixture as necessary to maintain the proper headspace. Wipe the jar rims; seal the jars with the two-piece caps, hand-tightening the bands.

4 Process the filled jars in a pressure canner at 10 pounds pressure for 15 minutes (pints) or 20 minutes (quarts). When the processing time is done, allow the pressure to return to 0, wait an additional 10 minutes, and then carefully open the canner lid. (Head to Chapter 9 for detailed processing instructions for pressure canning.)

5 Remove the jars from the canner with a jar lifter. Place them on a clean kitchen towel away from drafts. After the jars cool completely, test the seals (see Chapter 4). If you find jars that haven't sealed, refrigerate them and use them within two weeks. Boil the contents of each jar for 15 minutes before tasting or eating.

*Per ½-**cup serving:** Calories 159 (From fat 4); Fat 0g (Saturated 0g); Cholesterol 0mg; Sodium 14mg; Carbohydrates 40g (Dietary fiber 2g); Protein 1g.*

Spaghetti Sauce with Meat

Everyone seems to have his or her favorite recipe for spaghetti sauce. After much recipe testing, this is the one my (Amy's) family likes the best.

Preparation time: *2 to 2½ hours*

Processing time: *Pints, 1 hour 5 minutes*

Yield: *About 5 pints*

12 ounces Italian sausage, bulk or links, mild or hot

½ pound ground beef or turkey

2 medium onions, chopped

4 garlic cloves, minced

2 carrots, peeled and finely chopped

2 stalks celery, finely chopped

½ pound mushrooms, sliced

Two 6-ounce cans tomato paste

2 quarts canned stewed tomatoes, including the liquid

1 cup red wine

1 tablespoon fresh basil, chopped

1 cup chopped Italian flat-leaf parsley

1 teaspoon salt (omit if salt was added to your canned tomatoes)

Freshly ground pepper, to taste

1 Remove the sausage casings if you're using link sausage. Brown the sausage in a 5- or 6-quart pot over medium heat, stirring to break up the sausage. Add the ground meat and the onions; continue cooking until the meat is brown and the onions are translucent. Drain off any fat.

2 Add the garlic, carrots, celery, and mushrooms to the pan with the sausage and ground meat; cook an additional 2 to 3 minutes. Add the tomato paste, tomatoes, wine, basil, parsley, salt, and pepper. Bring the mixture to a boil over high heat; reduce the heat to medium low and simmer covered for 1½ to 2 hours, stirring often, until the sauce has thickened.

3 While the sauce is simmering, prepare your canning jars and two-piece caps (lids and screw bands) according to the manufacturer's instructions. Keep the jars and lids hot. (For instructions on preparing your jars, see Chapter 4.)

4 Ladle the hot sauce into the prepared jars, leaving 1-inch headspace. Release any air bubbles with a nonreactive utensil (refer to Chapter 3), adding more sauce as necessary to maintain the proper headspace. Wipe the jar rims; seal the jars with the two-piece caps, hand-tightening the bands.

5 Process your filled pint jars in a pressure canner at 10 pounds pressure for 1 hour 5 minutes. After the pressure in the canner has returned to 0, wait an additional 10 minutes and then carefully open the canner lid. (Head to Chapter 9 for detailed instructions on pressure canning.)

6 Remove the hot jars with a jar lifter. Place them on a clean kitchen towel away from drafts. After the jars cool completely, test the seals (refer to Chapter 4). (If you find jars that haven't sealed, immediately refrigerate them and use them within one week.) Boil the contents of each jar for 15 minutes before tasting or eating.

Vary it! *For a meatless sauce, follow all the recipe instructions, omitting the sausage and meat. Process your pints for 25 minutes at 10 pounds pressure.*

Per 1-cup serving: Calories 164 (From fat 66); Fat 7g (Saturated 3g); Cholesterol 28mg; Sodium 552mg; Carbohydrates 13g (Dietary fiber 3g); Protein 12g.

Rounding Out Your Meals with Beans

Beans are high in protein, calcium, phosphorus, and iron, and are a good source of fiber. The more your family eats them in their regular diet, the less they will suffer from any gassiness. There are very effective over-the-counter remedies that can be used in the meantime.

Baked Beans

Basic baked beans are the perfect accompaniment to any barbecue or outdoor meal.

Preparation time: *4 hours 15 minutes plus 12 to 18 hours soaking time*

Processing time: *Pints, 1 hour 20 minutes; quarts, 1 hour 35 minutes*

Yield: *About 6 pints or 3 quarts*

2 pounds dried navy beans	*⅔ cup packed brown sugar*
6 quarts water	*4 teaspoons salt*
½ pound bacon cut into pieces	*2 teaspoons powdered mustard*
3 large onions, sliced	*⅔ cup molasses*

1 Place the beans in a 6- to 8-quart pot. Add 3 quarts of water to cover the beans; allow them to soak, covered, for 12 to 18 hours. Drain the beans, but don't rinse.

2 Return the beans to the pot; cover with the remaining 3 quarts of water; bring the mixture to a boil over high heat. Reduce the heat; cover and simmer until the bean skins begin to split. Drain the beans, reserving the liquid.

3 Transfer the beans to a 4-quart or larger covered baking dish. Add the bacon and onions. Combine the brown sugar, salt, mustard, and molasses in a large mixing bowl. Add 4 cups of the reserved bean liquid (if needed, add water to make 4 cups). Pour the sauce mixture over the beans. Don't stir. Cover the beans and bake them in a preheated 350-degree oven for 3 to 3½ hours. The consistency should be like a thick soup. Add more liquid if the beans become too dry.

4 While the beans are baking, prepare your canning jars and two-piece caps (lids and screw bands) according to the manufacturer's instructions. Keep the jars and lids hot. (For instructions on preparing your jars, see Chapter 4.)

5 Ladle the hot beans into your prepared jars, leaving 1-inch headspace. Release any air bubbles with a nonreactive tool (refer to Chapter 3), adding more beans as necessary to maintain the proper a headspace. Wipe the jar rims; seal the jars with the two-piece caps, hand-tightening the bands.

6 Process your filled jars in a pressure canner at 10 pounds pressure for 1 hour 20 minutes (pints) or 1 hour 35 minutes (quarts). After the pressure in the canner has returned to 0, wait an additional 10 minutes, and then carefully open the canner lid. (Head to Chapter 9 for detailed instructions on pressure canning.)

7 Remove the hot jars with a jar lifter. Place them on a clean kitchen towel away from drafts. After the jars cool completely, test the seals (refer to Chapter 4). (If you find jars that haven't sealed, immediately refrigerate them and use them within one week.) Boil the contents of each jar for 15 minutes before tasting or eating.

Per 1-cup serving: *Calories 390 (From fat 39); Fat 4g (Saturated 1g); Cholesterol 5mg; Sodium 889mg; Carbohydrates 73g (Dietary fiber 12g); Protein 17g.*

Beans with Salt Pork

This basic staple item combines plain beans with the light taste of salt pork. You can use these as an add-in for any soups or stews. You'll find them handy to keep on hand year round for those unexpected guests who arrive just at mealtime.

Preparation time: *30 minutes plus 12 hours soaking time*

Processing time: *Pints, 1 hour 20 minutes; quarts, 1 hour 35 minutes*

Pressure level: *10 pounds*

Yield: *About 6 pints or 3 quarts*

1 pound dried beans	*Canning salt (optional)*
4 ounces salt pork, cut into the number of jars you are using (optional)	

1 Cover the dried beans with cool water and let them sit for 12 hours. (This is perfect task right before bed, letting the beans soak all night.) Drain the beans; then cover them with fresh water and bring them to a boil. Allow the beans to boil for 30 minutes.

2 While the beans are boiling, prepare the canning jars and two-piece caps (lids and screw bands) according to the manufacturer's instructions. Keep the jars and lids hot. (For instructions on preparing your jars, see Chapter 4.)

3 Place one piece of salt pork (if desired) into each prepared jar and ladle the hot beans and the resulting bean broth into the jars. If you're not adding salt pork, add ½ teaspoon canning salt to each pint jar or 1 teaspoon salt to each quart jar, leaving 1-inch headspace. Release any air bubbles with a nonreactive utensil (refer to Chapter 3), adding more beans and broth as necessary to maintain the proper headspace. Wipe the rims and adjust the caps.

4 Process your filled jars in a pressure canner at 10 pounds pressure for 1 hour 20 minutes (pints) and 1 hour and 35 minutes (quarts). After the pressure in the canner has returned to 0, wait an additional 10 minutes, and then carefully open the canner lid. (Head to Chapter 9 for detailed instructions on pressure canning.)

5 Remove the hot jars with a jar lifter. Place them on a clean kitchen towel away from drafts. After the jars cool completely, test the seals (refer to Chapter 4). (If you find jars that haven't sealed, immediately refrigerate them and use them within one week.) Boil the contents of each jar for 15 minutes before tasting or eating.

Per 1-cup serving: Calories 273 (From fat 103); Fat 12g (Saturated 4g); Cholesterol 12mg; Sodium 184mg; Carbohydrates 31g (Dietary fiber 9g); Protein 13g.

Part IV
Freezing

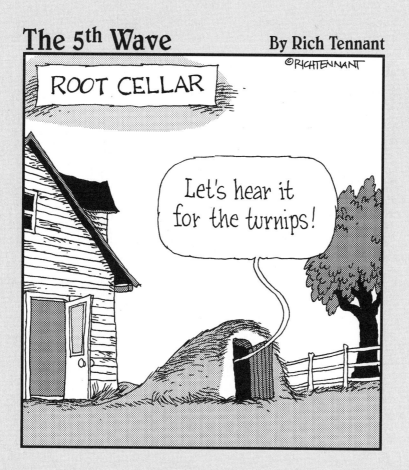

The 5th Wave   By Rich Tennant

©RICHTENNANT

ROOT CELLAR

Let's hear it for the turnips!

In this part . . .

Frozen food doesn't have to be limited to popsicles for the kids and leftovers you tossed in and forgot. With a little planning and few easy-to-follow (and remember) instructions, you can fill your freezer with foods you 1) recognize and 2) actually look forward to eating. This part includes a chapter on the basics of freezing, how to freeze food correctly for optimum flavor, and ideas for getting the most out of your frozen foods. You also find directions for freezing everything from fruits to vegetables to meats. Your freezer will become an important part of your pantry when filled with delicious foods that your family loves.

Chapter 13

Baby, It's Cold Inside!
Freezing Food

● ●

In This Chapter

▶ Exploring the freezing process

▶ Getting acquainted with the spoilers of frozen food

▶ Discovering packaging methods

▶ Perfectly thawing your frozen food

● ●

*W*elcome to freezing, the simplest and least time-consuming method for preserving food. Freezing works well for almost any food. With a minimum of planning and equipment (you may already have most of it), proper storage containers, and basic freezing techniques, keeping food from spoiling and tasting as if you just took it out of the oven or brought it home from the store is a piece of cake. This chapter gives you the basics. The remaining chapters in this part give detailed instructions on freezing particular foods.

Defining Freezing

Since the advent of home refrigeration, people have discovered the joys of prolonging the life of fresh food by freezing. Freezing food is easy, convenient, and relatively inexpensive. The results produced from freezing food are superior to canning or drying. When food is properly prepared, packaged, and quickly frozen, there's no better method for retaining its natural color, flavor, and nutritive value. The process of freezing lowers the temperature of the food to 0 degrees or colder. This low temperature halts microorganism activity by slowing the growth of enzymes. Freezing doesn't sterilize food or destroy the microorganisms; it only stops the negative changes in the quality of your frozen food. The goal with freezing is to preserve the fresh quality of your food.

Follow these tips for best freezing results:

✔ **Prepare your food quickly.** This means be ready to freeze your foods the same day you pick them or purchase them. Have your supplies ready, and the time set aside to freeze at the peak of freshness.

✔ **Package your food in moisture- and vapor-proof wrappings.** These products don't permit the penetration of air or moisture, two common spoilers. (To find out about other spoilers, head to the next section.)

✔ **Keep your freezer at 0 degrees or colder.** Frozen food stored at 15 to 20 degrees may appear as solid as food stored at 0 degrees or colder, but the quality of your thawed food stored at the warmer temperature is lower than food stored at 0 degrees or colder.

✔ **Properly thaw your food to preserve its quality and eliminate bacteria growth.** For thawing instructions, head to the later section "Thawing Out Your Frozen Food."

Meeting the Spoilers of Frozen Foods

Before getting started, you need to recognize the spoilers of frozen food. These spoilers reduce the quality, flavor, and freezer life of frozen foods. One or more of these may occur before, during, or after freezing. For detailed information on the spoilers, refer to Chapter 3.

Bacteria, molds, and yeast

All fresh food contains microorganisms or bacteria. When active microorganisms are present in food, they multiply quickly and destroy the quality of your food, sometimes right before your eyes. The best example of this is a loaf of bread that becomes covered with green mold.

Prevent the growth of bacteria, mold, or yeast in your food by following these guidelines:

✔ **Select food of the highest quality.**

✔ **Freeze your food at a temperature of 0 degrees or colder.**

✔ **Use sanitary conditions when handling and preparing your food.**

Bacteria are microorganisms that have no chlorophyll. Some bacteria may cause disease; other bacteria are actually good and are required for the fermentation process, such as that used for making beer.

Enzymes

Enzymes speed up the ripening process and change the color and flavor of your food. Use these methods to retain the colors and the flavors in fresh fruits and vegetables before the freezing process:

- ✓ **Add sugar and *antioxidants,* a commercial anti-darkening agent (see Chapter 5).** These keep fruit from darkening in color.

- ✓ ***Blanch* your veggies:** Briefly plunge them into boiling water and then into cold water to stop the cooking process.

Not all enzyme reactions are bad: When beef is *aged,* it sits in a chilled room for about one week. The enzymes naturally tenderize the meat, making it more desirable to consume. Fermenting foods, that is, allowing good enzymes to change a food's basic makeup, creates healthy and delicious new foods.

Freezer burn and oxidation

Freezer burn and oxidation result from air coming in contact with your frozen food. *Freezer burn* is a change in color, texture, and flavor in the food during the freezing period because the air in the freezer removes moisture from the food and dries it out.

Oxidation is a chemical change in your frozen food. The technical term is *lipid oxidation,* which occurs on an atomic level and has to do with hydrogen atoms and free radicals. What is important to know is that enzymes have a lot to do with oxidation. By blanching foods (most commonly vegetables) before freezing, you stop or at least slow down the enzymes' actions and delay oxidation. Other steps you take to prevent oxidation are to properly wrap foods, use suitable containers, and follow correct storage times. (Check out "Packaging Is Everything" later in this chapter.) Oxidized foods have a funny or off taste and color.

Ice crystals

When you think of ice crystals, you probably think of winter and snowflakes. But in the world of freezing, ice crystals aren't charming at all. They cause your frozen food to lose liquid and darken. Because the freezing process essentially turns the water in food to ice, the way to eliminate destructive ice crystals is to keep them as small as possible. This is accomplished by a fast freeze and keeping foods as cold as possible at a temperature of 0 degrees or lower.

Gearing Up to Fill Your Freezer

Whether food is fresh from your garden or fresh from a store, the selection choices you make have an effect on the quality of your food after it's thawed. Of course, packaging materials, packaging procedures, and thawing methods play an important role in your frozen-food quality, as well.

Knowing what should (and shouldn't be) frozen

In practice, any food can be frozen. In reality, not all foods freeze well because of their texture or composition. The key to being happy with the results of freezing is to make sure you select foods that freeze well. There are almost too many categories of good foods for the freezer, but in general, you can freeze most fresh vegetables and fruits, meats and fish, breads and cakes, and clear soups and casseroles.

Here's a list of foods that don't freeze well:

- ✔ **Cooked frostings and frostings made with fluffy egg whites and whipped cream.** These types of frostings become soft and *weep* (emit a thick liquid). *Note:* Butter-based frostings freeze well.

- ✔ **Cooked pasta:** Reheated cooked pasta is soft, mushy, and shapeless.

- ✔ **Custards and cream-pie fillings:** These foods turn watery and lumpy.

- ✔ **Egg whites and meringues:** These crack, toughen, and turn rubbery.

- ✔ **Mayonnaise:** This condiment breaks down and separates.

- ✔ **Raw fruits or vegetables with a high water content:** Foods with a high water content break down when frozen and become mushy beyond recognition when thawed. Some examples are lettuce, watermelon, citrus fruit, and cucumbers. Tomatoes are an exception to this if you're using them in cooked dishes, like stews. Tomatoes also become soft and watery, but usually this texture is desired in a soup or other cooked dish.

    When freezing fresh tomatoes, cut them into quarters. Package them in one-cup portions for quick freezing and easy measuring.

- ✔ **Sauces and gravy:** Thickened sauces and milk gravies separate when they're frozen. Freeze your *pan drippings;* the juices produced from cooking a roast or turkey freeze without adding a thickener.

- ✔ **Yogurt, cream cheese, and sour cream:** These tend to separate.

- ✔ **Soft cheeses, ricotta, and cottage cheese:** These tend to break down and separate when frozen.

✔ **Potatoes:** These become watery and grey when thawed. You could use them in a cooked dish, but even then the texture is so mealy that they're not recommended in your frozen foods list.

Evaluating your freezer

Before you embark of a freezing frenzy, you need to make sure your freezer is in good working order: that is, frost free and maintains a constant temperature of 0 degrees or lower.

✔ **Getting rid of frost:** Today, most freezers are *frostfree*, automatically defrosting any buildup of ice in the freezer. Freezers that don't automatically defrost require defrosting when the ice buildup is ¾ inch, or at least once a year. You need to empty your freezer before defrosting it. (Refer to your owner's manual for instructions for defrosting your freezer.)

Keep your freezer operating in top-notch condition with proper care and maintenance according to the manufacturer's recommendations (refer to your owner's manual). If you've misplaced your manual or have questions regarding maintenance or usage, contact your local appliance company or search on the Internet for the manufacturer's Web site.

✔ **Checking your freezer's temperature:** Adjust your freezer thermostat, as needed, to maintain a temperature of 0 degrees or colder. Purchase a freezer thermometer to monitor the internal temperature of your freezer.

Add no more food to your freezer than can freeze solid in 24 hours, about 2 to 3 pounds of food for each cubic foot of freezer space. Adding a large quantity of food to your freezer at one time may raise the temperature in the freezer above 0 degrees. This stops the quick-freezing process and may affect the quality of your frozen food.

Types of freezers

Select a freezer based on your needs, the size of your family, the space available to you, your budget, and the cost required for running the freezer.

Refrigerators with freezer compartments are the most common units in homes today. The preferred model has a separate door for the refrigerator and the freezer. This allows you to regulate the temperature in each compartment with individual built-in thermostats.

Upright freezers and chest freezers are made for freezing only. Upright freezers have a door on the front with shelves inside, while a chest freezer opens from the top and you reach into it. Sizes vary from 6 cubic feet of storage to 32 cubic feet of storage.

Packaging Your Food and Filling Your Freezer

Proper packaging is important for preserving the quality of your frozen food both during the freezing process and after it's thawed. Any excess air in your container may compromise the quality of your thawed food. Remove as much air as possible in bags and wraps, and allow the recommended headspace in rigid freezer containers.

Similarly, how you fill your freezer is also important. Put too much unfrozen food in at once and the temperature may rise above 0 degrees. Fail to rotate your food and you're more likely to use newer food before older food. The following sections explain how to package your food, pack your freezer, and keep everything organized.

It's a wrap! Choosing a container

Protecting foods during the storage period requires containers that are easy to seal, suitable for low temperatures, and, most importantly, moisture and vapor proof. Three types of packaging materials meet the criteria for properly freezing food: rigid containers, freezer bags, and freezer paper and wrap.

Rigid containers

Rigid containers are the perfect solution for freezing any soft or liquid food, such as casseroles and soups, and they're reusable. The most desirable material for rigid containers is plastic, although some glass jars are made for freezing. Container sizes range from ¼ of a cup to 1 quart with a variety of sizes in between. Purchase container sizes that fit your freezing needs.

Choose square- or rectangular-shaped containers. They save space and fit better in your freezer than round containers.

Rigid containers approved for freezing prevent the spoilers from attacking your food as well as stopping moisture and vapors from penetrating your food. When you use them, be sure to allow the proper headspace so that your food or liquid can expand without forcing the top off (you can find a table listing headspace guidelines in Chapter 15). A good rule: Allow ½ inch of head-space for shallow containers and 1 inch for tall containers. For freezing in freezer bags, always press all the air possible out of the bag.

Freezer bags

Freezer bags are readily available, reasonably inexpensive, require a minimum amount of storage space, and come in a variety of sizes. When using freezer bags (we prefer the locking zipper variety), purchase bags labeled for freezing, because the thickness is moisture proof and protects the flavor of your food.

After placing your food in the bag, force out as much air as possible by folding the filled part of the bag against the nonfilled portion of the bag, pressing the air out while sealing the bag.

Freezer paper and wraps

Freezer paper comes coated or laminated and protects your wrapped food from air and freezer burn. Other freezer papers include heavy-duty foil, clear plastic wrap, waxed paper, and polyethylene (plastic) sheets.

Vacuum sealing machines

A vacuum sealing machine is a handy appliance that's great for packaging foods for the freezer. Air is almost completely removed from the package through a suction process, the trademark of this appliance. Most vacuum sealing machines use materials that are freezer safe or even microwavable and boil-proof. (This is handy for single-serving meals for home or at work.)

Consider these additional items when you're purchasing a vacuum sealing machine:

- ✔ **Cost:** Electric plug-in types range from a low of $50 to upward of $300. There are new battery or hand-powered vacuum sealers that are available for as little as $10. Although relatively new to the market, the reviews look promising.

- ✔ **Replacement bags:** Most machines include bags to get you started. Consider the cost of replacement bags and the reputation of the manufacturer. Investing in a vacuum sealer that is limited by a certain make of bags may limit use of your machine in years to come.

- ✔ **Storage requirements:** Depending on the size of your kitchen, storing a vacuum sealing machine may or may not be an issue. The ideal location for a vacuum sealer is usually on a counter, where you can use it at a moment's notice.

To extend the life of your vacuum sealing bags, cut them larger than necessary and reseal them each time you remove some of the food inside. This works well for dry products. You can also refill and reseal the bags if the item inside was dry and fresh. This technique is not recommended for juicy foods or meats.

These papers and wraps are especially useful when packaging irregularly shaped foods, such as steaks and roasts. Freezer paper is primarily used for meat, because tight wrapping forces out excess air. To freezer-wrap something, follow these steps (see Figure 13-1):

1. **Tear off a piece of freezer paper about double the size of your food (to ensure there are no exposed areas).**

2. **Place the food on the paper as close to a corner as you can get it without overlapping the paper.**

3. **Fold the corner tightly over the meat.**

4. **Fold the sides tightly over the center, one at a time.**

5. **Roll the package over until you reach the end of your freezer paper.**

6. **Securely tape the ends with *freezer tape,* a tape suited for cold temperatures.**

Alternatively, you can use drugstore wrap, also shown in Figure 13-1.

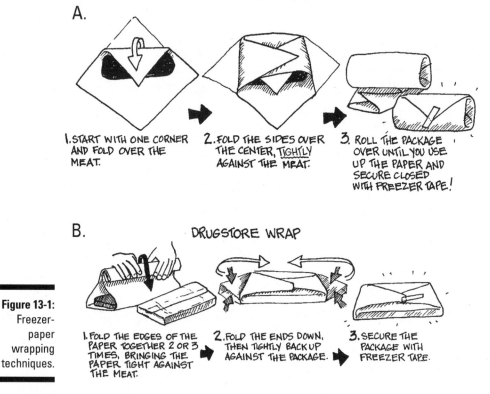

BUTCHER WRAP

A.

1. START WITH ONE CORNER AND FOLD OVER THE MEAT.

2. FOLD THE SIDES OVER THE CENTER, TIGHTLY AGAINST THE MEAT.

3. ROLL THE PACKAGE OVER UNTIL YOU USE UP THE PAPER AND SECURE CLOSED WITH FREEZER TAPE!

B. DRUGSTORE WRAP

1. FOLD THE EDGES OF THE PAPER TOGETHER 2 OR 3 TIMES, BRINGING THE PAPER TIGHT AGAINST THE MEAT.

2. FOLD THE ENDS DOWN, THEN TIGHTLY BACK UP AGAINST THE PACKAGE.

3. SECURE THE PACKAGE WITH FREEZER TAPE.

Figure 13-1: Freezer-paper wrapping techniques.

Tracking your frozen food trail

How many times have you looked in your freezer in astonishment that it's full and yet you have no idea what's taking up so much space? Have you ever defrosted what you thought was soup, only to discover you're now having stewed tomatoes for dinner? Solve the dilemma of freezer mystery food by following these simple tips:

✔ **Label each package with the item and the date before placing your food in the freezer.** Also include the weight of a roast, the quantity of cut-up tomatoes, your preparation method, or the number of servings. Use an indelible marker or a waterproof pen, which won't rub off.

✔ **Keep an up-to-date written record of food in your freezer to help with your meal planning.** Any sheet of paper works well. Make columns with the following headings: date, item (roast, spaghetti sauce, and so on), quantity or weight (1 cup or 3 pounds, for example), and any recipe or preparation ideas. Keep the list on your freezer door, crossing off items as you use them.

Packing your freezer

How you pack your freezer has an impact on the quality of your frozen foods. Follow these guidelines:

✔ **Cool your food to room temperature or chill it slightly before putting it in the freezer.** Doing this speeds up the freezing process (the freezer doesn't have to work so hard to get the prechilled food down to 0 or lower) and it uses less energy.

✔ **When you first place your foods in the freezer, pack them loosely.** Once they're frozen solid, you can pack them tightly. The extra space initially lets the cold air circulate and freeze the foods more quickly.

✔ **Rotate your food.** To rotate your food, simply add new frozen foods to the back of the freezer and bring the older foods up front. That way you can reach for the front of the group and get the oldest frozen food. Remember this acronym: FIFO (First In, First Out).

✔ **Use your frozen food within one year of freezing.** Table 13-1 lists approximately how long you can keep food in the freezer.

Table 13-1	Recommended Length of Time in the Freezer
Food	*Length of Storage at 0°F (–18C)*
Fruits and vegetables, excluding citrus	12 months
Citrus fruits	3 to 4 months
Poultry	12 months
Fish	2 to 3 months
Ground meat	3 to 4 months
Cured or processed meat	1 to 2 months

Thawing Out Your Frozen Food

Following the guidelines for freezing won't guarantee a great product without practicing proper thawing methods. So what's the big deal about thawing? Freezing only halts the growth of microorganisms. After thawing, bacteria and enzymes in your food are free to multiply as if they hadn't been frozen. Keep this growth at a standstill by thawing your food at a low temperature, preferably in a refrigerator, in its freezer container or packaging.

Thaw only what you need, using your food immediately upon thawing. If your food tastes funny or smells odd, harmful microorganisms may be present. Don't hesitate to dispose of any questionable food.

You don't need to thaw vegetables before adding them to a dish you're cooking. Instead, you can add them directly to the dish in the last 10 minutes of cooking. You can also place frozen unbaked goods directly into the oven to bake. Many previously prepared foods can be placed directly into the oven to reheat and bake as well.

Choices for thawing

Heat makes the spoilers grow faster, so the lower the temperature during the thawing period, the better for you and the quality of your food. Here are your best options for safely thawing and maintaining the quality of your food:

✔ **Thawing in your refrigerator:** This is the best and safest process for thawing your food because of the low temperature. Plan your meal the night before and place your choice in your refrigerator to thaw.

✔ **Thawing at room temperature:** Leave your frozen food at room temperature for 2 hours; then immediately place it in the refrigerator for the remainder of the thawing process. This option is a great alternative if you forgot to take your food out of the freezer the night before.

✔ **Thawing in the microwave:** Use this method only if your microwave has a defrost cycle. This is important because you want the food to defrost evenly, not be cooked in one portion and frozen in another part.

✔ **Thawing in water:** Immerse your packaged food in cold water, never hot or warm water. By maintaining the lowest temperature possible when thawing your food, you'll inhibit bacteria and enzyme activity.

Unplanned thawing

No matter how good technology is, everyone experiences a power failure at one time or another. This may be for a few minutes, a few hours, or, in the worst-case scenario, a few days. Don't panic, keep the freezer door closed, and resist the temptation to open the door to check the temperature.

A fully loaded freezer at 0 degrees or colder usually stays cold enough to keep your food frozen for up to two days. A freezer that's half-full may not keep your food frozen for more than a day because air space doesn't maintain a constant temperature as efficiently as a piece of solidly frozen food.

If you do have a power outage, follow these tips for saving the contents of your freezer:

✔ **Check with your electric company to estimate the length of your power outage.**

If you find that your freezer is the only electric appliance that isn't operating, check the electrical cord and plug for a good connection. If this isn't the problem, check your electrical panel for a blown fuse.

✔ **If you receive advance warning that your electricity will be off, set your freezer temperature to its coldest setting.** The colder temperature delays thawing during the time the electricity is off.

✔ **In the worst-case scenario, your freezer may be out long enough for your food to defrost.** Locate a supplier of dry ice and pack your food in the dry ice before it defrosts completely. (Ask your dry-ice supplier for safe packing and handling instructions.)

Dry ice is a refrigerant of solid carbon dioxide. Handle dry ice with care and never touch it with your bare hands. Even a short exposure to dry ice may cause frostbite.

To refreeze or not to refreeze thawed food

From time to time, even the best-laid plans change and your defrosted food doesn't get used when you planned. If your food is only partially defrosted, indicated by the presence of ice crystals, it may be refrozen.

We don't suggest refreezing food as a regular practice, but if you're considering it for any reason, keep these things in mind:

- ✔ Don't refreeze completely defrosted low-acid foods, such as vegetables or meat sauces, after they reach room temperature. These foods may not be safe to eat.

- ✔ You may refreeze high-acid foods and most fruits and fruit products if they're still cold.

- ✔ You may safely refreeze partially thawed foods containing ice crystals if the food was thawing in your refrigerator.

Refrozen foods have a shorter shelf life than when first frozen. They may also taste different. If you refreeze an item, make a note on the package including the refreezing date. Use refrozen food as soon as possible. Follow this simple rule when evaluating refrozen, thawed food: When in doubt, throw it out! Eating spoiled food can be quite dangerous.

Chapter 14

Meals and Snacks in a Snap: Freezing Prepared Foods

. . . .

In This Chapter

▶ Keeping frozen food as tasty as fresh food

▶ Saving time and money by freezing prepared foods

▶ Freezing meat, poultry, and fish

. . . .

*W*ork, children, school, after-school activities, and more! If you're like most people, you may struggle to get everything done and get a nutritious meal on the table. Filling your freezer with already-prepared or prepackaged meals and snacks allows you plenty of nutritious choices.

Freezing is a great option for taking advantage of buying food in large quantities at bargain prices, making large quantities of food, or saving leftovers. Taking a few minutes to package your food in meal-sized portions allows you flexibility in the amount of food you thaw. In this chapter, you get great tips on freezing food and hints for planning your meals.

The Whys and Wherefores of Freezing Food

There are many benefits of freezing food purchased from your supermarket or foods prepared in your home. These include:

✔ **Time saving:** Freezing food saves you time twice: First, when you plan to freeze a portion, you make extra. Making a double batch of something (like soup or spaghetti sauce, for example) takes less time than it takes to make the same recipe at two different times. Second, getting an already-made and previously frozen food on the table or in the cookie jar takes less time (and effort) than making the item from scratch.

If you make soup or a casserole, double your recipe and put one in the freezer. If you're baking cookies, freeze some for another day or freeze some of the raw dough and bake it later.

✔ **Cost saving:** By taking advantage of sale pricing and purchasing perishable food in large amounts, you can reduce your food costs. Watch your weekly food ads for specials, buy those items in bulk, and freeze them. This is a great way to keep the foods you enjoy on hand *and* protect your budget at the same time.

✔ **Convenience:** You'll always have a quick meal or quick dessert at hand for reheating, partial cooking, or complete cooking, depending on your time allowance.

Not enough pans? Here is a frugal tip: Line your pan with heavy-duty foil, prepare the dish and cover tightly with more foil. Freeze and then pop out the frozen meal. Label with name, date, and heating instructions. When you're ready to cook the frozen dish, just place it back into the original pan!

A guide to planning your meals

The best way to budget and be able to serve healthy foods is to plan your meals. No more coming home from a busy day to find something to throw together. With a meal plan, you'll never have to wonder what to fix, and everyone benefits from a home-cooked meal. Here are some tips for meal planning:

✔ **Review your schedule for the upcoming week to determine your time available for preparing meals.** Use prepared meals, like soups or stews, on busy days. Cook meat or bake casseroles on not-so-busy days.

✔ **Make a list of your planned meals, including snacks.** Keep a second list with a complete inventory of food in your freezer.

Create a basic list of 14 meals that are sure hits for your family. As long as you can pull out one of these favorites, you will always have a meal on hand.

✔ **Keep your lists (planned meals and freezer inventory) on the front of the refrigerator.** Cross off items as you use them and the meals as you make them.

✔ **Get your family involved in meal planning and meal making.** I (Amy) like to offer each person two or three choices for their meals. Once everyone chooses, I have plenty of ideas to rotate through the week and everyone feels like they have something special coming up.

A great way to allow children get involved with mealtime is to include reheating directions when you freeze your foods. Then all they have to do is follow the directions to be the cook!

The key to delicious frozen prepackaged food

Just as with any other food-preservation method (like canning or drying, for example), the quality of the food you choose and the care you take when storing it have a big effect on the quality of the final product. So keep these points in mind:

- ✔ Check your purchased foods for a sell-by or a use-by date. If the food is still on the shelf after the date, don't buy it. Just like fresh foods for canning, you want the freshest foods to go into the freezer as well. (Not all foods are dated. If you have a product that has no sell-by date, use the first in, first out plan and work these foods into your meal plan as soon as possible.)

- ✔ As Chapter 13 explains, excess air left in your freezer packaging is the number-one enemy causing damage in frozen food. Preserving the quality of your food during freezing requires quick freezing at a temperature of 0 degrees or colder. Unfortunately, packaged food from your store is rarely in moisture- and vapor-proof packaging. To preserve the quality of store-bought food, repackage your food following the guidelines in Chapter 13.

How you thaw your food also matters. (Yes, there's a correct process for thawing frozen food.) The preferred method is in the refrigerator, but there are exceptions. Some prepared frozen foods may be used in their frozen state; other foods may be used partially frozen. Check out Chapter 13 for details. (***Note:*** If there are special thawing instructions for the foods listed in this chapter, they're described within the section for that food.)

Freezing Convenience Meals

Meals of convenience include casseroles, soups, and sauces. Freezing them in family-sized portions or as single servings provides options for meals later. Always use masking tape or freezer tape, label the food, and write reheating instructions right on the container. This makes it easy for you or anyone else to pull out a meal and know how to prepare it without looking up the basics in a cookbook.

Main dishes

Prepare your recipe and transfer your food to rigid freezer containers. If you're making a casserole, prepare it in a baking dish (approved for the freezer) up to the point of baking. Wrap it in heavy-duty aluminum foil. Thaw the unbaked casserole in the refrigerator and bake it according to your recipe. These dishes stay fresh one to two months in the freezer. If freezing noodle dishes, undercook the noodles slightly for a better finish to the reheated product.

Soups, stews, and sauces

Ladle hot soup, stew, or sauce into rigid freezer containers, based on the portion you'll be using. Allow headspace of ½ inch for your pints and 1 inch for your quarts (head to Chapter 3 for more information on headspace). These items freeze well for 3 to 4 months. Here are some freezing tips:

- ✔ **Soups:** Use freezer containers no larger than 1 quart for quickly freezing your soups and preventing loss of flavor in your thawed product. If your workplace has a breakroom with a stove or microwave, freeze portions in single-serving containers and enjoy a hot lunch.

   Potatoes frozen in soup and stew may darken or become mushy or mealy after freezing. You can still use them if you don't mind this, or simply leave them out and add them when you reheat.

- ✔ **Stocks:** Use rigid freezer containers to store larger portions of stock; use ice-cube trays to store smaller portions (each cube is roughly equivalent to 1 ounce). Transfer the frozen stock cubes to a freezer bag for storing. Add one to a soup or sauce for added flavor. You can find a couple of delicious stock recipes in Chapter 12.

- ✔ **Sauces:** Package your sauces in rigid freezer containers in quantities suited to your family's usage.

   Clear soups and unthickened sauces freeze better than milk-based and thickened gravy dishes because the milk or thickener may separate during thawing. Make a note to add thickener to gravies when you reheat them or any other ingredients (like milk or cream) that you need to add before the meal is finished.

   Don't add cooked pasta to your spaghetti sauce before freezing or freeze liquids with cooked grains and rice; their flavor and texture will be lost.

Freezing Bread, Snacks, and Other Treats

Have your ever felt like you had to finish a birthday cake before it went bad or had a partial loaf of bread grow fuzzy, green mold? Well, here's the answer to these (and other) challenges: Freeze these foods to save them.

Bread, buns, muffins, and rolls

Bread and bread products freeze well. Repackage them in moisture- and vapor-proof paper or freezer bags. Divide your loaves into the number of slices that your normally use in a meal to prevent thawing and refreezing of the entire loaf. Bread can be frozen for 2 to 3 months and still remain fresh tasting when thawed.

When you're making muffins at home, make two or three varieties at the same time, wrapping them individually.

When making bread, prepare your loaves to the point of baking, including all of the rising periods. Place your dough into a baking container approved for the freezer; wrap it for freezing. To bake your bread, remove the wrapping, place the container of frozen dough into a preheated 250-degree oven for 45 minutes, and then bake your bread as stated in your recipe.

Cakes

Cakes with or without frosting may be frozen, but fillings can make your cake soggy. Butter-based frostings freeze well. Remove other types of frosting, including whipped-cream frosting, before freezing your cake. Cakes freeze well for two to three months.

Cheesecakes, whole or leftover, are a favorite for freezing. They keep about four months in your freezer. Thaw the wrapped, frozen cheesecake in your refrigerator for 4 to 6 hours and serve it chilled.

Freezing leftover cake in single-serving sizes keeps you from thawing more cake than you may want available to you at one time.

Cookies

Who can resist warm cookies fresh from the oven? You can freeze cookies in many forms: store purchased or home baked or raw dough to bake later. Use all of these within three months.

- ✔ **Store- or bakery-bought cookies:** Most purchased cookies freeze well, except cream- or marshmallow-filled cookies. Laying sheets of wax or parchment paper between your cookies keeps them from sticking together. Thaw them at room temperature.

- ✔ **Homemade cookies, baked:** Store cooled cookies in rigid freezer containers, placing layers of wax or parchment paper between the cookies. Thaw them at room temperature or place them on a baking sheet in a preheated 350-degree oven for two to three minutes to warm them.

- ✔ **Homemade cookies, raw dough:** Freeze raw dough in rigid freezer containers, freezer paper, or freezer bags.

  - For slice-and-bake cookies: Form your cookie dough into a log, wrap the dough in freezer paper, and freeze it. Thaw your dough slightly for easy slicing. Bake according to your recipe instructions.

  - For drop cookies: Drop your cookie dough onto a baking sheet, leaving 1 inch between each cookie. Place the baking sheet in your freezer and quick-freeze the dough. Place the frozen cookies in freezer bags for storage. To bake your cookies, place them (frozen is okay) on a baking sheet and bake them as your recipe states.

Label bags of frozen cookie dough with the baking temperature and time.

Pies

You may freeze pies at almost any stage in the preparation process. (Check out Chapter 6 for pie-filling recipes.)

- ✔ **Whole baked pies:** Wrap your pie with freezer wrap or place it in a freezer bag. Thaw it, wrapped, at room temperature for 2 hours; serve.

- ✔ **Whole unbaked pies:** This works best for fruit, mince, and nut pies. Prepare your pie in the pie pan you'll bake it in.

  To reduce sogginess in your crust: Brush the inside of the bottom crust with shortening, add your filling, and brush the top crust with shortening. Cut vents and glaze the top; then wrap it for freezing.

For baking: Remove the freezer wrap and place your frozen pie on a baking sheet in a preheated 450-degree oven for 15 to 20 minutes. Reduce the temperature to 375 degrees; bake 20 to 30 more minutes or until the top is golden brown.

✔ **Pie fillings:** If you love homemade pies, you'll find having frozen filling on hand a real timesaver for assembling pies, especially when you have a pie shell in the freezer, too. Simply prepare your favorite pie filling, ladle the hot filling into rigid freezer containers, allowing ½-inch head-space. Allow the filled containers to cool on your kitchen counter up to 2 hours. Then seal and freeze.

✔ **Pie shells, baked or unbaked:** Place your bottom piecrust in a pie pan for baking. Wrap the dough-lined pan in freezer wrap or place it in a freezer bag, stacking multiple filled pie pans on top of each other.

✔ **Pie dough, unrolled:** Form your pie dough into a flat, round disc. Wrap it tightly in a piece of plastic wrap and place it in a freezer bag.

When making dough for a double-crusted pie, separate it into two rounds before wrapping and packaging them for freezing.

To use your dough: Thaw it slightly in the refrigerator and roll it out while it's still chilled. This keeps your dough tender after baking.

Cream pies and meringue pies aren't suitable for freezing.

Freezing Dairy Products and Nuts

Buying butter and nuts at special prices can keep your food costs in line. Not all dairy products are suitable for freezing. Here are your best choices:

✔ **Butter:** Unsalted and salted butter freeze well. Use salted butter within three months because the salt flavor disappears during the freezing process.

✔ **Hard cheese:** Freeze hard cheese as a last resort because it crumbles after freezing. Use this cheese within six months.

✔ **Soft cheese (like blue cheese):** Soft cheese freezes better than hard cheese. Use soft cheese within one month.

Freezing is perfect for keeping nuts fresh and ready to use. Freeze any size of shelled nut, raw or toasted, in rigid freezer containers or freezer bags. The bags that nuts come in are usually not suitable for freezing. If toasted nuts are desired, toast them and let cool to room temperature before freezing.

Freezing Meat, Poultry, and Fish

Purchase meat, poultry, and fish from stores that practice sanitary handling procedures. If you're buying at a butcher store or fish market, ask them to wrap it for the freezer. If your food is prepackaged, repackage it for the freezer.

Packing hints

Divide your meat into meal-sized portions, always packaging steaks, chops, and chicken parts individually. Even though you may use more than one piece at a time, freezing and thawing time is less because you're working with a smaller mass. Freezer bags or freezer wrap are your best packaging materials for these foods.

Never freeze a whole stuffed bird because freezing time is increased and microorganisms may be passed from the poultry to the stuffing. If the stuffing doesn't reach a high enough temperature during cooking to kill the bacteria, it may be passed to your consumers, making them ill.

Fish and shellfish must be kept chilled from the time they're caught. Ideally, clean and freeze them immediately if you aren't using them within 24 hours. Prepare your fish for your freezer based on its size:

- ✔ If it's under 2 pounds, remove the tail, head, fins, and internal organs; freeze it whole.

- ✔ If it's over 2 pounds, clean it as above. Cut it into fillets or steaks and wrap each piece separately for freezing.

Thawing tips

Thaw your food in its freezer packaging in the refrigerator. For meat, allow 5 hours for each pound; for poultry, allow 2 hours for each pound; and for fish, allow 8 hours for each pound. If your time is limited, thawing it on the kitchen counter at room temperature will take about half the time of thawing it in the refrigerator, but this isn't the preferred method because bacteria may start to multiply at room temperature.

Chapter 15

Freezing Fruits, Vegetables, and Herbs

*F*reezing fruits and vegetables is the second-best preserving method after canning. Preparing and processing fresh fruits and vegetables for the freezer takes about one-third of the time of water-bath or pressure canning. You can also preserve fresh herbs in your freezer.

The equipment required for freezing food is more than likely already in your kitchen: a freezer, packaging materials (check out Chapter 13), pots, a colander, measuring cups, measuring spoons, and a food scale. After your equipment and food is in order, start freezing!

Mastering Freezing Fruit

When freezing fruit, follow these steps:

1. **Select fruit that is free of bruising and not overly ripe.**

2. **Work with small, manageable quantities, about 8 to 12 cups of fruit, which yields about 2 to 3 quarts frozen.**

   Note: Most of the recipes in this chapter use about 2 cups of fruit, which yields 1 pint. You can easily do multiple batches at a time to get the yield you want.

3. **Wash your fruit before packing it for freezing.**

4. **Prepare your fruit for freezing based on your final use.**

5. **If called for in your recipe, add an antioxidant (refer to Chapter 5).**

6. **Fill your container, allowing the proper headspace (refer to Table 15-2).**

7. **Label the package and let your freezer do the rest!**

The following sections offer more information on each step in freezing fruit.

Selecting your fruit

The key to a great frozen product starts with perfect, ripe fruit. Choose only perfect fruit, free of bruises and not overly ripe. Be prepared to process your fruit the day it's picked or immediately after bringing it home from the store.

Don't feel like you have to grow your own fruits and vegetables to get the best produce. Local farmer's markets, food producers, and your supermarket can assist you with selecting your food, telling you when it was harvested or how long it's been on the shelf.

Preparing your fruit

Fresh fruits require a minimum of preparation before packaging them for the freezer. First you need to wash them and then choose a packing method.

Fruits may be frozen raw, with added sugar, or with added syrup (a mixture of sugar and water). Although adding sugar to your fruit isn't necessary, it's preferred. Occasionally, you'll add an *antioxidant* (an anti-darkening agent) to the liquid to keep your fruit from discoloring.

Following are your packing choices:

- **Dry or unsweetened pack:** When you'll be eating the fruit or using it for pies, jams, or jellies, use this method. No sugar or liquid is added. There may be minor changes in the color, flavor, or texture of your fruit.

- **Dry sugar pack:** This is preferred for most berries unless you're making pies, jams, or jellies (see the preceding bullet). Place your washed fruit on a shallow tray or a baking sheet. Evenly sift granulated sugar over the fruit (a mesh strainer works well). Then transfer the berries to a bowl or a rigid freezer container and allow them to sit. The longer the berries sit, the more juice is drawn out. (It's not necessary for the sugar to dissolve as in the wet-pack-with sugar method, below.) When your berries are as juicy as you want them, transfer the berries, including the juice, to a rigid freezer container, allowing the recommended headspace (refer to Table 15-2).

- **Wet pack with sugar:** Place your fruit in a bowl and sprinkle it with granulated sugar. Allow the fruit to stand until the natural fruit juices drain from the fruit and the sugar dissolves. Transfer your fruit and the juice to a rigid freezer container, allowing the recommended headspace (refer to Table 15-2).

- **Wet pack with syrup:** Place your fruit in a rigid freezer container, adding syrup (see Table 15-1 for a variety of syrup concentrations) to completely cover the fruit and allowing the recommended headspace (listed in Table 15-2). Your fruit needs to be fully submerged in the syrup before sealing the containers.

To solve the problem of *floating fruit,* fruit rising to the top of the liquid in the jar, wad a piece of moisture-proof paper (foil works well) into a ball. Place it on top of the fruit to force the fruit to stay completely submerged when the container is sealed. Remove the paper after thawing your fruit.

Not all packing methods are suitable for all fruits. Only methods recommended for each fruit are supplied in the recipes in this chapter.

Selecting a storage container

Select your storage container size and fruit-packing method based on how you intend to use your final product. The best choices for fruit packaging materials are rigid freezer containers and freezer bags (see Chapter 13). Use rigid freezer containers when you add liquid to the fruit. Use freezer bags when no liquid is added to your fruit.

Syrup concentrations at a glance

As mentioned previously, syrup is a sugar-and-water combination. Table 15-1 lists the different types of syrups. To make the syrup, you simply dissolve the appropriate amount of sugar into water. You can use either cold or hot water. If using hot water, let the sugar syrup cool to room temperature before adding it to fruit.

The concentration of sugar syrup is up to you, but usually, a thin syrup is used to prevent a loss of flavor, especially if the fruit is naturally sweet or mild flavored. A medium to heavy syrup is used for sour fruits, such as sour cherries or grapes. Different recipes may call the syrup concentrations different things. Simply follow the concentrations as specified in the recipe you are using.

Table 15-1		Syrup for Freezing Fruit		
Type of Syrup	*Sugar Concentration*	*Sugar*	*Water*	*Syrup Yield*
Extra-light	20	1¼ cups	5½ cups	6 cups
Light	30	2¼ cups	5¼ cups	6½ cups
Medium	40	3¼ cups	5 cups	7 cups
Heavy	50	4¼ cups	4¼ cups	7 cups

Use these syrup estimates for planning the amount of syrup to make for filling your storage containers:

✔ **Sliced fruit or berries:** ⅓ to ½ cup of syrup for 1½ cups of fruit in a 1-pint container

✔ **Halved fruit:** ¾ to 1 cup of syrup for 1½ cups of fruit in a 1-pint container

Headspace guidelines

Headspace is very important when freezing foods. Food expands when frozen, and you need the extra space to allow for this. In addition, if you're using glass jars and don't have enough headspace to accommodate the expanding food, the jars can break. To avoid this problem, use the headspace recommendation for the size containers you have (see Table 15-2).

Table 15-2	Headspace Guidelines for a Dry or Wet Pack		
Packing Method	**Container Opening Size**	**Pints**	**Quarts**
Dry pack	Narrow mouth	½ inch	½ inch
Dry pack	Wide mouth	½ inch	½ inch
Wet pack	Narrow mouth	¾ inch	1½ inches
Wet pack	Wide mouth	½ inch	1 inch

Frozen Apples Packed in Sugar

Use crisp apples with a firm texture like Pippin or Golden Delicious. Because apples tend to get a little mushy when you defrost them, these are ideal for use in baked goods.

Preparation time: *20 minutes*

Yield: *1 pint*

1¼ to 1½ pounds apples

1½ tablespoons lemon juice

8 cups of water

½ cup granulated sugar

1 Peel, core, and slice your apples into 12 or 16 pieces, dropping the slices into 1½ tablespoons of lemon juice to 8 cups of water to keep them from turning brown as you finish them all. (If you prefer, you can use an ascorbic or citric acid solution instead of the lemon juice and water.)

2 Remove the apples from the antioxidant solution and place them in a shallow dish or on a baking sheet. Sprinkle the apple slices with granulated sugar, one part sugar to four parts apples. Let your apples be the guide here: Taste a slice with sugar to see if it is to your liking.

3 Fill your container and allow the proper headspace (refer to Table 15-2) and freeze.

Vary It! *You can also pack your apples in syrup. To do so, place your drained apple slices in rigid freezer containers, filling them with a cold heavy syrup (refer to Table 15-1), adding ½ teaspoon of an antioxidant solution to each container and allowing the proper headspace (refer to Table 15-2).*

Per ½-cup serving: *Calories 168 (From fat 3); Fat 0g (Saturated 0g); Cholesterol 0mg; Sodium 0mg; Carbohydrates 44g (Dietary fiber 2g); Protein 0g.*

Frozen Peaches Packed in Syrup

In addition to freezing peaches with this recipe, you can also freeze nectarines and apricots the same way — all varieties of these fruits freeze well. Use fully ripe fruit without any bruised areas.

Preparation time: *30 minutes*

Yield: *1 pint*

1 to 1½ pounds peaches   *¼ teaspoon antioxidant*

½ cup medium syrup

1 Blanch the peaches to remove the skin (don't leave the fruit in the boiling water for more than 1 minute).

2 Place ½ cup of cold medium syrup (refer to Table 15-1) and an antioxidant into each rigid freezer container. Slice or halve the fruit directly into the pint container, discarding the fruit pits.

3 Fill the container with additional syrup, allowing the proper headspace (refer to Table 15-2) and freeze.

Tip: *Use freestone peaches to make removing the pit much easier.*

Per ½-cup serving: *Calories 65 (From fat 1); Fat 0g (Saturated 0g); Cholesterol 0mg; Sodium 0mg; Carbohydrates 17g (Dietary fiber 2g); Protein 1g.*

Quick-Frozen Blueberries

Jams, jellies, and preserves made with frozen berries produce a product superior in color, flavor, and texture to one made with fresh berries. This recipe uses blueberries, but you can use any type of berry (except strawberries); they all freeze well with this method (the best way to freeze strawberries is to pack them in sugar, as explained in the later Frozen Strawberries Packed in Sugar recipe). Whatever berries you choose, make sure they're firm.

Preparation time: *15 minutes*

Yield: *1 pint*

1 to 1½ pounds blueberries

1 Gently wash the berries, removing any stems. Spread the washed berries onto a towel-lined cookie sheet and allow them to air dry (about 15 to 20 minutes) to prevent them from sticking together while freezing.

2 Spread your washed berries on a baking sheet, placing it in your freezer. (This process is known as *quick-freezing* or *flash-freezing*.) When the berries are frozen, transfer them to freezer bags or rigid freezer containers.

Vary It! *To pack your berries in syrup, place the berries into rigid freezer containers, covering them with cold medium syrup (refer to Table 15-1), allowing the proper head-space (refer to Table 15-2). If the berries float, add a ball of moisture-proof paper to keep the berries submerged.*

Per ½-cup serving: Calories 64 (From fat 4); Fat 0g (Saturated 0g); Cholesterol 0mg; Sodium 7mg; Carbohydrates 16g (Dietary fiber 3g); Protein 1g.

Frozen Strawberry Purée

Use frozen fruit purées for making fruit leathers (see Chapter 17), fruit sauces (by adding water, fruit juice, or a teaspoon of your favorite liqueur), as a concentrated flavor in fruit smoothies, or as a topping for your favorite ice cream. This recipe makes a strawberry purée, but you can make any kind of purée. Just use any amount of fruit you have on hand; 2 to 4 cups of raw fruit is a good working quantity, and add sugar to taste.

Preparation time: 30 minutes

Yield: 1½ pints

2 to 4 cups strawberries	*2 tablespoons granulated sugar (or to taste)*
¼ cup water	*1 tablespoon lemon juice (or to taste)*

1 Wash, hull, and slice the strawberries. Place them in a 2-quart saucepan. Add the water to prevent the berries from sticking. Cook the berries on medium heat until soft (about 20 minutes). Remove the pan from the heat and let the fruit cool.

2 Process the cooled fruit in a food processor fitted with a metal blade until pureed, or run it through a food mill. Add the granulated sugar and lemon juice to taste.

3 Return the mixture to the saucepan and bring it to a boil over medium-high heat, stirring constantly. Remove immediately from the heat.

4 Ladle the puree into 1-cup or smaller rigid freezer containers, allowing the proper headspace (refer to Table 15-2). Alternatively, freeze small amounts of fruit purée in ice-cube trays. Remove the frozen cubes from the trays and transfer them to a freezer-storage bag.

Per 2-tablespoon serving: Calories 16 (From fat 1); Fat 0 (Saturated 0g); Cholesterol 0mg; Sodium 0mg; Carbohydrates 4g (Dietary fiber 1g); Protein 0g.

Frozen Lemon Juice

Lemons (and limes) produce a superior juice that retains its flavor after juicing. Use freshly picked, fully ripe fruit. Because this recipes requires so little (just squeezing), you can make as much or as little as you prefer (or have on hand to do). You freeze lime juice the same way, so consider this recipe a two-fer.

Preparation time: *10 minutes*

Yield: *2 cups*

8 lemons

1 Squeeze the juice from the lemons into a measuring cup.

2 Pour the juice into 1-ounce freezer containers or ice-cube trays. After the cubes freeze, remove them from the ice-cube trays and store them in freezer bags.

   Tip: *If you prefer juice without pulp in it, place a small mesh strainer over the edge of your measuring cup; juice your fruit over the strainer.*

   Per 1-tablespoon serving: *Calories 4 (From fat 0); Fat 0g (Saturated 0g); Cholesterol 0mg; Sodium 0mg; Carbohydrates 1g (Dietary fiber 0g); Protein 0g.*

Frozen Mangoes Packed in Syrup

Choose fully ripe mangoes that are slightly soft yet firm to the touch with a strong mango aroma.

Preparation time: *20 minutes*

Yield: *1 pint*

2 to 3 medium mangoes   *½ cup cold light syrup*

1 Peel the skin from the fruit, slicing the flesh away from the seed (see Figure 15-1).

2 Measure ½ cup cold light syrup (refer to Table 15-1) into a rigid pint container. Slice the fruit directly into the container. Press the slices to the bottom of the container, adding additional syrup to achieve the proper headspace (refer to Table 15-2).

3 Add a ball of moisture-proof paper to keep the fruit submerged, secure the lid, and freeze.

   Per 1-cup serving: *Calories 101 (From fat 3); Fat 0g (Saturated 0g); Cholesterol 0mg; Sodium 0mg; Carbohydrates 26g (Dietary fiber 2g); Protein 1g.*

Figure 15-1:
Peeling and
cutting a
mango.

Frozen Pineapple Packed in Syrup

Selecting a ripe pineapple can be challenging because of the thick peel. Start by smelling the skin. A strong sweet pineapple aroma, with no alcohol undertones, means the fruit is ripe. Here's a little tip: The stem end develops sugar first, so check for yellow eyes around the base. Although it might seem tricky, getting the ripest pineapple is essential for a sweet juicy flavor.

Preparation time: *20 minutes*

Yield: *1 pint*

1 pound pineapple   1 cup cold light syrup

1 Peel and core the pineapple (see Figure 15-2), cutting it into wedges or cubes.

2 Pack your fruit into a rigid freezer container. Fill the container with the cold light syrup (refer to Table 15-1), allowing the proper headspace (refer to Table 15-2). Then seal and freeze.

Per ½-cup serving: *Calories 96 (From fat 0); Fat 0g (Saturated 0g); Cholesterol 0mg; Sodium 1mg; Carbohydrates 25g (Dietary fiber 1g); Protein 0g.*

Figure 15-2: Removing the rind and the core from a pineapple.

TRIM AND CUT PINEAPPLE

1. LAY THE PINEAPPLE ON ITS SIDE. CUT OFF THE TOP FRONDS AND A SLICE OFF THE BOTTOM.

2. WITH THE PINEAPPLE UPRIGHT, CUT OFF THE EYES WITH A KNIFE.

3. CUT IN HALF

4. CUT AGAIN INTO WEDGES OR SLICES.

Frozen Strawberries Packed in Sugar

Strawberries are put in a category of their own for freezing. Cut them and treat them with sugar or pack them in syrup.

Preparation time: *20 minutes*

Yield: *1 pint*

¾ to 1½ pounds fresh strawberries · *½ cup sugar*

1 Wash your strawberries in water, being careful to not bruise them. Remove the hulls (stems).

2 Slice the strawberries lengthwise into a bowl. Add ¾ cup granulated sugar for each quart of strawberries, stirring the berries to dissolve the sugar. Let the strawberries and sugar sit for 30 minutes for the juice to develop.

3 Transfer your strawberries to rigid freezer containers, allowing the proper headspace (refer to Table 15-2).

Vary It! *To pack your strawberries in syrup, place the sliced strawberries into rigid freezer containers. Fill the containers with a cold medium syrup (refer to Table 15-1), allowing the proper headspace (refer to Table 15-2).*

Per ½-cup serving: *Calories 121 (From fat 3); Fat 0g (Saturated 0g); Cholesterol 0mg; Sodium 1mg; Carbohydrates 31g (Dietary fiber 2g); Protein 1g.*

Thawing and using frozen fruits

For retaining the best quality of your fruit after freezing, refer to Chapter 13 and follow these guidelines:

✔ Open your container when a few ice crystals remain in your fruit.

✔ Use your fruit immediately after thawing.

✔ When cooking with sweetened, thawed fruits, you may need to reduce the amount of sugar your recipe calls for.

✔ Use your frozen fruit within one year.

Freezing Vegetables Like a Pro

Like fresh fruit, fresh vegetables are quick and easy to freeze. The key to great frozen vegetables is a process called blanching. *Blanching* scalds the vegetables in boiling water, slows down the enzymes and the spoiling process, and preserves the color, flavor, texture, and nutritive value.

Blanching isn't necessary if you're using your frozen vegetables, like onions, in foods when you're only concerned with flavor and not color.

Blanching perfect vegetables

Blanching requires 100 percent of your attention. Vegetables blanched for too short of a time won't stop the enzymes in the vegetables, and microorganisms start where they were stopped after the vegetables thaw. Vegetables left in the boiling water too long start cooking and may become limp.

Follow these steps for successful blanching:

1. **Wash and drain your vegetables; then remove any peel or skin, if needed. If you're not freezing your vegetables whole, cut them now.**

2. **Bring a 5- to 6-quart pot of water to a boil and fill a large mixing bowl with ice water.**

   Add ice cubes to the mixing bowl because the hot vegetables increase the temperature of the ice bath. Cold stops the cooking process.

3. **Add your prepared vegetables to the boiling water for the amount of time specified in the recipe.**

   Begin timing your vegetables as soon as they're in the boiling water; don't wait for the water to return to a boil.

   Blanch your vegetables in batches, no more than 1 pound of vegetables in 1 gallon of water.

4. **Remove your vegetables from the boiling water and plunge them into the ice-water bath, stirring the vegetables and circulating the ice water to stop the cooking process as quickly as possible.**

Don't leave your vegetables in the ice-water bath longer than they were in the boiling water.

5. **After the vegetables are chilled all the way through, remove them from the ice-water bath and drain them in a colander. If you're dry-packing them, roll them in or lay them on clean, dry kitchen towels to remove excess moisture.**

Packing your vegetables

Pack your vegetables immediately after preparing them. Moisture-proof, vapor-proof freezer bags are the best choice for your vegetables. Don't season them before freezing them.

Removing all excess air is important to avoid the spoilers, such as freezer burn (refer to Chapter 13). To remove air from your containers, follow these guidelines:

- **Freezer bags:** Package your vegetable pieces as close together as possible at the bottom of the bag, without bruising or squashing the vegetables. Fold the unfilled upper portion of the bag over the vegetables, gently pushing any air out of the bag. Seal the bag.

- **Rigid containers:** Use reusable containers when you're adding liquid to the vegetables. Allowing the proper headspace exhausts the air because the liquid in the container expands when it freezes. For headspace allowances, refer to Table 15-2.

After filling your bags, place them in a single layer in your freezer. Quick freezing is important to the thawed quality of your vegetables. After the packages are frozen solid, you may stack them on top of each other.

Step-by-step instructions for freezing vegetables

Follow these steps for freezing vegetables:

1. **Choose only perfect vegetables, free of bruises and imperfections, not overly ripe.**

2. **Work with small, manageable quantities, about 2 pounds at a time.**

3. **Wash and drain your vegetables and prepare them according to your recipe (which usually specifies blanching the vegetables).**

   Be sure to allow the vegetables to dry thoroughly before freezing to prevent them from sticking together when frozen.

4. **Chill your vegetables before packing them for freezing.**

5. **Fill your container, allowing the proper headspace if you're using rigid containers (refer to Table 15-2), or removing all of the excess air from freezer bags.**

6. **Label your package, adding it to your freezer.**

Frozen Asparagus

Asparagus is one of those vegetables that mean spring has arrived. If you are lucky enough to grow it yourself, you know that you can sometimes feel overwhelmed with what to do with the abundance. Try freezing it!

Preparation time: *20 minutes*

Yield: *1 pint*

1 to 1½ pounds fresh asparagus

1 Wash and drain the asparagus spears. Leave the spears whole or cut them into 1-inch pieces.

2 Blanch the spears or pieces for 1 to 4 minutes, depending on the size (thinner spears take less time). Take the time to test your spears after each minute to check for a slightly crisp texture. Cool the asparagus immediately in an ice bath. (See the earlier section "Blanching perfect vegetables" for complete blanching instructions.)

3 Place the cooled asparagus in quart-sized freezer bags — 1 pound of asparagus fits nicely into a quart bag — removing all excess air before sealing the bag and placing it in the freezer.

Per ½-cup serving: *Calories 25 (From fat 3); Fat 0g (Saturated 0g); Cholesterol 0mg; Sodium 12mg; Carbohydrates 5g (Dietary fiber 2g); Protein 3g.*

Frozen Wax Beans

Freezing beans is a great way to have them on hand for quick soups and stews. You can add the frozen beans directly to the dish 10 minutes before it is finished cooking. You can use the following recipe for many types of common beans: Green, string, Italian, or wax all work equally well.

Preparation time: *20 minutes*

Yield: *1 pint*

⅔ to 1 pound fresh wax beans

1 Wash and drain the beans. Remove the ends and strings, and cut them into 1-inch pieces.

2 Blanch the beans for 2 to 3 minutes; cool immediately in an ice bath. (See the earlier section "Blanching perfect vegetables" for complete blanching instructions.) Spread beans on a dry kitchen towel to dry thoroughly before freezing.

3 Place the cooled beans in quart-sized freezer bags, removing all excess air before sealing and placing the bag in the freezer.

Per ½-cup serving: *Calories 26 (From fat 0); Fat 0g (Saturated 0g); Cholesterol 0mg; Sodium 8mg; Carbohydrates 6g (Dietary fiber 3g); Protein 1g.*

Frozen Shell Beans

These beans are the base for many hearty dishes. It is always a good idea to have plenty on hand to add sticking power to your winter soups and stews. This recipe works equally well for lime, butter, or other shell beans.

Preparation time: *20 minutes*

Yield: *1 pint*

2 to 2½ pounds shell beans

1 Wash and drain the beans.

2 Blanch the beans for 2 to 4 minutes; cool immediately in an ice bath. Spread beans on a clean kitchen towel to absorb all excess moisture. (See the earlier section "Blanching perfect vegetables" for complete blanching instructions.)

3 Place the cooled beans in quart-sized freezer bags, removing all excess air before placing the bag in the freezer.

Per ½-cup serving: Calories 158 (From fat 12); Fat 1g (Saturated 0g); Cholesterol 0mg; Sodium 110mg; Carbohydrates 25g (Dietary fiber 9g); Protein 12 g.

Frozen Bell Peppers

For this recipe you can use green, red, orange, or yellow peppers. Peppers really make an otherwise boring meal sparkle. Try freezing multiple-colored peppers in the same package. Because bell peppers become a little mushy when you defrost them, they're perfect for use in any cooked recipe.

Preparation time: 15 minutes

Yield: 2 pints

1 to 3 pounds fresh peppers

1 Wash and drain the peppers. Remove the stems and seeds and slice the peppers into uniform pieces. (***Note:*** You do not blanch peppers before freezing.)

2 Place the bell peppers into a rigid container, leaving the appropriate amount of headspace (refer to Table 15-2). Seal and freeze.

Per ½-cup serving: Calories 15 (From fat 1); Fat 0g (Saturated 0g); Cholesterol 0mg; Sodium 1mg; Carbohydrates 4g (Dietary fiber 1g); Protein 1g.

Frozen Broccoli

Broccoli is such an undervalued vegetable. Use these perfectly prepared spears in all your soups and casseroles.

Preparation time: *20 minutes*

Yield: *1 pint*

1 pound fresh broccoli

1 Wash and drain the broccoli, removing leaves and damaged spots. Cut the broccoli spears into ¹/₂-inch pieces.

2 Blanch the broccoli for 3 to 4 minutes; cool immediately in an ice bath. (See the earlier section "Blanching perfect vegetables" for complete blanching instructions.)

3 Place the cooled broccoli pieces in freezer bags, removing all excess air before sealing the bag and placing it in the freezer.

*Per ¹/₂-**cup serving:** Calories 30 (From fat 0); Fat 0g (Saturated 0g); Cholesterol 0mg; Sodium 29mg; Carbohydrates 6g (Dietary fiber 3g); Protein 3g.*

Frozen Brussels Sprouts

Brussels sprouts can be a delicious treat — if they're picked at their freshest and processed right away. Try adding these to your roasted vegetable mix, with browned butter and garlic, or doused with balsamic vinegar for a new twist on this tasty vegetable.

Preparation time: *20 minutes*

Yield: *1¹/₂ pint*

1 pound fresh Brussels sprouts

1 Wash and drain the Brussels sprouts, removing the leaves and sorting by size for blanching (the smaller-sized sprouts use the shorter blanching time).

2 Blanch the smaller Brussels sprouts for 3 minutes, the larger for 5 minutes; cool immediately in an ice bath. (See the earlier section "Blanching perfect vegetables" for complete blanching instructions.) Spread the blanched Brussels sprouts on a clean kitchen towel to remove all of the excess moisture before freezing.

3 Place the cooled Brussels sprouts in freezer bags, removing all excess air before sealing the bag and placing it in the freezer.

Per ½-cup serving: Calories 32 (From fat 4); Fat 0g (Saturated 0g); Cholesterol 0mg; Sodium 17mg; Carbohydrates 7g (Dietary fiber 2g); Protein 2g.

Frozen Carrots

You can freeze carrots whole, sliced, or diced — in whatever form you'll need them later.

Preparation time: *20 minutes*

Yield: *1 pint*

1 pound carrots

1 Wash and drain the carrots, removing the tops and peeling the skin. Leave the carrots whole or slice (or dice) them into uniform-sized pieces.

2 Blanch the carrots for 2 minutes (sliced or diced carrots) or 5 minutes (whole carrots); cool immediately in an ice bath. (See the earlier section "Blanching perfect vegetables" for complete blanching instructions.) Dry the blanched carrots on a clean kitchen towel to remove all of the moisture.

3 Place the cooled carrots in freezer bags, removing all excess air before sealing the bag and placing it in the freezer.

Per ½-cup serving: Calories 51 (From fat 0); Fat 0g (Saturated 0g); Cholesterol 0mg; Sodium 58mg; Carbohydrates 12g (Dietary fiber 3g); Protein 2g.

Frozen Cauliflower

Cauliflower is great for adding to all your winter dishes. Frozen cauliflower also roasts well; just add with your potatoes and onions to the roasting pan. Don't let this delicious vegetable go unused!

Preparation time: *20 minutes*

Yield: *1 quart*

1¼ pounds cauliflower   *White vinegar*

Water

1 Wash and drain the cauliflower, removing the leaves and core and breaking the flesh into 1-inch pieces (do not cut).

2 Blanch the cauliflower in a water-vinegar mixture (1 tablespoon of vinegar to 1 gallon of water) for 3 minutes; cool immediately in an ice bath. (See the earlier section "Blanching perfect vegetables" for complete blanching instructions.)

3 Place the cauliflower pieces in freezer bags, removing all excess air before sealing the bag and placing it in the freezer.

*Per ½-**cup serving:** Calories 7 (From fat 1); Fat 0g (Saturated 0g); Cholesterol 0mg; Sodium 8mg; Carbohydrates 2g (Dietary fiber 1g); Protein 1g.*

Frozen Corn

You can never have enough corn in the pantry. An easy way to keep plenty on hand (and put the prefrozen, store-bought bags to shame) is to freeze your own. Add frozen corn to a soup or stew during the last 5 minutes of cooking. Make sure your corn is sweet when you buy it. It won't taste any sweeter after freezing.

Preparation time: *20 minutes*

Yield: *3 pints*

4 pounds corn (about 12 ears)

1 Remove the husks and the silk from the corn. Wash the ears.

2 Blanch the ears whole for 4 minutes; cool immediately in an ice bath. (See the earlier section "Blanching perfect vegetables" for complete blanching instructions.) Cut the kernels from the corn after cooling.

3 Place the corn in freezer bags, removing all excess air before sealing the bag and placing it in the freezer.

Per ½-cup serving: *Calories 47 (From fat 6); Fat 1g (Saturated 0g); Cholesterol 0mg; Sodium 8mg; Carbohydrates 10g (Dietary fiber 2g); Protein 2g.*

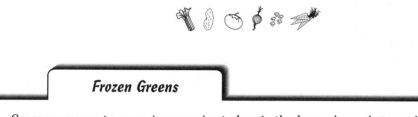

Frozen Greens

Greens are easy to grow, inexpensive to buy in the farmer's markets, and really pack a nutritional punch. Try keeping plenty on hand to add some extra flavor to your egg dishes, casseroles, and soups, when fresh vegetables are not available. *Note:* Your actual yield will vary depending on the type of greens you use. Spinach, for example, wilts much more than kale does and produces a smaller yield.

Preparation time: *20 minutes*

Yield: *1 pint*

1 to 1½ pounds greens (beet, spinach, or Swiss chard)

1 Wash the greens well, removing any thick stems.

2 Blanch the greens for 1½ minutes, stirring constantly to separate the leaves; cool immediately in an ice bath. (See the earlier section "Blanching perfect vegetables" for complete blanching instructions.)

3 Place the cooled greens in freezer bags, removing all excess air before sealing the bag and placing it in the freezer.

Per ½-cup serving: *Calories 36 (From fat 2); Fat 0g (Saturated 0g); Cholesterol 0mg; Sodium 320mg; Carbohydrates 7g (Dietary fiber 4g); Protein 3g.*

Frozen Okra

I (Amy) will be honest: I never thought I was going to like okra, until my oldest son started cooking. He bought some okra and cooked it before I could object. It is delicious! We now grow and keep as much as possible in our pantry. Give it a try.

Preparation time: 20 minutes

Yield: 1 pint

1 to 1½ pounds fresh okra

1 Wash the okra well, removing stems. Do not cut (you leave okra whole for blanching). (**Note:** Because larger pods can be tough, use only pods that are 2 to 3 inches in diameter.)

2 Blanch the okra pods and cool them immediately in an ice bath. (See the earlier section "Blanching perfect vegetables" for complete blanching instructions.) You can pack the okra whole or in slices. If you prefer sliced okra, slice it after it's cooled.

3 Place the cooled okra in freezer bags, removing all excess air before sealing the bag and placing it in the freezer.

Per ½-cup serving: Calories 40 (From fat 2); Fat 0g (Saturated 0g); Cholesterol 0mg; Sodium 6mg; Carbohydrates 9g (Dietary fiber 3g); Protein 2g.

Frozen Onions

Use either white or yellow onions for freezing. When thawed, their soft texture makes them suitable for adding to a dish or sautéing.

Preparation time: 10 minutes

Yield: 1 pint

1 large or 3 small whole onions

1 Peel and chop the onions. Do not blanch.

2 Place the chopped onion in freezer bags, removing all excess air before sealing the bag and placing it in the freezer.

Per ½-cup serving: Calories 14 (From fat 1); Fat 0g (Saturated 0g); Cholesterol 0mg; Sodium 0mg; Carbohydrates 3g (Dietary fiber 0g); Protein 0g.

Frozen Shelled Peas

There is nothing to compare to a fresh garden pea. To preserve their sweet flavor, add them to the dish during the last 5 minutes of cooking. Delicious!

Preparation time: *20 minutes*

Yield: *1 quart*

2 to 4 cups shelled peas

1 Rinse the peas in cold running water.

2 Blanch the loose peas for 1¹/₂ minutes; cool immediately in an ice bath. (See the earlier section "Blanching perfect vegetables" for complete blanching instructions.)

3 Place the cooled peas in freezer bags, removing all excess air before sealing the bag and placing it in the freezer.

Per ¹/₂-cup serving: Calories 29 (From fat 1); Fat 0g (Saturated 0g); Cholesterol 0mg; Sodium 1mg; Carbohydrates 5g (Dietary fiber 2g); Protein 2g.

Frozen Snow Peas

Snow peas are used in many stir-fried and Asian dishes. If you have them available, you will find different ways of bringing this spring-fresh flavor into your cooking. Try chopping them up and adding them to soup for a surprising boost in taste.

Preparation time: *20 minutes*

Yield: *3¹/₂ cups*

²/₃ to 1 pound snow peas

1 Wash the snow peas, removing the stems and blossom ends.

2 Blanch the whole peas for 1½ minutes; cool immediately in an ice bath. (See the earlier section "Blanching perfect vegetables" for complete blanching instructions.)

3 Place the snow peas in freezer bags, removing all excess air before sealing the bag and placing it in the freezer.

Per ¹/₂-cup serving: Calories 18 (From fat 1); Fat 0g (Saturated 0g); Cholesterol 0mg; Sodium 2mg; Carbohydrates 3g (Dietary fiber 1g); Protein 1g.

Frozen Summer Squash

Summer squash includes crookneck, patty pan, and zucchini squash. Are all unbelievably tasty vegetables. Once frozen, they lose their attractive look, but still hold onto that summer-fresh flavor. They are suitable for casseroles and egg dishes, soups and stews, and other dishes that benefit from their great taste.

Preparation time: *20 minutes*

Yield: *1 pint*

1 to 1¼ pounds summer squash

1 Wash the squash, remove the stems, and slice it into ½-inch pieces.

2 Blanch the squash for 3 minutes; cool it immediately in an ice bath. (See the earlier section "Blanching perfect vegetables" for complete blanching instructions.)

3 Place the cooled squash in a rigid container, leaving the appropriate amount of headspace. Seal and freeze.

Per ½-cup serving: *Calories 22 (From fat 0); Fat 0g (Saturated 0g); Cholesterol 0mg; Sodium 2mg; Carbohydrates 5g (Dietary fiber 2g); Protein 1g.*

Frozen Winter Squash

Winter squash includes banana, butternut, and Hubbard. Winter squashes are known for their creamy smooth flavor. They are usually cooked with brown sugar or honey and are a gorgeous bright orange or yellow color from the high vitamin A content. You can add them interchangeably to any bread, cake, stew, or pancake recipe calling for pumpkin. (***Note:*** You follow this same recipe to freeze pumpkin!)

Preparation time: *30 minutes*

Yield: *1 pint*

1 to 1½ pounds winter squash

1 Peel the outer skin of the winter squash, scrape out the seeds, and cut the flesh into chunks.

2 Place the squash in a 3-quart saucepan and add enough water to cover the bottom of the pan. Cook the squash over medium-low heat until the flesh is soft, about 10 to 30 minutes. or until a chunk slides off a fork. Remove the squash from the pan and mash it until smooth.

3 Place the mashed squash in a rigid container, leaving the appropriate amount of head-space (refer to Table 15-2). Seal and freeze.

Per ½-cup serving: Calories 43 (From fat 1); Fat 0g (Saturated 0g); Cholesterol 0mg; Sodium 3mg; Carbohydrates 11g (Dietary fiber 3g); Protein 1g.

Thawing and using your vegetables

Properly thawing your vegetables completes the cycle of preserving your fresh vegetables by freezing. Thawed vegetable results are best when thawed in your refrigerator rather than on your kitchen counter. A package of vegetables containing a single serving size takes less time to thaw than a package containing 1 pound of vegetables.

Of course, you don't have to thaw your vegetables. You can always add them directly to hot water or a recipe and allow them to thaw and cook with the rest of the ingredients.

Freezing Fresh Herbs

The flavors fresh herbs impart in just about any dish are truly a gift from nature. Frozen herbs are a great compromise when fresh herbs aren't available.

Thawed herbs are great in cooked dishes, but they aren't suitable as a garnish because they're limp after freezing and thawing. If you grow your own herbs, harvest them early in the day before the sun wilts the leaves. Some herbs that freeze well include basil, chervil, chives, cilantro, comfrey, dill, lovage, mint, parsley, savory, sweet fennel, and thyme.

To prepare fresh herbs for the freezer, follow these steps (see Figure 15-3):

1. **Clean the herbs.**

   Hold the bottom of the stems (don't remove the leaves from the stems) and swish the herbs in a bowl of cool water.

2. **Drain and dry the herbs, gently shaking off any excess water.**

3. **Lay the herb sprigs flat, not touching each other, on a piece of wax paper.**

4. Starting at one end, roll the wax paper snuggly over the herbs.

This keeps the herbs separate and easy to use one sprig at a time.

5. Place the rolled herbs in a freezer bag, label the package, and freeze.

There's no need to thaw the herbs before using them.

Some herbs, like basil, mint, parsley and cilantro, turn black if you freeze the leaves directly. For these herbs, purée them in just enough olive oil to make a paste and then freeze them in ice cube trays. They keep their fresh flavor and color.

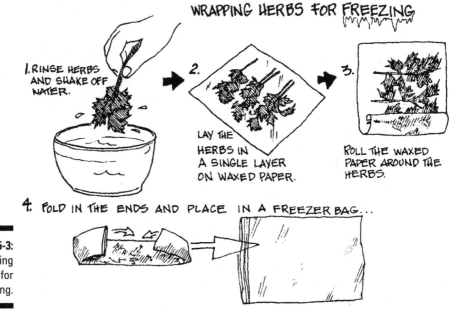

Figure 15-3:
Wrapping herbs for freezing.

If you're still stumped for more ways you can freeze fresh herbs, try the following:

✔ **Herb cubes:** After washing the herbs, remove the leaves from the stem and cut them into pieces. Place 1 teaspoon to 1 tablespoon of herbs in each opening of an ice-cube tray. Pour boiling water into the tray and freeze the herb cubes. After the cubes are frozen solid (usually 24 hours) pop them out of the tray and into a plastic freezer bag. When your recipe calls for 1 teaspoon or 1 tablespoon of an herb, add the ice cube to the dish and continue cooking!

✔ **Herbed butter:** Add chopped fresh herbs to one cube of softened, unsalted butter. For a mild herb flavor, start with ¼ cup of herbs, adjusting the amount to your personal taste. Transfer the flavored butter to an ice-cube tray sprayed with no-stick cooking spray and freeze the butter. After the butter is frozen (about 24 hours), remove the butter cubes, placing them in a labeled freezer bag. Serve the flavored butter with bread or add one to a casserole.

✔ **Herbed butter logs:** Flavor the butter as stated in the previous paragraph. Form the flavored butter into a log in a sheet of wax or parchment paper. Twist the ends, place the log in a freezer bag, and freeze it. Slice off what you need and return the log to the freezer.

Part V
Drying and Storing

The 5th Wave   By Rich Tennant

"I SAID, I DON'T KNOW WHY WE NEED A FOOD DEHYDRATROR WHEN WE ALREADY OWN A CLOTHES DRYER!"

In this part . . .

Food preservation is not all about canning and freezing. Part V shows you all about preserving your foods by drying them. Here you discover the art of drying foods, the different methods that work, as well as those that are no longer recommended. This part also includes plenty of recipes for drying fruits and vegetables for delicious snacking or to speed up a quick dinner, and instructions for drying assorted common herbs for teas and seasoning. You also discover alternative ways to store your foods without losing quality and flavor.

Chapter 16

Dry, Light, and Nutritious: Drying Food

*I*n the world of food preservation, sun-drying is the oldest method known. Although canning and freezing require exact applications of processing procedures, drying food isn't exact or precise. Don't be surprised if you find yourself working by trial and error when it comes to knowing how long it takes for your food to reach its degree of doneness. Just follow the general guidelines provided and make adjustments. Remember, drying isn't exact.

In this chapter, you can find basic techniques for drying food, the best drying methods, and how drying food prevents spoilage. Drying is simple and easy to do in your home. Most of the equipment and tools you need, except an electric dehydrator, are probably just waiting for you in your kitchen.

Opening the Door to Successful Food Drying

Drying food is also referred to as *dehydrating*. The goal in this technique is to remove moisture from your food. Achieving a successfully dried product requires removing 80 to 95 percent of the food's moisture. Removing moisture inactivates the growth of bacteria and other microorganisms but doesn't kill them.

Key factors in drying food

The following factors affect your finished product:

- ✔ **Heat:** The correct temperature is important in drying food. It must be high enough to force out moisture but not so high that it cooks the food. If your temperature is too high, your food exterior cooks or hardens before the interior of the food dries, trapping moisture in your food — known as *case hardening.* If your temperature is too low or the humidity too high, your food dries too slowly. Both of these dilemmas may cause your food to spoil before you consume it.

  The temperature guidelines for drying food are as follows: 125 degrees for vegetables, 135 degrees for fruit, and 145 degrees for meat. Always follow the instructions for the correct drying temperature for your food in your recipe or the owner's manual for your dehydrator.

- ✔ **Dry air:** Dry air absorbs moisture leaving the food in the drying process. The higher the humidity, the longer foods takes to dry because of the additional moisture in the air.

- ✔ **Air circulation:** Circulating air carries away moisture absorbed by dry air. This keeps the humidity level constant in the drying chamber.

- ✔ **Uniform size:** Pieces of food uniform in size and thickness contain about the same amount of moisture and therefore dry in the same general time, preventing some pieces from not being completely dried and spoiling the entire batch when stored.

Necessary equipment

After you decide which drying method you want to use, assemble your basic tools to aid you in completing the drying process. In addition to the basics every kitchen should have (knives, cutting board, vegetable peeler, grater, and so on; go to Chapter 2 for a whole list of basic supplies), consider the following, which are particularly useful when you're drying food:

- ✔ **Blender:** Use this for puréeing fruit. For a great fruit purée recipe, head to Chapter 17.

- ✔ **Food processor:** You'll make uniform slices in a blink of the eye.

- ✔ **Oven thermometer:** For safely drying food in your oven, it's critical to know the exact temperature of your oven chamber.

✔ **Racks and tray:** Your electric dehydrator provides the correct size of trays for your unit. For oven- or sun-drying, you can use oven racks, net-covered racks, or baking sheets. Racks with mesh bottoms or oven racks work well and provide air circulation. To prevent food from falling off the racks, tightly stretch and pin layers of cheesecloth or nylon netting over the racks. If you use baking sheets, you need to rotate the sheets and turn the food over for even drying.

Other tips for successful drying

Drying is one of the easiest ways to preserve food. Still, following a few suggestions can ensure your success:

✔ **Pick quality food:** Food of high quality that's ripe, mature, and in top condition is the best for drying. If you dry food during the peak of its season, you get high-quality food at a lower price because the food is more abundant.

✔ **Wash and eliminate blemishes.** Always wash your food to remove dust, dirt, grime, or insects. When you clean your food, start with a clean sink and clean utensils. Any residue from previous use may cross-contaminate your food. (For detailed information on bacteria and safe food handling, check out Chapter 3.)

✔ **Strive for uniform size.** It's important to prepare your food in uniform size and thickness for the food to be done about the same time. If you have two different-size pieces of the same fruit, spread like sizes on one tray. Because one tray of food with smaller or thinner pieces will finish drying before the other tray with larger pieces, you won't spend time sorting through the food and disrupting the drying process.

✔ **Place your food carefully on the drying trays.** Whether you're using an electric dehydrator, a conventional oven, or Mother Nature, make sure you arrange the food in a single layer and leave spaces between the pieces of food so that they're not touching each other or the edge of the tray.

✔ **Watch for spoilage while the food's drying.** The shorter the drying period, the less opportunity there is for mold to develop on your food. If mold does develop, remove the moldy pieces and then clean the area with a cloth moistened with distilled white vinegar with an acidity level of 5 percent to kill mold spores.

✔ **Test your food for doneness.** The length of time required for drying your food varies with the quality of your food, whether you're using a pretreating method, your climate and humidity, the size of the food pieces, the moisture content of the food, and the drying temperature. This all means you can't blindly follow the recommended drying time. Instead, you have to test your food for doneness. Here's how: Remove a piece from the tray and allow it to cool completely. Then check to see whether it matches the recipe's description of how the food should look and feel when what properly dried.

The easiest method for checking your dried food for doneness is touching and tasting it. This may sound overly simplified, but there's nothing like using your senses.

✔ **Store your cooled food in plastic bags, glass containers, or rigid plastic containers with airtight seals.** Make sure to label the container with contents and date. For more on storage containers and how to make your dried food last, head to the later section "Protecting the Life of Your Dried Food."

Choosing a Drying Method

The three approved methods for drying food are using an electric dehydrator, using a conventional oven, and drying in the sun. All methods work well when you follow basic food-drying procedures, use high-quality fresh food, and practice good sanitation for food preparation.

An electric dehydrator

If you dry a lot of food, an electric dehydrator is a great investment (see Figure 16-1). It's the most reliable method for achieving the most consistent results each time you dry food. This method dries your food evenly and quickly, doesn't tie up your oven, and produces great results in any weather.

An electric dehydrator dries your food by heating the air inside the chamber to a low temperature and circulating the warm air through the chamber with a fan, passing the heat evenly over your food for the entire drying process. After you place your food in your dehydrator, it needs little or no attention.

To use an electric dehydrator, follow these steps:

1. **Prepare your food according to the recipe and arrange it carefully on the drying trays.**

2. **Following the instructions for using your dehydrator, allow the food to dry for the specified period of time.**

   Turn the pieces of food and rotate the trays from bottom to top to ensure even drying of all the food in the dehydrator.

3. **Test your food for doneness and then label and store it in an airtight container.**

Each time you use your dehydrator, review the operating instructions including preheating the unit, filling the trays, setting the temperature, and the time recommended for drying your food. If you have any questions regarding the use or operation of your unit, contact the manufacturer. You can find this information in your owner's manual or check with the store you purchased it from.

Figure 16-1:
Two examples of electric dehydrators.

TWO ELECTRIC DEHYDRATORS

If you're purchasing a dehydrator, carefully assess your needs. Then consider the following factors when making your final decision:

✔ **Overall construction:** Purchase a unit that's approved for safe home use by the Underwriters Laboratory (UL). If the unit isn't UL approved, don't buy it — it may not be safe for use in your home. Choose one with insulated walls that's easy to clean and drying trays that you can move easily in and out of the dehydrator without disturbing the food.

✔ **Capacity:** Purchase a dehydrator big enough to hold the amount of food you'll dry at one time. Typically, the most common-sized food dehydrator has four trays. Each tray holds about ¾ to 1 square foot of food. Some dehydrators expand to utilize 30 trays at one time. Snack-size dehydrators with two trays are also available.

✔ **Heat source:** Select one with an enclosed heating element. Wattage needs to accommodate about 70 watts for each tray the unit holds.

✔ **Fan:** The fan circulates the heated air around your food. Purchase a dehydrator with a quiet fan, because it runs for long periods of time. If your unit isn't equipped with a fan, you need to rearrange the trays more often during the drying period for an even drying.

When buying a dehydrator secondhand, always plug it in to hear how it sounds when running. The level of noise is not an indicator of quality, but a loud dehydrator needs an out-of-the-way place to run, or it'll be too inconvenient to use.

✔ **Thermostat:** Purchase a dehydrator with an adjustable thermostat. Your temperature options need to range from 85 to 160 degrees.

✔ **Drying trays:** Check for trays that are sturdy and lightweight; made from a food-safe product like stainless steel, nylon, or plastic; and easy to clean. Some manufacturers offer dehydrator accessories like extra drying trays and trays for drying fruit leather and herbs.

✔ **Cost:** Dehydrator prices may start as low as $65 and go up to $200 or more.

✔ **Warranty:** Check out the warranty term (one year is a good average) and any restrictions the manufacturer has for your dehydrator.

A conventional oven

If you have an oven — gas or electric — that maintains a temperature between 130 and 150 degrees with the door propped open, you can use your oven to dry food.

Your oven must maintain a temperature of 130 to 150 degrees for 1 hour to safely dry food; maintaining these acceptable temperatures is difficult unless your oven can be set at less than the standard 200 degrees as the lowest temp. The problem with higher temperatures is that they cook — they don't dry — the food. To test your oven's temperature, put an oven thermometer in the center of your oven with the door propped open.

Oven-drying takes longer than using a dehydrator and costs more because the oven uses a greater amount of electricity than an electric dehydrator does. In addition, if you use your oven for drying, it isn't available for any other use during that time.

To dry food in a conventional oven, follow these steps:

1. **Preheat your oven to the temperature setting in your recipe.**

   Use a separate oven thermometer to check for accuracy. Check the oven frequently to be sure food isn't over- or underdried.

2. **Wash and prepare your food as directed in your recipe.**

3. **Place your filled trays in the oven and leave the door propped open to allow moisture to escape during the specified drying time.**

   If you use baking sheets or other trays without holes or openings in the bottom, you must turn your fruit to achieve an evenly dried product. After the first side of the fruit has absorbed all the liquid on the top of the food, turn it over and repeat this for the other side. After this has been done on both sides, turn the food occasionally until it's done.

4. **Test your food for doneness and then label and store it in an airtight container.**

The sun

Sun-drying is the oldest and least expensive of the three methods and it lets you dry large quantities of food at one time. But — and these are big buts — it's dependent on perfect weather conditions to produce a safely dried product and it can take days compared to hours in a dehydrator or a conventional oven.

Weather conditions must be perfect for sun-drying, making only a few climates suitable for this method. The ideal temperature for sun-drying fruit is 85 degrees or hotter for many consecutive days, with the humidity level low to moderate. If your temperature drops more than 20 degrees below your highest temperature during the drying period, your conditions are *not* suitable for this method. You also need good air circulation, a minimum of air pollution, and insect control around the food. Sun drying is even less attractive for drying vegetables because the temperature needs to be at 100 degrees or above for a number of days with the lowest evening temperature never dropping below 80 degrees (even at night) *and* the humidity level needs to be low.

Sun-drying isn't safe for meats and fish because the low-acidity level of the food, the low drying temperature, and the long drying period (taking many days) don't destroy the bacteria that cause your food to spoil.

If you're willing to deal with the variances in weather conditions and the lengthy drying time, follow these step-by-step instructions:

1. **Wash and prepare your food as specified in your recipe.**

2. **Line your drying trays or racks with a double layer of cheesecloth or nylon netting.**

3. **Place your food on the tray and cover your trays with a single layer of cheesecloth or nylon netting to protect your food from insects and dust.**

   Stretch the cover tightly over the trays, but don't let it touch the food.

4. **Place your filled trays on benches or tables in full sunlight and check regularly.**

   Check your trays at different times of the day, keeping them in full sun at all times. If your nighttime temperature varies more than 20 degrees from the temperature at the hottest part of the day, move your trays to a warmer area (indoors or an enclosed patio area) for the evening, returning them outside when they can be in full sunlight. Relocate the trays if it rains, regardless of the temperature.

   If you use baking sheets or other trays without holes or openings in the bottom, you must turn your fruit to achieve an evenly dried product. After the first side of the fruit has absorbed all the liquid on the top of the food, turn it over and repeat this for the other side. After this has been done on both sides, turn the food daily until it's done.

5. **Check your fruit daily for evidence of mold (refer to "Other tips for successful drying" earlier in this chapter).**

6. **Test your food for doneness and then label and store it in an airtight container.**

If one day is hot and sunny, yet the next is cloudy, you have a problem because mold can develop on partially dried foods before the weather turns back to hot and sunny again. In this situation, you need to use an alternative to sun-drying to finish the foods.

Protecting the Life of Your Dried Food

You'll receive many months of rewarding flavor from your dried foods when they're protected from air, moisture, light, and insects. Generally speaking, food dried and stored properly can be kept from six months to one year.

Cooler air provides a longer shelf life for your food. The best storage temperature is 60 degrees or colder. This will hold your food for at least one year. Temperatures between 80 and 90 degrees preserve the quality of your dried food for only about three to four months.

Check your unused dried food from time to time for any visible moisture or spoilage. If the food has signs of moisture, such as droplets of liquid in the containers, your food isn't completely dried. Use it immediately or repeat the dehydrating process and repackage it.

Suitable storage containers include the following:

- ✔ **Glass:** Home-canning jars with two-piece caps (see Chapter 2) are a perfect choice for storing dried food. Wash them with hot soapy water and rinse them well or wash them in a dishwasher. Dry and cool your jars completely before filling them and adding the two-piece caps. Reusing glass jars with lids also works well. Remove the cardboard liner that sometimes lines the underside of the plastic lid before washing and filling with herbs.

- ✔ **Plastic:** Heavy-duty (freezer) plastic bags with locking zipper-style seals work well. After placing your dried food in the bag, roll the bag to remove any extra air and press the seal together, making the bag airtight.

- ✔ **Metal:** If you buy coffee in cans, line the inside of a clean can with heavy plastic wrap, place your food inside, and add the tight-fitting lid.

- ✔ **Vacuum sealers:** If you own one of these units, now's the time to use it. Check your owner's manual for operating instructions and start packaging your dried food.

Always label your container with the type of food it contains, the date of processing, and, if you measure your food before placing it into the storage container or bag, list the amount.

 Because some pieces of fruit contain more moisture than others, be sure all your fruit is dried the same for storage. Try this tip from the Oregon State Extension Office: Fill a plastic or glass container with cooled, dried fruit about $^2/_3$ full. Cover or seal tightly. Shake the container daily for two to four days. The excess moisture in some of the fruit will be absorbed by the drier pieces. Vegetables dry almost completely, so you don't have to do this with them.

Chapter 17

Snacking on the Run: Drying Fruit

*T*his chapter discusses the rewarding process of drying fruit. Dried fruit has many uses — from snacks to sauces, dessert toppings to baked-good fillings. Many of the best fruits for this method oxidize and brown easily when their flesh is exposed to air. This chapter introduces you to the options available to you to prevent any color change in your fruit.

The times required for drying fruit may take anywhere from a few hours to many days. An electric dehydrator provides you with the shortest drying time and produces the best dried fruit of the three methods discussed in Chapter 16. Sun-drying is the lengthiest process and requires a lot of your attention as well as perfect weather conditions.

Putting Your Fruit in Order

Using the best, perfectly ripe fruit for drying is important for a dried fruit that's worthy of high marks and rave reviews. Most fruit is suited for this process with a few exceptions. Fruits *not* recommended for drying include avocados, citrus fruits (except for the peel), crab apples, guavas, melons, olives, pomegranates, and quinces.

Sizing up your preparation options

Drying time is determined by the moisture in your fruit, the size of your fruit pieces, the moisture in the air (even if you're using a dehydrator or an oven), and the pretreating method you choose. Larger pieces of fruit take longer to dry than smaller pieces of the same fruit. So the smaller you cut your peaches or the thinner you slice your bananas, the less time you need to produce a safely preserved dried product.

Pretreating your fruit

Pretreating makes your fruit look good by preventing *oxidation* and *discoloration,* the darkening of the fruit flesh after it's exposed to air. This process retards the enzyme activity in the fruit that causes it to ripen.

Pretreating only slows down the ripening process in fruit; it doesn't stop it.

Using a pretreating method before drying your fruit isn't as important as when you're canning fresh fruit. In fact, it's not necessary at all, but it does assist you with the drying process by shortening the drying time.

The following section explains your pretreating choices.

At one time, sulfuring fruit was popular for preserving fruit color and vitamins in dried fruit. Sulfur is unsafe for any drying method other than sun-drying because the sulfur produces dangerous fumes of sulfur dioxide when it's heated, which occurs when you dry fruit in an oven or a dehydrator. People with asthma or other allergies should avoid this product.

Water blanching

Water blanching is the best for maintaining the bright fruit color. Immerse the fruit in boiling water for a short period of time and then immediately plunge it into ice water to stop the cooking process started from the boiling water. Drain the fruit well.

Steam blanching

Steam blanching is the most common method used for fruit. The steam quickly heats the fruit, shortens the drying and rehydrating times, sets the color and flavor, and slows down the enzyme activity, in some cases killing microorganisms (refer to Chapter 3). In fact, fruit retains more of its water-soluble vitamins and minerals from steam blanching than water blanching.

To steam blanch, hang a colander on the inside edge of a pot of boiling water, making sure the colander doesn't touch the water. Place your fruit in the colander and heat it as directed in your recipe. Cool your fruit quickly in a bowl of ice water. Drain the fruit well.

Dipping in a solution

With this method, you immerse your fruit into a liquid or a solution to control darkening. Dipping the fruit helps it retain vitamins A and C that are lost during the oxidation process. You can use any of the following liquids:

- ✔ **Lemon or lime juice:** Fresh citrus juice is the most natural of the dipping solutions. Mix 1 cup of juice with 1 quart of water. Soak the fruit no longer than 10 minutes; drain thoroughly before drying.

- ✔ **Ascorbic acid:** This white, powdery substance is available in drugstores. Its common name is vitamin C. Dissolve 1 tablespoon of powder in 1 quart of water. Don't soak your fruit longer than 1 hour; drain it well before drying.

- ✔ **Commercial antioxidants:** These products are found in supermarkets or where canning supplies are sold. Some common brand names are Fruit-Fresh and Ever-Fresh. Follow the directions on the product package for making your solution and determining the soaking time.

Detailing Your Fruit-Drying Expertise

Properly dried fruit produces a superior product for use at a later time. After your fruit is dried, labeled, and stored (check out Chapter 16), you'll have delicious and healthful fruits at your fingertips all year round.

Fruit contains a lot of water, and you may be surprised at just how much volume you lose when you dry it. So don't be put off by the amount of fruit you start with, wondering where you're going to store it all. Four pounds of fresh blueberries, for example, makes 1¼ cup dried blueberries. And the best news? All the taste and nutrition is still there. The only thing missing is the water.

Evaluating dryness

Knowing when your fruit is properly dried is important. Normally, touching and tasting a cooled piece of fruit gives you the answer, but when you're in doubt and you positively, absolutely need to know the moisture in your fruit has reduced enough, follow these basic steps:

1. **Prepare your fruit and weigh the portion you'll be drying.**

2. **Look up the amount of moisture (water content) in your fruit.**

   You can find this information in the recipes list in this chapter.

3. **Determine the total water weight of your fruit.**

   Multiply the weight of your prepared fruit before drying by the water content percentage. For example, you have 20 pounds of prepared peaches with a water content of 89 percent:

   20 pounds of peaches × 0.89 water content = 17.8 pounds of water

4. **Calculate the amount of water (by weight) that needs to be removed from the fruit during the drying process.**

   Multiply your total water weight (your answer from Step 3) by 0.8 (the minimum amount of water you want to remove from your fruit during the drying process). Using the peaches example

   A total water weight of 17.8 × 0.8 = 14.24 pounds of water to remove

5. **Determine how much the fruit should way *after* drying.**

   Subtract the amount of the water you want removed (your answer from Step 4) from the total weight of the fruit you prepared for drying (your answer from Step 1). Example

   Twenty pounds of prepared fruit – 14.24 pounds of water to remove = 5.76 pounds of dried fruit as your goal

6. **Weigh your fruit when you think it's done.**

   If your fruit weighs the amount you calculated in Step 5 or less, your processing is successful. If your fruit weighs more than this amount, return it for more drying.

Properly dried fruit has 80 to 95 percent of its moisture removed, which means leathery, not crispy, results.

Drying fruit step by step

This procedure is simple and is detailed in Chapter 16 for the three drying methods. Here's a summary for drying fruit in a dehydrator or an oven:

1. Preheat your oven or dehydrator and prepare your trays.

2. Prepare your fruit as directed in your recipe.

3. Place your fruit on your prepared trays or racks.

4. Place the filled trays in your dehydrator or oven and begin the drying process.

5. Check fruit and rotate the trays periodically to ensure even drying of the entire batch.

6. At the end of your drying time, check your fruit for the proper degree of doneness as stated in your recipe.

7. Package your fruit in temporary containers, like plastic bags, and allow them to *condition* or *mellow*.

   This process distributes any moisture left in the fruit pieces to other, drier pieces, reduces the chance of spoiled fruit, and may take up to one week.

8. Package and label your product for storage.

Don't add fresh fruit to partially dried trays of fruit. The fresh fruit increases the humidity in the drying chamber and adds moisture back to your drying fruit. This adjustment in the humidity level affects drying and increases the drying time for both fruits.

Drying a Variety of Fresh Fruits

Patience is the key to successful drying. Preparation may take you less than an hour, but that's just the beginning of many hours until you have dried fruit.

If you're using an electric dehydrator, verify the correct drying temperature for your fruit in your owner's manual. If it differs from the guidelines given in your recipe or this section, use the temperature in your manual.

Dried Apples

Apples with tart flavors and firm texture dry best. Some good choices are Pippin, Granny Smith, Jonathan, and Rome Beauty.

Preparation time: *20 minutes*

Drying time: *6 to 8 hours*

Water content: *84 percent*

Yield: *1½ cups*

4 pounds firm apples

1 Wash, peel, and core your apples. Slice the apples into ¼- to ½-inch thick rings (see Figure 17-1). Dip the apple slices in your choice of dipping solution (refer to "Pretreating your fruit" in this chapter for your options and detailed instructions).

2 Arrange the apple slices on your trays and dry in a conventional oven or dehydrator for 6 to 8 hours at 130 to 135 degrees, rotating the trays occasionally to facilitate even drying. (Sun-dry for 2 to 3 days.)

3 Test for doneness: The apples should be soft, pliable, and leathery.

Per ¼-cup serving: Calories 147 (From fat 7); Fat 1g (Saturated 0g); Cholesterol 0mg; Sodium 0mg; Carbohydrates 38g (Dietary fiber 5g); Protein 0g.

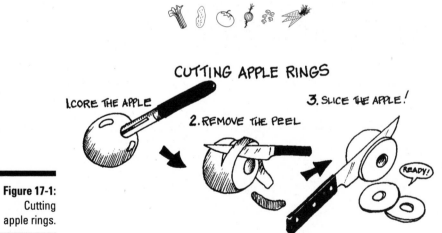

CUTTING APPLE RINGS

1.CORE THE APPLE

2.REMOVE THE PEEL

3. SLICE THE APPLE!

READY!

Figure 17-1:
Cutting
apple rings.

Dried Apricots

Even though apricots are one of the most naturally sweet-tasting fruits right off the tree, dehydrating makes them taste even better!

Preparation time: *20 minutes*

Drying time: *18 to 20 hours*

Water content: *85 percent*

Yield: *2 cups*

6 pounds fresh apricots

1 Wash the apricots and then them cut in half, discarding the pits. Dip the apricot halves in your choice of dipping solution (refer to "Pretreating your fruit" in this chapter for your options and detailed instructions).

2 Arrange the apricot halves on your trays, skin side down, cut side up. Dry them in a conventional oven or dehydrator for 18 to 20 hours at 130 to 135 degrees, rotating the trays occasionally to facilitate even drying. (Sun-dry for 2 to 3 days.)

3 Test for doneness: The apricots should be pliable and leathery with no moisture pockets.

Per ¼-cup serving: *Calories 152 (From fat 11); Fat 1g (Saturated 0g); Cholesterol 0mg; Sodium 3mg; Carbohydrates 35g (Dietary fiber 8g); Protein 4g.*

Dried Bananas

Use ripe, yellow-skinned fruit with a few brown speckles.

Preparation time: 20 minutes

Drying time: 10 to 12 hours

Water content: 85 percent

Yield: ¾ to 1 cup

2 pounds fresh bananas

1 Peel and slice the banana to ¼-inch thickness. Dip the banana slices in your choice of dipping solution (refer to the section "Pretreating your fruit" earlier in this chapter for your options and detailed instructions).

2 Arrange the slices on your trays and dry in a conventional oven or dehydrator for 10 to 12 hours at 130 to 135 degrees, rotating the trays occasionally to facilitate even drying. (Sun-dry for 2 days.)

3 Test for doneness: The bananas should be pliable and crisp, almost brittle.

*Per ¼-**cup serving:** Calories 134 (From fat 6); Fat 1g (Saturated 0g); Cholesterol 0mg; Sodium 2mg; Carbohydrates 34g (Dietary fiber 4g); Protein 2g.*

Dried Blueberries

Blueberries will make a nice surprise for your family. Use them in place of raisins and listen to them rave! Use plump berries that aren't bruised.

Preparation time: 20 minutes

Drying time: 24 hours

Water content: 83 percent

Yield: 1¼ cups dried blueberries

4 pounds fresh blueberries

1 Drop the blueberries into boiling water for 30 seconds. Remove them from the water and drain. Place the drained berries on paper towels to remove any excess water.

2 Place the blueberries on your trays and dry in a conventional oven or dehydrator for about 24 hours at 130 to 135 degrees, rotating the trays occasionally to facilitate even drying. (Sun-dry for 2 to 4 days.)

3 Test for doneness: The blueberries should be leathery and hard, but shriveled like raisins.

Per ¼-cup serving: Calories 203 (From fat 12); Fat 1g (Saturated 0g); Cholesterol 0mg; Sodium 22mg; Carbohydrates 51g (Dietary fiber 10g); Protein 2g.

Dried Cherries

Drying cherries only enhances their rich taste. They taste great out of hand or in your next muffin recipe. Any sweet or sour cherries work well.

Preparation time: 20 minutes

Drying time: 14 to 28 hours

Water content: Sweet cherries, 80 percent; sour cherries, 84 percent

Yield: 2 cups

6 to 8 pounds fresh cherries

1 Wash the cherries in cold water. Then cut them in half and remove the pits.

2 Place the cherry halves on your trays skin side down, cut side up. Dry them in a conventional oven or dehydrator for 2 to 3 hours at 165 degrees, or until there is a slightly leathery appearance to the skin and cut surface. Then reduce the heat to 135 degrees and dry for an additional 12 to 25 hours. (Sun-dry for 2 to 4 days.). Rotate the trays occasionally to facilitate even drying.

3 Test for doneness: The cherries should be leathery, hard, and slightly sticky.

Per ¼-cup serving: Calories 220 (From fat 27); Fat 3g (Saturated 1g); Cholesterol 0mg; Sodium 0mg; Carbohydrates 51g (Dietary fiber 7g); Protein 4g.

Dried Citrus Peel

Dried citrus peel make a great addition to your tea. It gives a fruity zip to desserts and sweetbread recipes. Try citrus peel in muffins and cakes. Use grapefruit, lemon, lime, oranges, or tangerines with unblemished skin. Don't use fruit with color added.

Preparation time: *20 minutes*

Drying time: *1 to 2 hours*

Water content: *86 percent*

Yield: *⅛ cup*

1 pound fresh oranges

1 Wash the citrus fruit and remove a thin layer of peel with a vegetable peeler. Be careful not to get any of the white, bitter pith. If you do, don't use that part of the peel.

2 Arrange the peel on your trays and dry in a conventional oven or dehydrator for 1 to 2 hours at 135 degrees, rotating the trays occasionally to facilitate even drying. (Sun-drying is not recommended.)

3 Test for doneness: The peels should be crisp, but not brittle.

Per 1-teaspoon serving: Calories 2 (From fat 0); Fat 0g (Saturated 0g); Cholesterol 0mg; Sodium 0mg; Carbohydrates 1g (Dietary fiber 0g); Protein 0g.

Dried Grapes

Everyone loves raisins! Making your own is a fun way to get kids involved with healthy, delicious eating. Try different varieties to see which ones you like the best. Thompson seedless grapes make the best-tasting raisins. **Note:** If you use seeded grapes, cut them in half and remove the seeds before drying. If you're using seedless grapes, you need to split the skins to allow the grapes to dry more quickly (otherwise, the skin holds the moisture in).

Preparation time: *20 minutes*

Drying time: *24 to 48 hours*

Water content: *81 percent*

Yield: *1¼ cups*

4½ pounds fresh grapes

1 If you're using seedless grapes, hold them by the stem and dip the grapes in boiling water for 30 seconds to split the skins. Drain grapes on paper towels and remove the stems. If you're using seeded grapes, cut each grape in half and remove the seeds.

2 Arrange the grapes on the tray (if you're drying grape halves, place them skin side down, cut side up, on the tray). Dry the grapes in a conventional oven or dehydrator for 24 to 48 hours at 130 to 135 degrees, rotating the trays occasionally to facilitate even drying. (Sun-dry for 3 to 6 days.)

3 Test for doneness: The grapes (now raisins) should be pliable with no moisture pockets.

Per ¼ cup serving: Calories 279 (From fat 21); Fat 2g (Saturated 1g); Cholesterol 0mg; Sodium 8mg; Carbohydrates 70g (Dietary fiber 4g); Protein 3g.

Dried Peaches

ny ripe fruit works well. Clingstone or freestone varieties, where the fruit separates asily from the pit, are easier to work with. ***Note:*** Although this recipe uses peaches, ou follow the same steps to dry nectarines.

eparation time: 20 minutes

ying time: Halves, 24 to 36 hours; slices, 14 to 16 hours

ter content: Peaches, 89 percent; nectarines, 82 percent

ld: ½ cup

½ fresh peaches

prepare peaches, remove the peel, cut the fruit in half, and remove and discard the . Leave the fruit in halves or slice them into ¼-inch pieces. (Prepare nectarines the ne way, except leave the peel on.) Dip the fruit in your choice of dipping solution fer to the section "Pretreating your fruit" earlier in this chapter for your options and tailed instructions).

rrange the fruit on your trays (if you're drying halves, place them skin side down, cut de up). Dry in a conventional oven or dehydrator 24 to 36 hours (halves) or 14 to 16 ours (slices) at 130 to 135 degrees, rotating the trays occasionally to facilitate even rying. (Sun-dry for 2 to 6 days.)

Test for doneness: The fruit should be leathery, pliable, and shriveled with no moisture pockets.

Per ¼-cup serving: Calories 42 (From fat 1); Fat 0g (Saturated 0g); Cholesterol 0mg; Sodium 0mg; Carbohydrates 11g (Dietary fiber 2g); Protein 1g.

Dried Pears

Use dried pears in any recipe calling for dried apples. Your family will enjoy eating these sweet slices just as much as they do apples.

Preparation time: *20 minutes*

Drying time: *12 to 18 hours*

Water content: *83 percent*

Yield: *1½ cup*

4 pounds fresh pears

1 Wash, peel, and core the pears. Cut them into halves, quarters, or ¼-inch slices. Dip the pear pieces in your choice of dipping solution (refer to the section "Pretreating your fruit" earlier in this chapter for your options and detailed instructions).

2 Arrange the fruit on your trays and dry in a conventional oven or dehydrator for 12 to 18 hours at 130 to 135 degrees, rotating the trays occasionally to facilitate even drying. (Sun-dry for 2 to 3 days.)

3 Test for doneness: The pear pieces should be leathery with no moisture pockets.

Per ¼-cup serving: Calories 164 (From fat 10); Fat 1g (Saturated 0g); Cholesterol 0mg; Sodium 0mg; Carbohydr 42g (Dietary fiber 7g); Protein 1g.

Dried Pineapple

If you have never tasted a dried pineapple, you're in for a huge surprise! Drying cre a chewy morsel that is packed with sweet flavor. Use fully ripe fruit.

Preparation time: *20 minutes*

Drying time: *12 to 18 hours*

Water content: *86 percent*

Yield: *1½ cups*

6 pounds fresh pineapple

Fruit	Preparation	Pretreat	Drying Time	Testing a Cooled Piece
Apples	Peel, remove ends and core; slice into ¼ to ½-inch-thick rings.	Yes	8 hours	Soft, leathery, pliable
Apricots	Wash, cut in half, discard pits.	Yes	18 to 24 hours	Soft, pliable, slightly moist in center
Bananas	Peel, cut into ¼-inch slices.	Yes	10 to 12 hours	Leathery and pliable
Figs	Leave on tree until ripe and ready to drop; wash, cut in half or leave whole.	No	24 to 36 hours	Leathery but pliable exterior, slightly sticky interior
Grapes	Wash, cut in half.	No	16 to 24 hours	Wrinkled like raisins
Nectarines and peaches	Wash, cut in ¼-inch slices, discard pits; peeling is optional.	Yes	13 to 16 hours	Soft, pliable, slightly moist in center
Pears	Wash, peel, cut into ¼-inch slices.	Yes	12 to 18 hours	Soft, pliable, slightly moist in center
Persimmons	Wash, cut into ½-inch-thick rings.	No	8 to 24 hours	Leathery

Enjoying the Labors of Your Drying

Most dried fruit is used just as it's stored after the drying process. It's great added to hot or cold cereal or baking batters. It's perfect if you're always on the go: It travels well and can be eaten right out of the container. For a fun twist to your teas, add a few dried berries to your teapot before steeping. The berries will lightly infuse the pot of tea with sweetness.

If you prefer your dried fruit a bit chewier, soften or rehydrate it. *Rehydrating is the process of adding moisture back to the fruit.* Use rehydrated fruit right away because it's not dry enough to go back on the shelf without spoiling.

Your rehydrating options are

- ✔ **Boiling water:** Place the desired amount of fruit in a bowl. Cover the fruit with boiling water, allowing it to stand for 5 to 10 minutes to plump, or add moisture, to your fruit. Use this method when adding fruit to jams, chutney, or baked goods. Substitute fruit juice or wine for water.

- ✔ **Steaming:** Place your fruit in a steamer or a colander over a pot of boiling water (refer to steam blanching earlier in this chapter). Steam your fruit for 3 to 5 minutes or until the fruit plumps.

- ✔ **Sprinkling:** Put your fruit in a shallow bowl. Sprinkle the fruit with water or fruit juice. Allow it to soak in the moisture. Repeat the process until the fruit reaches the level of moistness you desire.

When chopping dried fruit, spraying your knife with no-stick cooking spray keeps the fruit from sticking to your knife.

Dried Fruit Medley

A great blend for a quick and nutritious snack, make up small packages to grab and go.

Preparation time: 15 minutes

Yield: 4½ cups

½ cup toasted almonds

½ cup sunflower seeds

½ cup dried apples, cut into ½-inch pieces

½ cup dried apricots, cut into ½-inch pieces

½ cup dried banana slices

½ cup dried pears, cut into ½-inch pieces

½ cup dried pineapple, cut into ½-inch pieces

½ cup raisins

1 Place all the ingredients in a large bowl; stir to combine and distribute the fruit and nuts evenly.

2 Store your mix in home-canning jars or other airtight containers.

Vary It! Mix in a little bit of chocolate, such as M+M-type candies.

Per ½-cup serving: Calories 267 (From fat 83); Fat 9g (Saturated 1g); Cholesterol 0mg; Sodium 5mg; Carbohydrates 47g (Dietary fiber 6g); Protein 6g.

Fruit and Bran Muffins

Personalize this hearty muffin by using **your favorite dried fruits and nuts.**

Preparation time: *25 minutes*

Baking time: *20 to 25 minutes*

Yield: *16 to 20 muffins*

1½ cups whole-bran cereal (not bran flakes)	*1½ cups mixed dried fruit, your combination choice*
½ cup boiling water	*½ cup chopped macadamia nuts*
1 egg, lightly beaten	*½ cup whole-wheat flour*
1 cup buttermilk	*¾ cup all-purpose flour*
½ cup honey	*½ teaspoon kosher salt*
¼ cup melted unsalted butter	*1¼ teaspoon baking soda*

1 Preheat the oven to 425 degrees. Spray a muffin pan with nonstick cooking spray.

2 Combine the bran cereal with water in a large mixing bowl. Stir to moisten the cereal. Cool the mixture until it's lukewarm. Stir in the egg, buttermilk, honey, butter, dried fruit, and nuts; mix well. Set aside.

3 Combine the flours, salt, and baking soda in a small mixing bowl. Add this to the wet ingredients, stirring just until the ingredients are evenly moist. Spoon the batter into your prepared muffin pan, filling each cup about ¾ full.

4 Bake the muffins for 20 to 25 minutes or until a toothpick inserted in the center of a muffin comes out clean. Cool the muffins for 5 minutes in the pan; remove them from the pan and place them on a rack to cool completely. Wrap them individually in plastic wrap or store them in an airtight container.

Per 1-muffin serving: Calories 199 (From fat 87); Fat 10g (Saturated 4g); Cholesterol 29mg; Sodium 225mg; Carbohydrates 28g (Dietary fiber 3g); Protein 3g.

Fruit Leather

Fruit leather is dried puréed fruit rolled up in plastic (see Figure 17-2). The result is a chewy, fruity, taffylike treat. Some good choices for fruit leathers are apples, apricots, berries, cherries, nectarines, peaches, pears, pineapple, and plums. If you try drying nothing else, fruit leather is a *must* have. It is so delicious, your family will never guess how nutritious it actually is.

Preparation time: *20 minutes or longer, depending on the amount and type of fruit*

Drying time: *Depends on the amount of moisture in your fruit; allow 6 to 8 hours in an electric dehydrator or up to 18 hours in a conventional oven. Sun-drying isn't recommended.*

Yield: *4 cups of fruit purée makes 8 to 12 servings; 2½ cups covers an 18-x-14-inch area, ¼-inch thick*

One of any of the following fresh fruits:

> *2 to 3 pounds apples (about 8 to 12)*
>
> *3 to 4 pound apricots (about 24)*
>
> *3 to 4 pound peaches (about 8 to 12)*
>
> *4 pints strawberries*

Water or fruit juice (optional)

Corn syrup or honey (optional)

⅛ teaspoon ground spices (optional): choose fro[m] allspice, cinnamon, cloves, ginger, mace, nutme[g] or pumpkin pie spice

¼ to ½ teaspoon pure extract flavors (optional): choose from almond, lemon, orange, or vanilla

1 Cover your drying trays or baking sheets with a heavy-duty, food-grade plastic wrap. If your dehydrator comes with special sheets for your trays, use those.

2 Wash your fruit and remove any blemishes. Prepare your fruit as directed in the guidelines for preparing fruit in this chapter.

3 Purée the fruit in a blender until smooth. Strain out any small seeds, if desired, with a mesh strainer or a food mill. If your purée is too thick, add water or fruit juice, 1 tablespoon or less at a time. If your purée is too tart, add corn syrup or honey, 1 teaspoon at a time. If you're adding spices or other flavorings, add them now.

4 Spread the purée onto the prepared trays to a thickness of ⅛-inch in the center and ¼-inch-thick around the edges (you want the edges thicker than the center because the edges dry faster). If you use cooked fruit, it must be completely cool before spreading it on the trays.

5 Dry your fruit leather at a temperature of 135 degrees in a dehydrator or 140 degrees in a conventional oven. Dry the fruit until it's pliable and leatherlike with no stickiness in the center.

6 Roll the warm fruit leather, still attached to the plastic, into a roll. Leave the rolls whole, or cut them into pieces with scissors. Store the rolls in a plastic bag or an airtight container.

Note: The spice flavoring will intensify as this dries. Use a light hand, and no more than ⅛ of a teaspoon total in each batch.

Per ½-cup serving of apple purée: Calories 55 (From fat 3); Fat 0g (Saturated 0g); Cholesterol 0mg; Sodium 0mg; Carbohydrates 14g (Dietary fiber 2g); Protein 0g.

Per ½-cup serving of apricot purée: Calories 76 (From fat 6); Fat 1g (Saturated 0g); Cholesterol 0mg; Sodium 2mg; Carbohydrates 18g (Dietary fiber 4g); Protein 2g.

Per ½-cup serving of peach purée: Calories 64 (From fat 1); Fat 0g (Saturated 0g); Cholesterol 0mg; Sodium 0mg; Carbohydrates 16g (Dietary fiber 3g); Protein 1g.

Per ½-cup serving of strawberry purèe: Calories 43 (From fat 5); Fat 1g (Saturated 0g); Cholesterol 0mg; Sodium 1mg; Carbohydrates 10g (Dietary fiber 3g); Protein 1g.

ROLLING FRUIT LEATHER

1. AFTER YOU REMOVE THE PEEL, STEMS OR CORES, BLEND THE FRUIT TO A SMOOTH PASTE.

2. SPREAD THE PURÉE EVENLY ON A LINED BAKING SHEET WITH TURNED UP SIDES.

3. DRY THE PURÉE UNTIL IT FEELS LEATHER-LIKE AND PLIABLE. REMOVE IT FROM THE TRAY WHILE IT'S STILL WARM. ROLL IT !

4. CUT EACH ROLL INTO 4 TO 6 PIECES. WRAP EACH PIECE IN PLASTIC WRAP OR WRAP EACH WHOLE ROLL IN PLASTIC WRAP.

Figure 17-2: Preparing and rolling fruit leather.

Chapter 18

Drying Vegetables for Snacks and Storage

Drying foods is a super way to store a large amount of food in a surprisingly small space. If you are short on pantry space or lack more than a small freezer in the kitchen, drying may be the perfect storage solution for you.

In this chapter, you find out how to choose the best vegetables for drying, what they look like, and how they appear when fully dried. You will be able to mix and match your family's favorite vegetables and create easy to store and use vegetables for your pantry.

Note: The per serving nutrition analyses in this chapter represent the nutrition information for the food *before* it's been rehydrated. Once rehydrated, the vegetables plump up again and the quantity at least doubles.

Your Vegetable-Drying At-a-Glance Guide

Traditionally, drying meant using the sun's warmth and a lot of time. You would bring in the screen-covered trays at night, before the cool night air could cause condensation. Flies and other wildlife were a cause for concern, and you had no way to know whether airborne bacteria were present until you ate the food and got sick because of it. Of course, you can still dry foods that way, but there are easier ways: in an oven or with a dehydrator (refer to Chapter 16 for a basic explanation of these drying methods).

For vegetables, a food dehydrator is your best bet because a controlled, clean heat combined with constantly moving air results in a completely dried vegetable. To use a dehydrator, you simply layer your vegetables onto stacked trays and turn on the unit. Some dehydrators have fans that blow the warmed air over the drying food. Other units have a heating element at the bottom, and as the warm air rises, it filters through all the trays, drying the produce in the process. If you're serious about drying vegetables, look for one that has both a fan and heating element, as well as a thermostat that you can set at just the right temperature.

Drying know-how

Although drying seems pretty, well, cut and dried (pick the freshest vegetables you can find, prepare them as necessary, and put them in a food dehydrator for the required time and temperature), you can ensure that you'll end up with a tasty, edible veggie by following some basic rules:

- ✔ Not all vegetables need to be peeled before drying. Leaving on clean, washed skin increases the final nutritional content. Peels often contain fiber and other nutrients that only add to the overall benefit of the vegetable. You can find the best prep method in the drying instructions.

- ✔ While your vegetables are drying, switch the trays around to ensure they all get even heat. For best results, be sure to cut all the food into evenly sized pieces and spread the pieces in a thin layer on the drying trays.

- ✔ Some vegetables dry faster than others due to the water content of the vegetable while fresh. When setting up your trays, don't mix juicy vegetables with those that are drier.

  Vegetables with different water content can have much different drying times. If you dry them all together, you can end up with mildew because some may not get completely dehydrated.

- ✔ Make sure the vegetables are completely dried before sealing. To know that, you need to know what a properly dried vegetable looks and feels like. Not all are crispy when dried. Often, a vegetable is dried properly and yet remains pliable. (You can find out how to tell whether a vegetable is properly dried in the vegetable-specific sections that appear later in the chapter.)

The drying process involves many factors: moisture in the food that is being dried, the accuracy of the thermostat in the dehydrator, how full the trays are, and the humidity on the day you are drying. You may have to experiment a bit to figure out what works best. The drying process is not as accurate as other methods in this book, like canning and freezing. The final goal is to remove enough moisture so that organisms that spoil food cannot grow.

Storing and using your dried produce

When you take the vegetables from the dehydrator, they're ready to be stored in an airtight container in a cool, dry place out of direct sunlight.

For best results, store batches of vegetables together, but keep them in separate containers. For example, keep all dried tomatoes in a gallon jar, but inside the jar, divide them into separate storage bags, with each bag holding tomatoes dried on different days. This way, if something isn't quite right about a particular batch of vegetables, your entire season's storage isn't ruined.

You can store dried vegetables for up to a year as long as they are kept dry and out of sunlight.

Dried vegetables can be used for snacking and adding to soups and stews in the last few minutes of cooking. To rehydrate your dried vegetables add 1½ cups boiling water to 1 cup of dried vegetables. Let them stand for 20 to 30 minutes to absorb the water. If all the water is absorbed and they're not as plump as you'd like, add about 2 cups additional water and let them stand until most of the water is absorbed. Use the vegetables as you would raw ones; cook them or add them to a soup or stew. A good rule of thumb is 1 cup of dried vegetables equals two cups of reconstituted vegetables.

Avoid pouring or sprinkling vegetables over a steaming pot, straight from the storage container. Doing so can cause the moisture from the steam to condense in the container and promote mold. Always pour dried vegetables into a separate dish or your hand before adding to your recipe.

Signs of trouble: Good vegetables gone bad

Although it doesn't happen often — especially if you follow instructions carefully — sometimes your vegetables don't dry properly. Or maybe they dried all right, but something happened during storage. Here are the warning signs for dried vegetables that aren't safe to eat:

✔ **Black or brown specks suddenly showing up on food.** This is mildew on the surface that can make you sick.

✔ **Moisture building up inside the storage container.** Whether you store your dried produce in a bag or glass jar, no moisture should *ever* be inside the container, even when the food's been stored for a long time.

✔ **An off odor to the vegetables.** You can detect this when first opening the storage container or by holding a handful of vegetables up to your nose and sniffing. This is a sign of mildew, due to moisture being present.

✔ **Vegetables sticking together after being stored.** There should not be any stickiness to the vegetable pieces when stored; they should remain loose and easily separated throughout the storage life.

Drying Common Vegetables

Having dried vegetables in your pantry makes good sense. They are quick to fix, and they let you keep that summer-fresh flavor year round. Dried vegetables take up much less room, too, than their nondried counterparts. Your family will marvel at these fresh-tasting foods when the snow is flying!

The recipes in this section assume you have an electric dehydrator with an adjustable temperature gauge. If your dehydrator doesn't have a thermostat, check your vegetables periodically for doneness and evaluate their appearance, using the information in the recipes as a guide.

Beans, shelled

Shell beans are those that grow all season and are picked at the same time. The beans in this category can include soybeans, navy beans, kidney beans, lentils, and more. All require the same drying process.

Dried beans are a wonderful addition to the pantry. They add protein and bulk to many types of foods and make recipes go farther with little change in the overall taste. Once cooked, dried beans can be made into thick, creamy dips and sandwich spreads.

TIP

Leave these beans on the vine until the pods are dry and shriveled. When you can hear the beans rattling inside the dry pods, it's time to pick them. Many times, dried beans in the pod are available at your local farmer's market, where you can buy them inexpensively by the pound.

Dried Shell Beans

Dried shell beans take up little room on the pantry shelf. Store yours in quart-sized jars because they look so pretty and are easy to pour from.

Preparation time: *10 minutes*

Drying time: *6 to 8 hours*

Yield: *1¹/₂ cups*

1 pound of shell beans of your choice

1 Remove the pods and collect the beans. Place the beans on the dehydrator tray(s) in a single layer, adding enough to fill, but be sure that the beans are in a single layer on the trays.

2 Set your dehydrator temperature to 120 degrees and dry the beans for 6 to 8 hours, or until you can break a bean in half by hitting it with a hammer or other heavy object. Rotate the trays occasionally to facilitate even drying.

3 Remove your dried beans from the trays, place them in a tightly sealed container, and freeze them overnight to kill any tiny bug eggs that may be hiding in them.

4 Store your dried beans for up to one year.

Per ¹/₂-cup serving: Calories 129 (From fat 10); Fat 1g (Saturated 0g); Cholesterol 0mg; Sodium 37mg; Carbohydrates 26g (Dietary fiber 6g); Protein 12g.

Beets

Beets are naturally sweet and even more so when dried. They are great to eat out of hand, or dipped in a vegetable dip. Beets are also wonderful when reconstituted in boiling water.

Dried Beets

For drying beets, choose young, firm beets. Avoid large ones that can be fibrous. To use dried slices, eat them as-is or boil for 30 minutes in plain water, until soft once again.

Preparation time: *10 minutes*

Drying time: *8 to 10 hours*

Yield: *2 cups*

2 pounds of beets

1 Cut off the leaf and root ends of your beets and cook the beets in boiling water just long enough to slip the skins off easily (this may take from 5 to 15 minutes). Thinly slice the beats and arrange them in a single layer on your dehydrator trays.

2 Set your dehydrator temperature to 120 degrees and dry the beets for 8 to 10 hours, or until the slices are hard. Rotate the trays occasionally to facilitate even drying.

3 Place the dried beets in an airtight container and store for six months in a cool dry place, out of direct sunlight.

Tip: *An easy way to get the skin off a beet is to drop each boiled beet into ice water for a few seconds before pulling off the skins.*

Per ½-cup serving: *Calories 65 (From fat 2); Fat 0g (Saturated 0g); Cholesterol 0mg; Sodium 119mg; Carbohydrates 15g (Dietary fiber 4g); Protein 2g.*

Cabbage

Dried cabbage is a great way to add bulk and flavor to soups and stews. You can use cabbage in everything from tomato-based to clear broth soups. Your family probably won't know what that filler in the soup is, but they'll know that it tastes great.

Dried Cabbage

Select the brightest and heaviest cabbage heads to dry. To use the dried cabbage, measure out the amount desired and sprinkle it directly into boiling soups or stews.

Preparation time: *10 minutes*

Drying time: *6 to 10 hours*

Yield: *2 cups*

1½ pounds fresh cabbage

1 Remove any tough outer leaves; then core and shred the cabbage. Blanch the shredded cabbage for 2 minutes in boiling water and cool immediately in ice water. Drain well. Place the cabbage shreds in a thin layer on the dehydrator trays.

2 Set your dehydrator temperature to 120 degrees and dry the cabbage shreds for 6 to 10 hours, stirring every few hours to keep them from sticking together and rotating the trays occasionally to facilitate even drying. Start checking for doneness after 4 hours. Completely dried cabbage will shrink quite a bit and feel brittle.

3 Store the dried cabbage in glass jars or plastic bags, in a cool, dry place.

Per ½-cup serving: Calories 43 (From fat 4); Fat 0g (Saturated 0g); Cholesterol 0mg; Sodium 31mg; Carbohydrates 9g (Dietary fiber 4g); Protein 2g.

Carrots

Carrots are a well-known vegetable, loved by everyone. They are also prolific in the garden and easy to find at farmer's markets. If you're lucky enough to buy or grow bunches of them, drying carrots is easy and works very well.

Dried Carrots

The best carrots for drying are young and tender. You can add dried, shredded carrots as-is to sweetbreads and cakes for added fiber and natural sweetness; they'll absorb moisture and become delicious during the cooking process. You can also add dried slices to any soup or stew and simmer until tender, about 30 minutes. Or try sprinkling shredded carrot directly into eggs when making omelets. They'll cook as the eggs do and add a colorful look to the dish.

Preparation time: *10 minutes*

Drying time: *8 to 10 hours*

Yield: *1 cup*

1 pound fresh carrots

1 Scrub the carrot skin with a vegetable brush to remove any trace of dirt. Cut off the tops and about ¼ inch of the carrot itself to remove any of the green, bitter part of the carrot. Then cut the carrots into ⅛-inch slices or shred finely. Blanch the slices or shreds for 2 minutes in boiling water and then cool immediately in ice water. Drain well. Layer carrot slices or shreds in a single layer on your dehydrator trays.

2 Set the temperature on your dehydrator to 120 degrees and dry the carrots for 8 to 10 hours, or until they're tough and leathery, stirring at least once to ensure that the pieces don't stick and rotating the trays periodically to facilitate even drying.

3 Store the dried carrots for up to one year in a tightly sealed container.

Tip: *To remove as much water as possible from the blanched carrots, especially for shreds, use paper towels.*

Per ½-cup serving: *Calories 102 (From fat 0); Fat 0g (Saturated 0g); Cholesterol 0mg; Sodium 116mg; Carbohydrates 23g (Dietary fiber 6g); Protein 3g.*

Corn

Corn is another popular vegetable. It is not often dried at home, due to the availability of it frozen. Yet drying corn is an easy way to take advantage of the abundance in spring.

Dried Corn

Select young, milky ears of corn for drying. To use dried corn, bring water to boil in saucepan and add the corn. Simmer for about 45 minutes or until the corn is once again tender.

Preparation time: 10 minutes

Drying time: 5 to 7 hours

Yield: 1 cup

2 pounds fresh corn

1 Husk the corn ears and blanch them in boiling water for 3 minutes. Cool immediately and drain. Cut the kernels from the cob, taking care to cut cleanly and not go over the same area more than once with your knife. (This keeps the cut corn from becoming too sticky with corn milk.) Layer the kernels in a single layer on trays.

2 Set the temperature on your dehydrator to 120 degrees and dry the corn for 5 to 7 hours, stirring every 2 hours to prevent sticking and rotate the trays to facilitate even drying. Dried kernels will be hard and brittle throughout.

3 Store the dried corn up to one year in a tightly sealed container.

Per ½-cup serving: Calories 272 (From fat 29); Fat 3g (Saturated 1g); Cholesterol 0mg; Sodium 43mg; Carbohydrates 63g (Dietary fiber 7g); Protein 8g.

Green Beans

Green beans have a special place in my pantry. I (Karen) remember when I lived in my cabin, and dried my beans, strung like beads onto string, over my woodstove. They were a staple vegetable for my winter meals. I now use my dehydrator and although not as interesting a story, they still come out perfect.

Dried Green Beans

Select young, smooth beans; avoid those that have grown enough to develop seeds inside. To use dried green beans, drop dried beans into simmering soup and cook until softened, about 30 minutes. Although there are recipes for it, we don't recommend rehydrating plain green beans. The results are always mushy.

Preparation time: *10 minutes*

Drying time: *8 hours*

Yield: *½ cup*

2 ½ pounds fresh green beans

1 Wash and trim the beans as you usually would to eat. Blanch them for 2 minutes in boiling water and then chill immediately in cold water and drain well. Arrange the beans in a single layer on your drying trays.

2 Set the temperature on your dehydrator to 120 degrees and dry the beans for 8 hours, stirring at least once to prevent sticking and rotating the trays occasionally to facilitate even drying. Properly dried beans are leathery and shriveled.

3 Store the dried beans up to one year in a tightly sealed container.

Per ¼-cup serving: Calories 155 (From fat 5); Fat 1g (Saturated 0g); Cholesterol 0mg; Sodium 30mg; Carbohydrates 36g (Dietary fiber 17g); Protein 9g.

Greens

Greens are powerhouses of nutrition in a small package. If your family is not used to eating greens, you can use them as a flavorful addition to any soup or stir fry. You can add dried greens to your tomato sauce to add a lot of nutrition. Your family will not even notice.

Dried Greens

Select young, fresh greens for drying. To use, crumble dried greens into broth, tomato-based sauces, stews, and any other dish that you want to add some nutritional punch to.

Preparation time: *10 minutes*

Drying time: *4 to 6 hours*

Yield: *¼ cup*

1 pound fresh greens

1 Trim and wash the greens thoroughly to remove any fine grit. Blanch the greens until they are limp, about 2 minutes. Spread them in a thin layer onto your drying trays.

2 Set the temperature on your dehydrator to 120 degrees and dry the greens for 4 to 6 hours, or until the greens are crispy, stirring once to keep them from sticking together and rotating the trays occasionally to facilitate even drying.

3 Store your dried greens for up to one year in a tightly sealed container.

Note: *Check drying greens carefully to ensure they are layered loosely enough to fully dry. Greens that are stuck together may hold moisture and develop mold.*

Vary It!: *You can create a powder to add as-is to any sauce or baked good. Simply pulverize the dried greens in a food processor and then dry them in your dehydrator for at least 4 hours.*

Per ¼-cup serving: *Calories 227 (From fat 29); Fat 3g (Saturated 0g); Cholesterol 0mg; Sodium 195mg; Carbohydrates 45g (Dietary fiber 9g); Protein 15g.*

Onions

Onions are a familiar vegetable, even dried. They are a tasty addition to many foods, and if added in dried, tiny pieces, often are overlooked by those who claim to not like them.

Dry onions separately from other vegetables or their strong odor will permeate throughout. Once dried, they don't overpower other foods and can be mixed with other vegetables when making your own blends. You may also want to dry them in an out-of-the-way area. The drying process makes the onions smell quite strong.

Dried Onions

Select firm, unblemished onions for drying. You can add dried onions to any dish that you normally use onions in. If needed, simply add hot water to dried onion, soaking for 15 minutes, before adding to your dish.

Preparation time: *10 minutes*

Drying time: *12 hours*

Yield: *¼ cup*

1 pound fresh onions (3 large or 4 to 5 medium)

1 Thinly slice your onions or chop them evenly so that the pieces are of uniform size to facilitate even drying times. Arrange the onion slices or chunks in a thin layer on your drying trays.

2 Set the temperature on your dehydrator to 120 degrees and dry until brittle, about 12 hours, rotating the trays every 4 hours or so to ensure even drying.

3 Store your dried onions for up to one year in a tightly sealed container.

Per ¼-cup serving: Calories 172 (From fat 6); Fat 1g (Saturated 0g); Cholesterol 0mg; Sodium 14mg; Carbohydrates 39g (Dietary fiber 8g); Protein 5g.

Peas

Peas make a great addition to your dried pantry. They blend well in many recipes and add a bright pop of color and flavor. Peas are one vegetable that many children love.

Dried Peas

Choose young green peas when they are at their peak of flavor. They shrivel up quite a bit when dried but plump up nicely when added back to water or broth. Add dried peas to broth or stew and simmer for 30 minutes.

Preparation time: 5 minutes

Drying time: 9 to 12 hours

Yield: ¼ cup

1 pound fresh peas

1 Shell and blanch your peas for 2 minutes in boiling water; then chill in ice water and drain. Arrange the peas in a thin layer on your drying trays.

2 Set the temperature on your dehydrator to 120 degrees and dry until the peas are shriveled and hard, about 9 to 12 hours, stirring at least once to prevent sticking and rotating the trays periodically to facilitate even drying.

3 Store your dried peas for up to one year in a tightly sealed container.

Per ¼-cup serving: Calories 367 (From fat 16); Fat 2g (Saturated 0g); Cholesterol 0mg; Sodium 23mg; Carbohydrates 66g (Dietary fiber 23g); Protein 25g.

Peppers, sweet

Drying peppers is a great way to add this tasty vegetable to your cooking. It only takes a few pieces to really turn up the flavor. Another nice thing about drying peppers is that when dried, they take up only a tiny portion of space, versus freezing. Be sure to dry at least one batch of these for your winter pantry.

Dried Sweet Peppers

Select heavy, unblemished peppers for drying. To use, add peppers directly to any dish calling for pepper, without rehydrating. If desired, soak pieces in boiling water for 30 minutes, until soft. Use the same as fresh.

Preparation time: *10 minutes*

Drying time: *8 to 10 hours*

Yield: *1 cup*

5 pounds fresh sweet peppers

1 Wash, core, and remove all of the white membrane and seeds from your green peppers. Chop or slice the peppers, making sure that the pieces are of uniform size for even drying. Arrange the peppers in a single layer on your drying trays.

2 Set the temperature on your dehydrator to 120 degrees and dry the peppers until they are leathery and dry throughout, about 8 to 10 hours, stirring at least once and rotating the trays to facilitate even drying.

3 Store the dried peppers for up to one year in a tightly sealed container.

Tip: *Depending on the size of the dehydrator, you may need to divide and dry the bell peppers into two batches.*

Per ½-cup serving: *Calories 251 (From fat 16); Fat 2g (Saturated 0g); Cholesterol 0mg; Sodium 19mg; Carbohydrates 60g (Dietary fiber 19g); Protein 8g.*

Potatoes, white or sweet

Potatoes are a great dried vegetable. Having these on hand and ready saves time and work by cutting out almost all of the prep time taken in peeling and slicing.

When you dry potatoes, make sure that they're *completely* dry; otherwise, they'll mildew during storage.

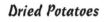

Dried Potatoes

Select young, unblemished potatoes for drying. Because they have such a long drying time, plan on drying potatoes overnight. To use dried potatoes, cover them with water and bring to a simmer until soft again — about 45 minutes. Dried sweet potatoes make a great snack as-is.

Preparation time: *10 minutes*

Drying time: *10 to 12 hours*

Yield: *¾ cup*

1 pound potatoes (about 4 to 5 medium)

1 Wash and peel the potatoes. Cut them into ½-inch strips for shoestring potatoes, or ⅛-inch slices, making sure all pieces are of uniform size for even drying. Blanch the potatoes for 5 minutes and drain. Arrange them in an single layer on your drying trays.

2 Set the temperature on your dehydrator to 120 degrees and dry the potatoes until they're hard and brittle, at least 10 to 12 hours, stirring after the first 4 hours to prevent sticking. Rotate the trays occasionally to facilitate even drying.

3 Store the dried potatoes for up to one year in a tightly sealed container or in plastic freezer bags.

Tip: *To prevent your potatoes from turning brown during drying, dip them in a mixture of 2 tablespoons lemon juice to 1 quart of water prior to drying.*

Per ¼-cup serving: *Calories 108 (From fat 1); Fat 0g (Saturated 0g); Cholesterol 0mg; Sodium 6mg; Carbohydrates 25g (Dietary fiber 2g); Protein 2g.*

Sweet Potato Crunch Sticks

These potatoes are a kid-friendly favorite. If you are looking for a fun, healthy alternative to chips for your next brown-bag lunch, this is it! Once you try this recipe, mix up some of your favorite seasoning to add your personal touch.

Preparation time: *10 minutes*

Drying time: *12 hours*

Yield: *8 servings*

1 pound sweet potatoes, washed, peeled and sliced into shoestrings	*1 tablespoon olive oil*
	½ teaspoon sea salt

1 Blanch the shoestring sweet potatoes in boiling water for 5 minutes and dip in ice cold water. Drain well. Dry the potatoes on paper towels to remove any outside moisture.

2 Place the sweet potatoes in an 8-quart bowl and add olive oil. Toss well to coat. Spread the shoestring pieces in a single layer on your drying trays. Sprinkle with salt.

3 Set the temperature on your dehydrator to 120 degrees and dehydrate the shoestring potatoes until they're crispy, at least 12 hours. Rotate the trays occasionally to facilitate even drying.

4 Store (if you can!) in a cool, dry place.

Vary It! *For a slightly different flavor, add an additional seasoning you like at Step 2.*

Per serving: *Calories 50 (From fat 16); Fat 2g (Saturated 0g); Cholesterol 0mg; Sodium 291mg; Carbohydrates 8g (Dietary fiber 1g); Protein 1g.*

Pumpkin

Pumpkin is a great item for your pantry. Its naturally sweet flavor is also rich in vitamins. Try using pumpkin in place of zucchini for sweetbread, in muffins and cakes, as a side dish, with cinnamon and sugar for the holidays, and as a creamy base for soups. Drying pumpkin is a great way to have enough on hand all year.

Dried Pumpkin

Select unblemished pumpkin for drying. Pumpkin's flavor only improves after drying. You can use dried pumpkin in dessert breads and other sweet dishes, or include it in soups and stews for added color and richness. You can also simply simmer it until soft again and eat it as a side dish.

Preparation time: *45 minutes*

Drying time: *12 to 18 hours*

Yield: *¼ cup*

1 pound fresh pumpkin (about 1 medium pumpkin)

1 Cut the pumpkin in half, remove the seeds, and slice it into workable-size pieces. Peel each piece and cut into 1-inch pieces. Blanch the pieces in boiling water for 2 minutes and then dip in cold water. Drain well. Spread the blanched pieces in a single layer on trays.

2 Set the temperature on your dehydrator to 120 degrees and dry the pumpkin for 12 to 18 hours, turning the pieces at least once to prevent them from sticking and rotating the trays to facilitate even drying. Pumpkin is dried enough when it is leathery throughout the entire piece.

3 Store for up to one year in a tightly sealed container.

Vary It! *Make a pumpkin purée: Cook cubes in boiling water until tender and mash until smooth. Spread the mashed pumpkin on trays covered with plastic wrap to prevent dripping. Dry for 6 hours, or until you can easily peel off the plastic layer from the pumpkin purée. Flip over the purée, and dry it until the pieces are brittle enough to snap when bent. You can use this dried purée as an ingredient in any recipe that calls for puréed pumpkin. To rehydrate, pour 1 cup boiling water over 1 cup of dried pumpkin purée and let stand for 30 minutes or until soft.*

Per ¼-cup serving: *Calories 118 (From fat 4); Fat 0g (Saturated 0g); Cholesterol 0mg; Sodium 5mg; Carbohydrates 30g (Dietary fiber 2g); Protein 5g.*

Tomatoes

Once again, tomatoes are the highlight of the dried food pantry. They are loved by almost everyone, dry easily, taste delicious, and have the ability to add a tasty kick to any dish. Great for many a meal, try drying as many tomatoes as you can. You will be surprised at how many you use!

You can also season plain tomatoes to work with either Italian- or Mexican-flavored dishes. Prepare a jar of both flavors, using the Tomato Two Way recipe. You will always have a quick meal on hand if you keep these in your pantry.

Dried Tomatoes

Choose firm, ripe but not overripe tomatoes. This recipe works with both paste style and slicing tomatoes, but the drying times are much shorter for paste style. Sprinkle dried tomatoes directly into simmering soups or stews or grind them up to add to dips and sauces.

Preparation time: *5 minutes*

Drying time: *20 to 34 hours*

Yield: *⅛ cup*

2 pounds fresh Roma or paste-style tomatoes (about 10 to 12)

1 Dip tomatoes in boiling water for 1 minute, and then plunge them into icy water for 30 seconds. Slip off the skins and core. (***Note:*** If you're using slicing tomatoes, remove the seeds.) Cut the tomatoes into ⅛-inch slices or ¼-inch cubes. Take care to cut uniform pieces. Place slices or cubes onto trays, in a single layer.

2 Set the temperature on your dehydrator to 120 degrees and dry your tomatoes for 14 to 16 hours. Remove the trays, flip all slices over or stir the cubes well, and dry again for another 6 to 8 hours or until brittle. Rotate the trays occasionally to facilitate even drying.

3 Store for up to one year in a tightly sealed container.

Per ⅛-cup serving: Calories 191 (From fat 27); Fat 3g (Saturated 0g); Cholesterol 0mg; Sodium 82mg; Carbohydrates 42g (Dietary fiber 10g); Protein 8g.

Tomato Two Way

These two blends are considered staples. Try making them as spicy or bland as your family likes and use in your dishes for preseasoned flavor. They also make wonderful gifts, if tied with a ribbon and a recipe attached.

Preparation time: *10 minutes*

Yield: *3 cups*

1 cup dried chopped green pepper

1 cup dried chopped onion

1 cup dried chopped tomatoes

For Italian-flavored vegetables, mix and add the following:

   ½ teaspoon dried oregano

   ½ teaspoon dried marjoram

   ½ teaspoon dried basil

½ teaspoon dried rosemary

For Mexican-flavored vegetables, mix and add the following:

   1 teaspoon ground cumin

   1 teaspoon oregano

   1 teaspoon powdered garlic

   ¼ to ½ teaspoon chili powder

1 In a large bowl, combine the green pepper, onions, and tomatoes. Sprinkle your choice of flavoring over the vegetables and toss the ingredients well to mix.

2 Transfer the mixture to a 1-quart container and store in a cool dry place.

Per ½-cup serving: *Calories 208 (From fat 18); Fat 2g (Saturated 0g); Cholesterol 0mg; Sodium 39mg; Carbohydrates 48g (Dietary fiber 13g); Protein 7g.*

Zucchini

Zucchini is always plentiful in any garden. The trick is to pick it often and do not let it grow to gigantic proportions. Young zucchini has a tender skin and doesn't need to be peeled before drying. One fun way to enjoy zucchini is to make zucchini chips.

Because dried zucchini is virtually tasteless in your dishes, you can easily add nutrients to a dish without changing the flavor.

Dried Zucchini

Select young, small- to medium-size zucchini. To use, sprinkle directly into your soup or stew and cook until tender. Add shredded zucchini directly into any baked goods without rehydrating.

Preparation time: *10 minutes*

Drying time: *8 hours*

Yield: *1½ cup*

10 pounds fresh zucchini (about 30 medium)

1 Shred the zucchini or slice it in ⅛-inch slices — blanching first isn't necessary — and place the cubes or slices in single layer on your drying trays.

2 Set the temperature on your dehydrator to 120 degrees and allow the zucchini to dry for 8 hours, stirring at least once to prevent sticking. Rotate the trays occasionally to facilitate even drying. Properly dried zucchini is crisp.

3 Store the dried zucchini for up to one year in a tightly sealed container.

Per ½-cup serving: *Calories 302 (From fat 29); Fat 3g (Saturated 1g); Cholesterol 0mg; Sodium 30mg; Carbohydrates 66g (Dietary fiber 29g); Protein 18g.*

Zucchini Chips

These crispy chips are the perfect way to use up the piles of zucchini you always end up with during the summer. Keep in mind, though, that they absorb moisture from the air quickly. Once opened, use them as quickly as possible to avoid them becoming soft.

Preparation time: *10 minutes for preparing, 15 minutes for marinating*

Drying time: *12 hours, or until crisp*

Yield: *4 servings*

1 pound zucchini (about 3 medium)   *¼ cup Italian-style salad dressing*

1 Wash and slice the zucchini into ⅛-inch thin slices. Place the slices in a large bowl or gallon-size plastic, sealable storage bag. Pour the Italian-style dressing over the slices and toss to coat. Marinate the zucchini in the dressing for 15 minutes. Place marinated slices in a single layer on your drying trays.

2 Set the temperature on your dehydrator to 120 degrees and dry the zucchini slices for 12 hours (or until crisp), turning at least once. Rotate the trays occasionally to facilitate even drying.

3 Store the zucchini chips for up to three months in a 1-gallon, sealable plastic storage bag.

Per serving: Calories 91 (From fat 66); Fat 7g (Saturated 1g); Cholesterol 0mg; Sodium 118mg; Carbohydrates 6g (Dietary fiber 2g); Protein 11g.

Soup and Stew Mix

This is a wonderful way to have the basics for soups and stews on hand. Dry each vegetable separately, as explained in the preceding sections, and then store together. For a vegetable soup, add these to a simple broth base. Fast and easy! *Note:* If you don't have dried potatoes, dried carrots, dried peas, or dried onions on hand, use the instructions in the earlier recipes to dry each vegetable and then proceed with this recipe.

Preparation time: *10 minutes for mixing*

Yield: *4 cups*

1 cup dried potatoes	*1 cup dried peas*
1 cup dried carrot slices	*1 cup dried onions*

1 Combine the dried vegetables in a large bowl.

2 Store the stew mix in a moisture-proof container in a dark, cool place.

3 To use, measure out the amount of vegetables you want and then simply add them to your broth and simmer until tender, about 30 to 40 minutes.

Per ½-cup serving: Calories 188 (From fat 6); Fat 1g (Saturated 0g); Cholesterol 0mg; Sodium 40mg; Carbohydrates 38g (Dietary fiber 10g); Protein 9g.

Chapter 19

Drying Herbs

In This Chapter

▶ What makes a good drying herb

▶ Creating blends for cooking

▶ Making your own herb tea

Drying herbs is a wonderful way to be sure you have the freshest seasoning possible for your cooking. Because you pick herbs throughout the growing season, you can collect the finest herbs again and again, drying them as you go. Drying herbs is also an easy way to create your own signature blends for cooking and herbal tea. You will always have your favorites on hand if you dry them yourself.

This chapter shares the most common herbs that dry well and some recipes for making herbal blends that everyone can enjoy.

Drying Common and Not-So-Common Herbs

Herbs are one of the most important and expensive ingredients in any dish. Drying them can save you a lot of money and give you much fresher and fuller flavor than any found on a store shelf.

The best herbs for drying are those that are *resinous,* or contain the most oils. The oils are where the scents and flavor come from. Herbs that have very juicy stems and overly thick leaves don't dry well.

If you find that your herb of choice seems to become tasteless or dries to a black mess, try freezing that herb instead. Two herbs that are commonly used in cooking but do not dry well are chives and basil. Some have luck drying basil at a low temperature, but we don't recommend it for those just starting out. Blend in a little olive oil with these too fussy herbs and freeze instead (go to Chapter 15 for details).

The best herbs for drying are those you grow in your own garden. If you don't have a green thumb, the next best thing is to buy your herbs from a farmer's market that sells produce grown without chemical sprays and picked as recently as the day you buy it.

✔ **If you grow your own herbs:** Start small, growing only what you can easily care for because you'll have to pick your herbs many times over the gardening season. You can simply dry them as they become ready, and combine the fully dried herbs with the ones dried before.

Harvest your herbs just after the morning dew has dried, but before the hot, noonday sun has hit them. The heat from the sun drives the fragrant oils out of the leaves and blossoms, so the herbs have less flavor.

✔ **If you choose herbs from a farmer's market:** Look for fresh, vibrant leaves, a strong smell, and clean, healthy-looking plants. Avoid buying wilted or shriveled herbs, as they have been picked too long ago. Don't hesitate to ask for a taste of a leaf. You may also want to crush a piece of leaf in your hand, to see if it smells strongly of the fresh herb.

The following sections outline several herbs that are easy to dry. When selecting your herbs, choose those that you're familiar with first.

You can use either an oven or a dehydrator set between 115 and 125 degrees. This temperature is just high enough to heat but not cook the herbs. Don't set the temperature any lower than 115 degrees though, because it takes too long and sometimes allows mildew.

Store your dried herbs in small containers. Glass jars with tight-fitting lids work best. For your herbs to maintain the best flavor during storage, keep them away from heat, light, and your refrigerator.

Air-drying fresh herbs

An electric dehydrator and oven aren't your only options when it comes to drying herbs. Air-drying them is an easy alternative. Follow these steps to air-dry herbs and check out the figure as well:

1. **If you're harvesting herbs from a garden, cut the stems, don't pick them, leaving an extra inch or two for tying them in bunches.**

   Harvest the herbs in the morning after any moisture on the leaves has dried.

2. **Rinse your herbs quickly by dipping them in a bowl of cool water and shaking off the excess water.**

   Pat them dry with a paper towel, making sure they're completely dry to prevent mildew.

3. **Tie the herb stalks near the cut part of the stem in small bunches (no more than five or six stems) with cotton string or thread.**

Don't mix your herb bunches because flavors transfer during the drying process.

4. Either hang the herbs upside down in a warm room (the kitchen works well) near a south-facing window and out of direct sunlight or place the tied herb bundle in a paper bag with holes or slits cut in it for air circulation before hanging the bag in a warm room. Place the herb bundle upside down in the bag with the stems toward the top opening of the bag. Tie the top of the bag closed. The bag protects the herbs from light and catches any loose seeds for replanting your herbs.

Your herbs will dry in two to three weeks with good air circulation.

Herbs are dry when they crumble easily. Remove the leaves from the stems. Crush soft leaves (like basil, sage, and oregano) by hand. Store harder leaves (like rosemary, tarragon, and thyme) whole, crushing them with a rolling pin before using them.

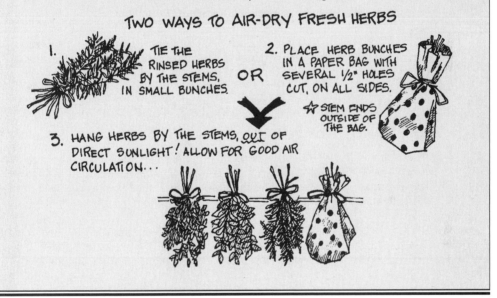

TWO WAYS TO AIR-DRY FRESH HERBS

1. TIE THE RINSED HERBS BY THE STEMS, IN SMALL BUNCHES.

OR

2. PLACE HERB BUNCHES IN A PAPER BAG WITH SEVERAL ½" HOLES CUT, ON ALL SIDES.

☆ STEM ENDS OUTSIDE OF THE BAG.

3. HANG HERBS BY THE STEMS, OUT OF DIRECT SUNLIGHT! ALLOW FOR GOOD AIR CIRCULATION...

Chamomile

Chamomile is a delicate flower that is as lovely as it is useful. Harvesting chamomile, however, is difficult in a major scale, making it loved by home gardeners but expensive as an herb farm crop.

Chamomile has a lightly fruity taste. Because the taste differs slightly from variety to variety, tasting is the best way to find the right chamomile for your garden.

To harvest chamomile for drying, pick the individual chamomile flowers as they bloom and just after the dew has dried in the morning. This is very important because chamomile's delicate scent is easily lost if you're not careful. Some leaves are fine to include because they also have some chamomile flavor.

To dry chamomile, follow these steps:

1. **Lay the flowers in a single layer on trays.**

2. **Set your oven or dehydrator temperature to between 115 and 125 degrees and dry for 3 to 5 hours, checking carefully after 4 hours and rotating the trays periodically to facilitate even drying.**

   You don't want to overdry them. Flowers are fully dry when the tiny petals curl inward, and the center of the blossom is totally dry.

3. **Store in a airtight container, out of sunlight.**

To use your dried chamomile, pour 1 cup of boiling water over 1 tablespoon dried flowers; then cover and steep for 3 minutes. (Don't steep chamomile too long; it can produce a bitter taste.)

Dill

Dill, an herb that grows anywhere, has tiny leaves and a large, flowering seed head. Harvest the leaves any time you want. Use dill leaves in dressings and pickle mixes. It makes a refreshing dip for vegetables and tastes great added to your summer salads.

Dill can quickly become an invasive plant. Once the plant goes to seed, it starts popping up everywhere. Be sure to keep it in check by trimming off the flowers and seeds before the plant makes itself a permanent member of your garden.

Drying dill is super easy. Follow these steps:

1. **Lay the dill leaves in a single, loose layer on trays.**

2. **Set your oven or dehydrator temperature to between 100 and 115 degrees and dry 3 to 5 hours, rotating the trays periodically to facilitate even drying.**

   Properly dried dill leaves are crispy.

3. **Store dried dill in airtight containers, out of light.**

   This herb loses its delicate flavor quickly if left in sunlight for too long.

Chewing a few dill seeds can help with indigestion. Historically, dill was an ingredient in gripe water for colicky infants.

Marjoram

Marjoram is sometimes mislabeled as oregano, and the two do look surprisingly similar. Marjoram, sometimes called sweet marjoram, is the perfect addition to any recipe that calls for oregano. Many people dislike the bitter taste that oregano can have, and using marjoram takes care of this problem. I (Amy) find that marjoram's taste has much more depth than oregano, too. (I am a true convert to this delicious herb!)

If you're growing your own marjoram, harvest its leaves when they are young. Cut the soft stems in the morning, after the dew has dried and before the sun becomes too hot. If you're buying marjoram at a farmer's market, look for young, small leaves with a bright green color and aromatic scent.

To dry marjoram, follow these steps:

1. **Lay the marjoram stems on trays, allowing room between them for proper air circulation.**

2. **Set your dehydrator's temperature to between 115 and 125 degrees and dry your marjoram for 3 to 5 hours, checking carefully after 3 hours and rotating the trays periodically to facilitate even drying.**

   Properly dried marjoram leaves crumble easily.

3. **Store the stems, whole, in a cool dry place, away from sunlight.**

To use dried marjoram, crumble leaves in your hand before adding to the dish and add the herb in the last 10 minutes of cooking to keep its flavor.

For the best flavor, remove flowering tops of marjoram as they appear. Once it flowers, the scent and flavor fade. Harvesting just before flowering, however, produces the strongest flavor of all.

Mint

Mint is arguably the herb most people are familiar with and also the easiest herb to grow. It only requires sunlight and water to thrive. Yes, you can grow mint on a counter in a glass of water — forever!

Mint comes in dozens of flavors, with more being created all the time. From citrus to chocolate, mints are available for any palate. Grow as many varieties as you want, but keep them contained! And harvest them often, throughout the growing season, for drying.

Mint is a highly invasive herb and will overtake a garden within one growing season if left to spread on its own. Plant mint in a container to keep from having it go wild (literally). If you grow more than one variety of mint, plant them at least 10 feet apart to avoid cross-pollination. Although you will still get mint, it will no longer be true to the original scent you planted, if cross-pollinated.

To dry mint, follow these steps:

1. **Cut the stems that seem to want to straggle, and lay them on a drying tray.**

2. **Set your dehydrator or oven temperature to between 115 and 125 degrees and dry for 3 to 5 hours, rotating the trays periodically to facilitate even drying.**

   Properly dried mint leaves easily crumble in your hand.

3. **Store mint in airtight containers.**

Try making it into tea or adding a few leaves, crumbled, to boiled potatoes.

Oregano

Oregano is another easy-to-dry herb. Used in any tomato-based dish, oregano adds a distinct flavor to your meals. By drying oregano, you ensure that you have plenty of this popular flavoring available throughout the winter months. Use only young leaves, as older oregano has a tendency to taste bitter.

To dry oregano, pick the young leaves once the dew has dried in the morning and then follow these steps:

1. **Remove any leaves that have insect damage or have been crushed while harvesting.**

   These sometimes turn an unappealing black when drying.

2. **Arrange in a single layer on trays, but don't fill them too full. You want air to flow around them.**

3. **Set the temperature on your dehydrator to between 115 and 125 degrees and dry the oregano for 3 to 5 hours, rotating the trays periodically to facilitate even drying.**

   Properly dried oregano is dry and crumbly.

4. **Store dried oregano in its whole form until ready to use.**

To use dried oregano, crush the leaves in your hand just before adding to the dish. Add oregano to the dish in the last 10 minutes of cooking to preserve the flavor.

Rosemary

Rosemary is a centerpiece to any herb garden. Its scent is recognizable by nearly everyone, and its lovely bluish flowers are truly special. Rosemary can be harvested throughout the season. To dry, cut the smaller, side stems where they branch off from the main stem and then follow these steps:

1. **Lay the whole stems onto the drying trays.**

2. **Dry the herb for 6 to 8 hours at a temperature between 110 and 115 degrees, rotating the trays periodically to facilitate even drying.**

   They're done when the leaves slightly shrivel and release from the stem easily.

3. **Remove the leaves by holding the stem over a dish or container and running your fingers along the stem.**

   The leaves come off with a gentle touch and you are left with a clean stem.

4. **Store rosemary leaves whole, and only break them up right before adding to your recipe.**

   This keeps most of the flavor inside until needed.

 Save the dried rosemary stems for making kabobs. They contain plenty of the rosemary flavor, and make a unique presentation. Use the stems as you would skewers.

Sage

Sage is an easy-to-grow herb that is available as seeds or plants that quickly grow into small, lovely bushes. You can use any variety of garden sage for drying. Some offer a stronger flavor than others, so be sure to taste it before purchasing to find your favorite. To dry sage leaves, harvest them as they become large enough (½ inch or more in length) and then follow these steps:

1. **Lay out your sage leaves in a single layer on your drying trays.**

   Be sure to leave room between the leaves for even drying.

2. **Dry the herb for 6 to 8 hours at a temperature between 115 and 125 degrees, rotating the trays periodically to facilitate even drying.**

   It's dry enough if a leaf crumbles in your fingers.

   Be careful to dry these leaves thoroughly; they are slightly thicker than many other herbs and require careful attention.

3. **Store the dried leaves in their whole form until needed.**

If you find that you use rubbed sage often, dry the whole leaves and rub them through a mesh strainer to create a fluffy sage powder perfect for cooking.

Stevia

Stevia may not be as widely known as some of the others in this list, but it is a very useful herb. It's been used for hundreds of years in other parts of the world as a replacement for sugar. Stevia users have found that it has a slight licorice aftertaste. You may find that your family enjoys stevia as much as sugar!

To dry, pick the stevia leaves as needed throughout the growing season and then follow these steps:

1. **Lay the leaves on your drying trays in a single layer.**

   Be careful to not overlap, as they can mold quickly if left in a warm place without adequate circulation.

2. **Set your oven or dehydrator temperature to between 115 and 125 degrees and dry for 4 to 6 hours, rotating the trays periodically to facilitate even drying.**

   Properly dried stevia leaves crumble easily in your hand.

3. **Store in an airtight container, away from direct sunlight.**

To make stevia sweetener, steep the dry leaves in boiling water and leave them to cool. You can then measure the resulting "tea" by the drop into any drink that requires a sweet taste. Be warned, it is extremely sweet — 300 times sweeter than table sugar, in fact — so start with a drop at a time.

If you find that you always sweeten a particular herb tea, try adding ½ teaspoon of dried stevia to the original recipe. Taste the sweetness of the tea and adjust the dried herb as needed.

Tarragon

Tarragon is an herb that, sadly, many people overlook. Tarragon has a slight anise flavor, dries well, and makes any chicken, egg, or cheese dish sing. The next time you serve a meal including this beautiful herb, your family will ask what that secret flavor is.

To dry tarragon, pick young tarragon leaves throughout the growing season and then follow these steps:

1. **Remove the stems that have become woody and place leaves in a single layer on your drying trays.**

   If you find that the leaves slip through the holes in your trays, leave the stems on during drying to prevent this.

2. **Set your oven or dehydrator temperature to between 115 and 125 degrees and dry for 4 to 6 hours, rotating the trays periodically to facilitate even drying.**

   Properly dried tarragon leaves crumble easily in your hand.

   Be careful not to overdry. Check carefully after the first 2 hours, and every 30 minutes after that.

3. **Store in a cool, dry place, out of direct sunlight.**

   Tarragon loses its flavor rapidly, so be sure to dry just what you need for the winter months.

To avoid tarragon leaves becoming an unappetizing black, pick them quickly and dry them right away.

Thyme

Thyme has many uses: It tastes great mixed with other herbs for flavoring Italian dishes and it can hold its own when paired with poultry. Thyme comes in many varieties, but the drying technique is the same. Follow these steps:

1. **Snip off stems as soon as your plants are large enough for drying and lay them whole, in a single layer, on your drying tray.**

2. **Set your oven or dehydrator temperature to between 110 to 115 degrees and dry the thyme for 4 to 6 hours, rotating the trays periodically to facilitate even drying.**

   Properly dried thyme leaves are dry and crisp.

3. **Store dried thyme, stems and all, in a cool, dry place away from sunlight.**

   Thyme loses its flavor quickly when left in sunlight.

When it comes time to use your dried thyme, crush the tiny stems right along with the leaves. If stems are too woody, strip leaves off, right before use.

The next time you have a cough or cold, make a tea out of dried thyme leaves. Thyme tea tastes very soothing when you are congested.

Getting Creative with Herb Cooking Blends

Creating herbal blends for cooking is a matter of using your senses to choose what smells and looks best. If you match the types of foods you eat most often with herbs that compliment these foods, you will be able to create your own signature blends.

Dry each herb separately as explained in the preceding sections before combining. Once your herbs are dry, you can experiment with different combinations of flavors to see what tastes the best.

 Freshly dried herbs have far more flavor and aroma than those dried and sold in a grocery store. So use a light hand when you season with freshly dried herbs. Add your herbs at the end of the cooking process to make the most of the flavor.

 In addition to the herb mix recipes that follow, try creating an herb-butter blend: Combine your favorite herbs and roll a cube of butter in them to coat the stick, or soften the butter to room temperature and mix the dried herbs directly into the butter. Chill the butter; cut it into slices or make rounds with a melon baller for serving.

Italian Herb Mix

From pizza to salad dressing, this mix is the taste that gets used the most in my (Amy's) house. Mix it with olive oil and baste on grilled chicken, sprinkle it on any Italian foods, and add it to your favorite soups.

Preparation time: *10 minutes*

Yield: *1 cup*

¼ cup dried marjoram, crumbled

¼ cup dried oregano, crushed

¼ cup dried rosemary leaves, crushed

¼ cup dried thyme leaves, crushed

1 Combine all the ingredients in a medium-size bowl and mix well.

2 Transfer the herb mix to an airtight container and store in a cool, dry place.

Per 1-tablespoon serving: Calories 11 (From fat 3); Fat 0g (Saturated 0g); Cholesterol 0mg; Sodium 2mg; Carbohydrates 2g (Dietary fiber 1g); Protein 0g.

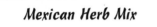

Mexican Herb Mix

If your family loves Mexican food as much as mine (Amy's), you may end up making this mix quite often. It has just the right amount of kick that everyone can enjoy. Add it to ground meat for tacos, burritos, and Mexican-themed soups and dips.

Preparation time: *10 minutes*

Yield: *1 cup*

½ tablespoon chili powder (adjust for desired heat)

⅛ cup dried epazote leaves, crushed

⅛ cup dried basil leaves, crushed

¼ cup dried oregano leaves, crushed

¼ cup cumin seeds, ground just before use

¼ cup dried coriander seeds, ground just before use

1 Combine all the ingredients in a medium-size bowl and mix well.

2 Transfer the herb mix into an airtight container and store in a cool, dry place.

Tip: *You can find epazote leaves at large grocery stores in the ethnic foods section or online from most herb suppliers.*

Per 1-tablespoon serving: Calories 16 (From fat 7); Fat 1g (Saturated 0g); Cholesterol 0mg; Sodium 6mg; Carbohydrates 3g (Dietary fiber 2g); Protein 1g.

Rice Mix

A great way to use dried herbs is to use them in ready-to-make mixes. These are much better than the standard mixes you find at the store. To prepare the rice, add the rice mix to 2 cups of water in a 2- to 3-quart saucepan. Bring the rice to a boil over high heat, stir, cover, and reduce the heat to medium-low. Cook for about 30 minutes (don't lift that lid to peek). Remove the rice from the heat and let the rice stand for 30 minutes. Fluff the rice with a fork and serve immediately.

Preparation time: *10 minutes*

Yield: *1¼ cups rice mix*

1 cup long-grain rice

2 teaspoons chicken bouillon granules

2 to 3 teaspoons dried herbs of your choice

¼ teaspoon kosher salt

1 Combine all the ingredients in a medium sized bowl.

2 Transfer the mix to a glass container or clear food-safe bag. Seal the jar or tie the bag closed.

Vary It! *Instead of chicken bouillon, use beef or vegetable for a slightly different taste.*

Tip: *Make up a cooking instruction card and keep it with the mix.*

Per ½ cup serving of prepared mix: *Calories 139 (From fat 3); Fat 0g (Saturated 0g); Cholesterol 0mg; Sodium 490mg; Carbohydrates 30g (Dietary fiber 1g); Protein 3g.*

Herbs for Teas

Nothing is more enjoyable or relaxing than a cup of steaming hot tea. Nothing, that is, except relaxing with a special herbal tea you've made yourself. In this section, you find out how to create your own tea blends. Make distinct recipes for any occasion, and pick the perfect herb for the job.

Like seasoning a dish, herbal tea is a matter of blending herbs that taste great together to create a new flavor you love. The same recipes that you use for hot tea work equally well for cold tea. You can keep a pitcher of iced, herbal tea in the refrigerator for the family during the summer and serve it hot in the winter. Mix up your favorite tea blends and keep them on hand for quick, tasty drinks when the kids want something other than water. They are fast to make and naturally sweet.

Make ice cubes from your leftover hot tea. Use these frozen tea cubes to cool down another ice tea. You will not dilute your delicate tea while cooling it, and using a second flavor to make your ice cubes with makes the entire glass taste great!

Cover steaming tea while it steeps to contain the volatile (and tasty) oils that make the tea so delicious.

Lemon Lover Tea Blend

This fruity, bright tea blend tastes great hot or iced. To make a cup of tea, pour 1 cup of boiling water over 1 tablespoon of the Lemon Lover Tea Blend; then cover and steep for 3 to 5 minutes. Turn it into a great party drink by floating slices of citrus fruit in it. Or mix equal parts tea and fruit juice for a refreshing drink.

Preparation time: *10 minutes*

Yield: *1 cup of tea mixture*

¼ cup dried lemon balm leaves   ¼ cup dried lemon verbena leaves

¼ cup dried chamomile flowers   ¼ cup dried lemon thyme leaves

1 Combine all the ingredients in a medium bowl and mix well.

2 Transfer the tea blend to an airtight container and store it in a cool, dry place.

Per 1-tablespoon serving: *Calories 5 (From fat 0); Fat 0g (Saturated 0g); Cholesterol 0mg; Sodium 2mg; Carbohydrates 1g (Dietary fiber 1g); Protein 0g.*

Mint Lover Herb Tea Blend

This minty, fresh tea is a great beginner tea blend. Drying mint leaves is easy, and everyone enjoys the taste. Surprise your family with this tea at your next meal. The lemon balm works well with the mint flavors and is a nice addition. To make a cup of tea, pour 1 cup boiling water over 1 tablespoon the Mint Lover Herb Tea Blend. Cover and steep 3 to 5 minutes.

Preparation time: *10 minutes*

Yield: *1 cup of dried, herb tea mix*

¼ cup dried peppermint leaves	¼ cup dried catmint leaves
¼ cup dried spearmint leaves	¼ cup dried lemon balm, crushed

1 Combine all the ingredients in a medium-size bowl and mix well.

2 Transfer the tea blend to an airtight container and store in a cool, dry place.

Vary It: *Don't like the lemon balm? Then increase the other mints and leave it out.*

Per serving: *Calories 5 (From fat 0); Fat 0g (Saturated 0g); Cholesterol 0mg; Sodium 6mg; Carbohydrates 1g (Dietary fiber 1g); Protein 0g.*

Chapter 20

Root Cellars and Alternative Storage Spaces

An often overlooked storage idea is underground storage. The traditional root cellar is an efficient way to keep many foods fresh throughout the winter months. Keeping your harvest at its best through cold storage is easier than you think! If you're not lucky enough to have a place for an actual root cellar, there are all sorts of other creative ways you can keep foods at the proper temperature.

In this chapter, you discover creative ways to store your produce and find out how to select the best foods to keep in cold storage.

Finding the Perfect Place for Cold Storage

Before refrigeration and artificial preservatives, cold storage was the way to go if you needed to store produce over the winter. The basic idea behind cold storage is that you can prolong the shelf life of both fresh and canned produce by keeping them in a cool, dark place under just the right conditions.

By combining the perfect mix of temperature and humidity, you can expand your storage to a large variety of foods. Temperature and humidity aren't the only considerations, however. An area used for cold storage also needs to have proper ventilation to keep the food as fresh as possible. And ease of access is vital, too.

✔ **Temperature:** Cold storage temperatures range from 32 to 60 degrees. The right temperature for any given food is one that slows the enzymes responsible for decay. Different foods require different storage temperatures. Beets, for example, need temps just above freezing; pumpkins and squashes, on the other hand, need temps in the 50- to 60-degree range.

✔ **Humidity:** Depending on the foods you want to store, your root cellar or alternative cold storage area needs a humidity range from 60 to 95 percent. Foods such as carrots, parsnips, and turnips store best at 90 to 95 percent humidity. Sweet potatoes and onions, on the other hand, do much better at a humidity of no more than 70 percent.

If you plan to store foods that require very different humidity and temperature levels, you need to use more than one storage area. It's not uncommon to have a dry cold storage area with lower humidity (like you'd get in an area that has a cement floor) and a higher humidity area (which you get in an area with a dirt or gravel floor)

To keep track of temperature and humidity level in the air, buy a simple thermometer unit, called a *hydrometer* (see Figure 20-1).

✔ **Ventilation:** No matter what type of storage area you choose, it must be able to let warm air out and cool air in.

✔ **Ease of access:** Because you have to regularly check your stored food, you need a place that is easy to get into and that allows you to easily move things around.

Read on to find out what your cold-storage options are, and head to the section "Preparing Foods for Cold Storage" to discover the optimum humidity levels and temperatures required for specific foods.

Tried and true: The traditional root cellar

Root cellars have had a long and important place in the history of food storage. Root cellars were most often the actual cellar of old homes and farmhouses. These older houses had cellars with dirt floors, perfect for keeping foods cool and the humidity higher than average.

If you're lucky enough to have an actual dirt-floor root cellar, all you need to do to store your produce there is provide sturdy shelving and rodent-proof the area by covering any holes or potential rodent-friendly entryways with wire mesh. You can also place rodent bait in out-of-the-way areas and check often for rodent activity.

A preexisting root cellar usually contains some sort of air vent or pipe located at the top of the area to allow warm air to rise and escape. If you don't have a preexisting air vent, periodically open a window or door to the outside to allow warm air out and fresh air in.

Figure 20-1:
A hydrometer for checking temperature and humidity.

In modern homes, cellars (or basements) often have concrete floors and are generally too warm and dry for food storage. Carefully measure your temperature and moisture content before placing your produce in a cellar that may not have optimum conditions.

DIY storage spaces

If you don't have a cellar with a dirt floor, there are alternatives. Take a look at your cellar layout and consider the areas suggested in the following sections.

Stairwells

Does a stairwell lead from your basement to the outside? If so, add an insulated door to separate the stairwell from the main room, and voilá, you have a cold storage space that has built-in shelves: the stairs! Just place bins of produce on each step and pans of water under the stairs for moisture, and you have an efficient storage area (see Figure 20-2).

A stairwell is particularly good because the stairs create areas with varying temperatures, allowing for a wide array of conditions that can benefit many different kinds of foods.

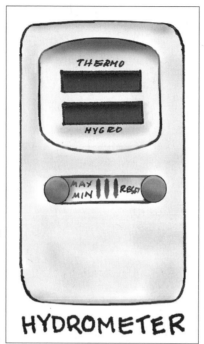

Figure 20-2:
A stairwell
converted
into a cold
storage
area.

Be sure to place a hydrometer in this area, as well as a few, inexpensive thermometers on different steps, to gauge the best conditions for your stored foods. There will be quite a variation in temperature as you go up the stairs.

Storm shelters

Do you have a storm shelter (also called a storm cellar)? In the Midwest, storm shelters are often underground cellars separate from the house or basement. (Think of Dorothy in *The Wizard of Oz,* when she runs through the yard to get to the storm cellar during the tornado.) These shelters are perfect for adding some shelves and neat bins of produce. They're below the frost line, have adequate ventilation, and are weatherproof. Whether your home had a storm shelter when you moved in or you decided to build one yourself, be certain to block any ventilation pipes with fine screen to keep out rodent activity.

Your stored foods will be used up long before the storm season approaches. Even so, keep your cold storage organized and neat.

Straw-bale storage

If you have a small area in your yard, you can construct a simple straw-bale storage area (see Figure 20-3) to hold your root crops, like potatoes, rutabagas, turnips, and parsnips.

The best location for straw-bale storage is one that tends to stay dry. Don't place these storage areas in high moisture areas (where you generally have a buildup of snowdrift, for example, or where water tends to puddle after storms). Also, don't build one close to buildings that protect the area from winter temperatures. You want the straw bales to be able to stay freezing cold on the outside and yet insulate the produce inside.

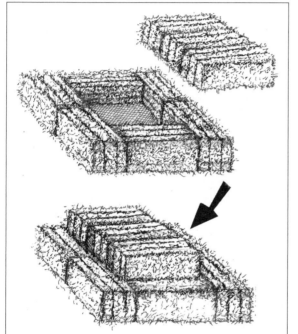

Figure 20-3:
Straw-bale
storage

Once you've found a suitable location, follow these steps to build your storage area:

1. **Place two bales of straw in a line, with the ends touching; about 16 inches away, place two more bales parallel to the first two.**

   The spacing is adequate for the bales that are laid on top to cover the open space completely.

2. **Place one straw bale on each of the remaining ends to enclose a box shape in the center.**

   You've just made a large square in the center.

3. **Cover the ground in the center of the square with a screen.**

   You don't have use the screen, but doing so helps keep your produce protected from critters that may be inclined to dig under the whole thing.

4. **Layer some soft straw on the bottom of the square to cushion the produce.**

   If you put a screen in the center, place the straw over the screen.

5. **Layer your root crops, very gently, into the bin.**

   Take care to not dump or toss your vegetables. Bruised food quickly turns to spoiled food.

6. **When the bin is full, layer another couple of inches of straw onto the food.**

7. **Place bales of straw across the top of the now-filled bin.**

   Your food is now protected from winter in a breathable storage bin.

To check on or access the food inside, simply remove the top two bales. Replace the bales carefully and evenly to cover the hole each time. In the late spring, or when the straw-bale storage area is empty, simply take the bin apart, and use the straw as mulch for your garden.

Some people use hay bales for these storage bins, but we don't recommend it. Hay molds rather quickly, sometimes spoiling the produce inside. Hay bales also seem to absorb more moisture than straw bales. If you use hay, check periodically for moisture damage, and remove the offending produce immediately.

Rubber trash cans

You can bury these up to their rims in the ground, place your produce inside, put on the lid, and then cover the whole thing with a thick layer of straw for a simple cold storage arrangement. These bins are easy to wash and the tight lids keep the foods fresh and sanitary and keep rodents out.

Following Simple Storage Rules

Underground storage is the fastest and possibly easiest way to store foods. There are, however, some rules to follow, no matter what variety of food you want to keep over the winter:

  ✔ **Be careful about the quality of the food you store:** Foods must be in perfect condition — not too ripe or picked too early. Overly ripe fruit is extremely fragile and in the last stage before naturally decaying. Food that's too green doesn't do particularly well, either. These foods may change color or become agreeably soft in storage, but they won't truly ripen and develop their best flavor in these conditions.

Make sure you pick your food at just the right ripeness, as fresh as possible, and store it immediately. *Don't* allow it to sit at room temperature while you decide what you are going to do with it.

✔ **Be careful about how you pair foods:** Some foods produce gases that make other foods spoil. For instance, apples produce a gas that makes potatoes start to sprout. Put these two together, and you'll end up with potatoes that are soft and inedible. Cabbage is a very strongly scented food that is better stored in an outside area, away from more delicately flavored items.

✔ **You must care for the foods, even while in storage.** Weekly checking for bruising, decay, dryness, and mold is essential. The old adage about a rotten apple spoiling the barrel definitely applies here. As the winter progresses, remove any produce that has blemishes. Your remaining foods will continue to last longer.

Rearrange your produce carefully. If you're like me (Amy), after a month, you may discover that you've used enough of your stored produce to enable you to bring the bottom layer up to the top. Be careful of excess handling though; gently place each food back in place to avoid bruising.

✔ **Pick the right storage container:** Choose containers that let you keep things neat and very organized. Some ideas:

- **Rubbermaid-style tubs:** These can be stacked when not in use, their covers fit tightly, and they can easily be filled with damp sand for foods needing increased humidity. Use clear bins to avoid colors leaching into foods and so that you can easily see all the produce inside.

- **Wooden bins or boxes:** Recycle these from thrift stores and some grocery stores. Even if you have to pay a few dollars each, they will give years of service and allow for neat, tidy stacking. If stacking wooden boxes, place the first row in a line, place a couple of sticks across the boxes for air circulation, and then place the next boxes. You want to let the moisture and gases escape, which allows the food to last longer.

- **Five-gallon pails:** You can find these for next to nothing from bakers and other restaurants. You don't need to include the lid; in fact, for cold storage, it is best not to. Fill the clean, dry bucket with produce, layer a damp cloth on the top and you can stack these buckets in a pyramid shape, allowing plenty of airflow between.

- **Old dressers:** You can arrange these unconventional pieces against a wall and use the drawers to keep your produce in a dry and safe place. Line the drawers with newspaper for easy cleaning. Keep them slightly ajar for proper air circulation.

Preparing Foods for Cold Storage

Foods that store well are generally the less juicy and delicate things, like root vegetables and firm fruits. The following sections list several fruits and vegetables that keep very well in cold storage. They are foods that many families enjoy; they provide a fresh taste when bland winter fare abounds; and they extend your food pantry to include fresh, tasty choices. (***Note:*** You may be able to extend the life of more tender foods, like eggplant or broccoli, but don't count on them lasting for months as the other foods will. You can keep these treats in storage about two weeks, but no longer.)

As a general rule, harvest root crops as late as you can in the season and don't wash the dirt from the roots. Simply use your hand or a rag to remove some of the loose soil.

Apples

Apples store very well. Choose a variety that is known for storage. Kept well, apples can last throughout the entire winter — four to six months! Toward the end of that time, a perfectly good apple may become slightly shriveled. This is simply from the loss of moisture, not nutrition.

Choose apples that are unblemished and firm (they shouldn't give at all when pressed). Check in bright light for dents and soft spots.

To store, layer the apples carefully in very cold temperatures (between 30 and 35 degrees), with a high humidity between 80 and 90 percent. (Place a pan of water in the area where they're stored.)

Try covering your bin of apples with a damp (not dripping) cloth, which remains damp for at least a day. And make it a habit to replace the cloth every couple of days when you check other stored produce.

Beets

Beets are prolific and inexpensive to grow, meaning you'll end up with plenty for storage if you plant a few rows. Harvest beets late in the season, after the nights become freezing cold. If you're buying beets at a farmer's market, look for fresh, crisp tops. This is the best indication that the beets are just picked.

To prepare the beets for storage, cut off the tops, leaving the beet itself intact (don't wash them). Then place the beets in your coldest storage, temperatures just above freezing, 32 to 40 degrees, with 90 to 95 percent humidity. To increase humidity naturally, place the beets on moist sand.

Some gardeners recommend leaving beets in the ground, covered with a thick layer of straw. They say beets and other root crops can be harvested directly from the ground into the coldest part of the winter. Be aware, though, that rodents may destroy root crops before you get a chance to harvest them. So before you follow the advice of the "leave 'em in the ground" crowd, make sure you — and not rodents — will be the benefactors.

Cabbage

Cabbage adds bulk and crunch to many winter dishes. Keeping cabbage in storage requires a few extra precautions, however, to ensure that it remains useable throughout the winter and doesn't ruin other food nearby.

First, cabbage gives off a strong odor while in storage, which is normal (don't confuse this smell with spoilage). The problem with the smell is that apples and other fruits can absorb the flavor of cabbage. The key is to make sure you don't store cabbage too closely to these other types of foods. If you must store cabbage close to other foods, wrap individual heads with newspaper to contain the odor.

The longer cabbage remains in storage, the stronger the taste when it's cooked. If your family does not like the stronger taste, plan on using up cabbage early in the storage season.

Second, cabbage needs to be stored in a damp area. If you store cabbage in a place that's too dry, the heads dry out, and the dry, wilted leaves are wasted. Fortunately, you can take care of this tendency with a simple pan of water.

To prepare cabbage for storage, choose unblemished cabbage that has not been picked for long. Remove the tough outer leaves. Wrap each head in newspaper and store it where temperatures are just above freezing, 32 to 40 degrees, and the humidity levels are between 80 to 90 percent. Place a pan of water near the cabbage to provide enough moisture during storage.

Carrots

Carrots are another root vegetable that stores well and tastes sweet and crisp throughout the winter months. Just as you do with beets, pick carrots as late as possible in the season. Avoid any that have grown too large and pithy, however, because these carrots have used up their natural sweetness and will taste bitter.

To prepare carrots for storage, trim off the tops, leaving the carrot itself intact. Don't wash them; simply brush off excess soil if you want to. Place carrots with beets in coldest storage of 32 to 40 degrees with high humidity of 90 to 95 percent. Carrots do especially well in moist sand.

Garlic

You can never have enough garlic, especially since garlic is so easy to store. If you're growing your own garlic, simply pull the bulbs once the tops have dried and fallen over. Allow the garlic bulbs to dry thoroughly out of direct sunlight until the outside of the bulbs has become dry and papery. Purchased garlic bulbs have already been dried. Look for the papery outer layer that you always see on a store-bought bulb.

Dry bulbs on newspaper outside during the warm summer days, but bring them in during the cool nights to prevent condensation. Repeat this process for a few days, until the garlic is completely dry.

When the garlic is thoroughly dry, tie bunches of tops together, braid in attractive garlic braids. Alternatively, do what I (Amy) do: Trim tops from bulbs and place them in women's stockings, tying a knot between bulbs. You can hang this long chain of bulbs on a nail in a cool and slightly damp area. I have luck placing my garlic in a cool coat room, instead of an actual root cellar. They are in a convenient location for cooking, and let's face it, they make quite a conversation piece! If you do keep them in cold storage, place them in 30 to 45 degrees with a humidity level of 60 to 70 percent.

Onions

Most onions keep very well in cold storage. Some varieties, such as the extra sweet onions, however, don't last long. When planting, choose varieties that say they work well for storage (you'll see the term "good keeper"). These onions last throughout the storage season.

Harvest onions the same as garlic. Pull them when the tops turn brown and fall over. Once pulled, they must also be cured, like garlic: Place them on newspaper to dry during the warm days, bringing them in during the cool night hours to avoid condensation buildup. When storing purchased onions, you don't have to worry about this step. They are already dried for you.

To store, gently place onions in a crate, loose mesh bag, or ladies' stockings, tying a knot between each onion. To prevent mildew on onion skins, air circulation is vital, so make sure your cold storage has adequate ventilation (see the earlier section "Finding the Perfect Place for Cold Storage"). The ideal storage conditions are temperatures of 35 to 40 degrees and humidity of 60 to 70 percent. If, throughout the season, you find onions with some mildew on them, simply use those onions first. Generally the mildew is on the outer layers, leaving the inside onions fresh.

Pears

Pears store very well and make a nice change from apples. In years when apples are affected by blight or scald and are too expensive, pears can be more available.

Pick pears you plan to store when they're just ripened. (Don't choose pears that are too ripe, or soft; simply leaning against each other can cause them to bruise.) To help protect the fruit, wrap each pear in a sheet of newspaper before storing. Keep temperatures cold, 30 to 35 degrees, with high humidity (80 to 90 percent). Pears can keep for several months in this manner.

Potatoes

Potatoes are the easiest of all fruits and vegetables to store. To prepare for storage, harvest late in the season. Don't wash the potatoes; instead remove excess soil with your hand or a soft rag. Inspect them carefully for bruising or nicks in the skin (fresh potatoes have a more delicate skin than those that have been harvested for a few days). If you find any bruising or nicks, keep these potatoes out of storage and use them within a few days.

Store potatoes in complete darkness at 32 to 40 degrees and 80 to 90 percent humidity. Every week, check them for damage. At least once a month, turn and rearrange them. Finally, don't let them freeze. A frozen potato is a ruined potato; it can't be saved.

The most important rule for storing potatoes is to store them in complete darkness. First, the darkness signals dormancy for the potato, and it won't sprout. Second, potatoes subjected to light become bitter over time. Other than perfect darkness, potatoes really do well in almost all storage conditions.

Turnips

Turnips are an underappreciated root crop. They are easy to grow: You simply plant them early in the season, weed them a few times, and harvest them late in the season, after the nights become freezing cold, sometime in November.

To prepare turnips for storage, don't wash them. Simply brush off any excess soil with your hand or a rag, and trim off the turnip tops.

Store them in your coldest storage area; just above freezing is ideal (temperatures of 30 to 40 degrees). The humidity should be high; between 90 to 95 percent is optimal. Turnips are another food that stores well in damp sand.

Consider turnips a crop that provides two separate foods: the greens and the root. So, after you trim the tops to prepare the root for cold storage, don't throw away the greens. You can dry them for use later. To see how to keep turnip tops, head to Chapter 10 for instructions for canning greens and Chapter 18 for info on drying greens.

Tomatoes

You may be surprised to see tomatoes, which are both fragile and juicy, in this list of good cold-storage vegetables. Tomatoes can, however, be kept for a limited period of time in cold storage.

When you store tomatoes, you store the whole plant, not just the individual tomatoes. So at the end of the growing season, select any tomato plants that have fruit with the slightest hint of ripening (any color change, from slight yellow to orange) and follow these steps:

1. **Remove any fruits from the plant that are still fully green or too small to ever ripen.**

2. **Pull the entire plant out of the ground and hang it upside down in temperatures between 55 and 70 degrees, with moderate humidity of 60 to 70 percent.**

   An unheated garage or cellar stairwell works great for this.

The tomatoes will ripen slowly over time, right on the vine. You will be amazed at the vine-fresh flavor.

Part VI
The Part of Tens

The 5th Wave   By Rich Tennant

"Quit moping. You won first place in the meatloaf category, and that's good. I'm the only one who knows it was a carrot cake you entered."

In this part . . .

1 f you wonder where you can find all the things for food preservation that you need, Part VI provides the answer. Here you'll also find a handy top-ten list that helps you troubleshoot and solving canning problems.

Chapter 21

Ten (Or So) Troubleshooting Tips for Your Home-Canned Creations

Canning and preserving is a science and, like any science, you must be precise when working in your lab, which in this case, is your kitchen. Although you follow your recipe instructions to the letter, accurately measure your ingredients, and properly process your filled jars, you aren't guaranteed a perfect product.

This chapter fills you in on some problems you may encounter in canning and what you can do to remedy the situation and avoid these troubles in the future.

Jars That Don't Seal Properly

There may be several reasons your jar didn't seal after processing: Maybe you didn't follow the manufacturer's instructions for using the jars and two-piece caps; maybe a particle of food was left on the jar rim; maybe a piece of food was forced out of the jar during processing; maybe the processing timing was calculated incorrectly; or maybe your filled jars weren't covered by 1 to 2 inches of water in your water-bath canner.

Eliminate these problems by reviewing and following the manufacturer's instructions for preparing and using your jars and two-piece caps, cleaning the rims after filling your jars, leaving the proper headspace in the jar, timing your processing after reaching a boil or the correct pressure, and covering your filled jars with 1 to 2 inches of water in your water-bath canner.

But what if your jar seals and then comes open? If this happens, check for hairline cracks in the jar. If you find a crack in the jar, discard the food (just in case there's a piece of glass in it) and the jar. If your food wasn't processed correctly, microorganisms may be active. They'll produce a gas in the jar that expands and forces the seal to break loose. Because this indicates food spoilage, don't taste the food or use it; dispose of it properly (refer to Chapter 9 for instructions).

Jars That Lose Liquid During Processing

Starchy food absorbs liquid — this is normal, and there's no way to correct it. Raw, unheated food also absorbs liquid during processing. Eliminate liquid absorption by using the hot-pack method.

Trapped air bubbles released during processing increase the air space in the jar while lowering the liquid level. Always release air bubbles before sealing and processing your jars (refer to Chapter 3).

Longer-than-suggested processing times cause a loss of liquid in your jars. If you're water-bath canning, prevent this by covering your jars with 1 to 2 inches of water for processing. If you're pressure canning, keep the pressure constant during processing; then let the pressure drop to 0 and wait 10 minutes before opening the canner.

Jars with Cloudy Liquid

Cloudy liquid occurs from using water with lots of minerals, salt containing additives, or ground spices. Remedy these problems by using soft water, pure salt (like canning and pickling salt), and whole spices.

If you used the right kind of water, salt, and spices and your jar's liquid is still cloudy, you probably have spoiled food. Dispose of it without tasting it.

Dark Spots on Your Jar's Lid

Occasionally, naturally occurring compounds (like acids and salts) in some food cause a brown or black deposit, along with some corrosion, on the inside of the lid. This deposit is harmless and doesn't spoil your food. You can go ahead and eat the food, and, because you dispose of the lids anyway, the spots won't matter in the future.

Jelly with the Wrong Consistency

Although you can still safely eat a batch of jelly that didn't set up or is too stiff, you obviously want to avoid the same problems in the future.

If your jelly is soft, runny, or syrupy

- ✔ **The proportions of sugar, acid, and juice may not be correct.** Accurately measure your ingredients.

- ✔ **Work with smaller amounts of juice, no more than 4 to 6 cups at one time.** Working with larger amounts of juice won't allow the juice to heat fast enough to reach its gel point, which can result in runny jelly.

- ✔ **Store your sealed jars in a cool, dark place with a temperature between 50 and 70 degrees.** Jelly may *break down* (become runny) in less-than-ideal storage conditions.

Stiff jelly, on the other hand, results from using too little sugar or cooking the jelly too long before it reaches the gel point. When your recipe doesn't call for adding pectin, your proportion guideline for sugar and juice (for most fruit) is ¾ cup of sugar to 1 cup of fruit juice.

Cloudy Jelly or Jelly with Bubbles

There's no solution for fixing cloudy jelly, but rest assured, it's safe to use. Poor straining is the most common cause of cloudy jelly. In the future, carefully strain your fruit through a damp jelly bag (or cheesecloth). This keeps pulp out of the juice. Don't squeeze the jelly bag; let it drain slowly by gravity.

Another likely cause is overcooking. Overcooking fruit breaks down fruit pulp, and broken pulp is small enough to pass through your strainer. Be sure to cook your fruit just until it's tender.

And finally, don't allow your jelly to cool before filling your jars.

Although cloudy jelly isn't anything to worry about, moving bubbles (bubbles that actually move through the product) in jelly indicates spoilage. This occurs when living microorganisms in the jar break the vacuum seal during storage. Discard your food without tasting it. Review the step-by-step instructions for preparing your food, readying and filling your jars, and processing your food. (***Note:*** It's not uncommon to see a few small air bubbles lodged in a thick jam or butter. It's the moving bubbles you need to be concerned about.)

Moldy Jelly

Mold on your jelly indicates an improper or a broken seal. Don't use or taste the jelly — just throw it out (see Chapter 9 for disposing of spoiled food). To avoid this problem in the future, always clean your jar rims, allow the proper headspace, and process your jars for the correct amount of time.

Jelly with Very Little Fruit Flavor

Jelly with weak flavor results from using fruit that's not ripe or fruit that's been stored too long after being picked. You can't add flavor to your jelly, but the next time, use tree-ripened fruit; store your sealed jars in a cool, dark, dry location; and consume your jelly within one year.

Glasslike Particles in Your Jelly

As long as your jar didn't break, you can safely use your jelly. What you're seeing isn't actually glass but undissolved sugar. Slow cooking evaporates liquid and allows particles to form in the jelly. Quickly heat the jelly to its gel point; then ladle, don't pour, your jelly from the pot into the jars. Pouring transfers any undissolved sugar crystals from the inside edge of the pot into your jars.

Hollow, Shriveled, Discolored, or Slippery Pickles

Occasionally, pickling cucumbers develop hollow interiors as they grow or if they wait too long between harvesting and pickling. You can't fix hollow pickles, but you can identify them because they float when they're put in a sink of water. (Don't throw out the hollow pickles; use them for making relish.)

If your pickles are shriveled, too much salt, sugar, or vinegar was added at once to the cucumbers. Start with a weaker solution and gradually add the full amount of ingredients called for in your recipe.

Discolored pickles may be from using hard water with minerals in it. Use soft water for your brine solution as well as for the liquid for filling your jars. Reactive metals like brass, iron, copper, aluminum, or zinc in pots and utensils cause darkening as well. Use nonreactive equipment such as enamelware with no chips or cracks, glass, stainless steel, or stoneware. Finally, your pickles may have absorbed ground spices. Prevent this by using whole spices rather than ground ones. These problems don't indicate spoilage, but your pickle flavor may be altered slightly.

Mushy or slippery pickles indicate spoilage. Discard the pickles without tasting them. Prevent these problems by accurately measuring your salt, using a vinegar with 5 percent acidity, and completely covering your pickles with liquid during the brining process and in your filled jars.

Remove the scum from your brining solution daily, use a modern-day recipe, follow your recipe to the letter, and use a heating period long enough to destroy any microorganisms.

White Sediment at the Bottom of the Pickle Jar

Soft pickles in a jar with white sediment indicate spoilage. Don't taste these; simply discard them. But, if the pickles are firm, they're safe to eat. The sediment is a harmless lactic acid or yeast that develops in the jar and settles to the bottom.

Food That Floats in the Jar

Fruit weighs less than the syrup you pack it in. If your fruit isn't packed snuggly, it'll float to the surface. Use ripe, firm fruit, and pack it tightly — but don't crush it. Fill your jars with a light to medium syrup. You can't sink floating fruit, but with practice, you can improve your packing skills.

Raw-packed vegetables shrink during processing. This doesn't indicate food spoilage. Reduce shrinkage by packing your vegetables tightly or blanching or precooking them prior to packing them in the jars. Floating food is still fine to eat, however.

Food with an Off Color

Fruit near the top of the jar may darken if it's not covered with liquid. This doesn't indicate food spoilage. Completely cover your fruit with liquid using the correct headspace for the fruit and the liquid. Too much headspace seals excess air in the jar. Trapped air bubbles change the liquid level in sealed jars when they're released during processing. Next time, leave the correct headspace and release any trapped air bubbles in the jar before sealing it.

If your fruit darkens after removing it from the jar, active enzymes may be to blame. You can still eat the fruit because it's in a sterile environment until you open the jar. But to avoid this problem in the future, make sure you process your filled jars for the required length of time stated in your recipe to inactivate these enzymes. Start counting your processing time when the water in your kettle reaches a full, rolling boil, with your jars covered by 1 to 2 inches of water.

You may notice your apples, pears, or peaches turning color during processing. Heat causes chemical changes in fruit that may alter the color of the food. Don't be surprised if these fruits turn pink, blue, red, or purple — there's no way to avoid it. So just sit back, admire the colors, and enjoy your food.

Fruits and vegetables turn dark when the natural chemical substances in food (such as acids, tannins, or sulfur compounds) react with minerals in the water. Food making direct contact with reactive utensils (utensils made from brass, copper, iron, aluminum, zinc, or chipped enamelware) experiences a color change. Prevent this by using soft water and nonreactive equipment, like stainless steel, glass, or enamelware with no chips or cracks.

Heating green vegetables breaks down *chlorophyll,* the green coloring in plant materials. If your green vegetables lose their bright-green color, you can't do anything about it. You have to expose your canned food to heat to produce a safe vacuum seal.

Green vegetables can turn brown if they're overcooked before they're heated again during processing. Accurately monitor your precooking time.

Chapter 22

Ten (Plus) Sources for Canning and Preserving Supplies and Equipment

● ●

In This Chapter

▶ Locating suppliers for canning and preserving gear

▶ Discovering suppliers of seeds and spices for the home-canner

● ●

*I*n this chapter are places where you can find anything and everything you need for canning and preserving without leaving the comfort of your home. The best part? When you shop by catalog or online, you never have to worry about finding a parking place or getting to the store before it closes!

Alltrista Consumer Products Co.

From the Alltrista Consumer Products Co., the canning jar company that makes Ball canning jars, you can find a great newsletter, canning basics, and plenty of recipes. Alltrista also sells containers for freezing that make great storage for dried foods as well.

14611 West Commerce Road
P.O. Box 529
Daleville, IN 47334
Phone: 800-240-3340
Web site: www.homecanning.com

HomeandBeyond.com

Home and Beyond offers all sorts of supplies for all sorts of food-preservation methods. You can find canning supplies (enter "canning" in the search box), food sealers, kitchen supplies, and much more. The product line is incredibly thorough and the prices are competitive.

61 Executive Avenue
Edison, NJ 08817
Phone: 866-961-3360
Web site: www.homeandbeyond.com

Cooking.com

Go to Cooking.com for all your kitchen needs. The site offers out-of-the-ordinary canning jars for special gift-giving, pressure canners, and just about anything you can think of for your food-preservation needs. To find what you need, type what you're looking for in the product search bar at the top of the page.

4086 Del Rey Avenue
Marina Del Rey, CA 90292
Phone: 800-663-8810 or 310-450-3270
Web site: www.cooking.com

Baker Creek Heirloom Seeds

Whether you have a garden or are new to gardening, Baker Creek is a fantastic place to find the perfect seeds for your garden. One way to really make a bright and cheerful-looking jar of veggies is to can some of the brightly colored varieties the company offers. The customer service is impeccable and the catalog is gorgeous.

2278 Baker Creek Road
Mansfield, MO 65704
Phone: 417-924-8917
Web site: www.rareseeds.com

Your local extension office

Your local extension office is the place to go to have your canner's safety checked, find new recipes and techniques, and locate the best produce for canning in your area. So how do you find your local extension office? Through the USDA's Cooperative State Research, Education, and Extension Office:

1400 Independence Avenue SW., Stop 2201
Washington, D.C. 20250-2201
Phone: 202-720-4423
Web site: www.csrees.usda.gov/Extension

KitchenKrafts.com

Get ready to be amazed! Kitchen Krafts is a specialty canning store with just about anything you can think of and plenty more than you'll want to have. Fast service and super-helpful customer service make this the place to browse for all the canning supplies you'll ever need. Order a free catalog and take your time making out your wish list.

Phone: 800-776-0575
Web site: www.kitchenkrafts.com

CanningUSA.com

A huge resource for canning preserving foods, CanningUSA.com is a store that teaches as well as sells everything for canning. If you are very visual, check out the video sections to see just how to can almost anything. CanningUSA's prices are often less expensive than many other canning supply stores, making this a must-have link. Don't let the name fool you, CanningUSA also offers a UK shopping site.

Web site: www.canningusa.com

Excalibur Products

Excalibur Products specializes in dehydrators. I (Amy) have used my Excalibur dehydrator for many years, all year around, and it's never failed me. The company offers units for home and commercial use, recipes and information for every need, and also a great newsletter for keeping updated with the newest techniques and tips for dehydrating.

6083 Power Inn Road
Sacramento, CA 95824
Phone: 800-875-4254
Web site: www.excaliburdehydrator.com/

Mountain Rose Herbs

Mountain Rose Herbs carries an extensive line of high-quality spices, herbs, and seasonings. The company offers pickling spices as well as every herb you can imagine for cooking and tea-making. Don't forget to sign up for its newsletter.

PO Box 50220
Eugene, OR 97405
Phone: 800-879-3337
Web site: www.mountainroseherbs.com

Pressure Cooker Outlet

Full of canning and preserving supplies, the Pressure Cooker Outlet is a one-stop shop for buying those hard-to-find pieces that make preserving food easy. Because the company carries all brands of canning jars, if you have a canning jar favorite, go here.

1035 Sylvatus Highway
Hillsville, VA 24343, USA
Phone: 800-251-8824
Web site: www.pressurecooker-outlet.com

Tupperware Corporation

Tupperware is well known for its line of plastic containers and other supplies for your home and kitchen. The Tupperware line includes rigid containers designed for the cold temperatures of your freezer. Choose from a wide variety of shapes and sizes. I (Amy) collect vintage Tupperware for my everyday kitchen use. It's that durable.

Phone: 800-366-3800 (or check your phone book for a local number)
Web site: www.tupperware.com

Appendix

Metric Conversion Guide

* *

*N*ote: The recipes in this book were not developed or tested using metric measures. There may be some variation in quality when converting to metric units.

Common Abbreviations

Abbreviation(s)	What It Stands For
C, c	cup
g	gram
kg	kilogram
L, l	liter
lb	pound
mL, ml	milliliter
oz	ounce
pt	pint
t, tsp	teaspoon
T, TB, Tbl, Tbsp	tablespoon

Volume

U.S. Units	Canadian Metric	Australian Metric
¼ teaspoon	1 mL	1 ml
½ teaspoon	2 mL	2 ml
1 teaspoon	5 mL	5 ml
1 tablespoon	15 mL	20 ml
¼ cup	50 mL	60 ml
⅓ cup	75 mL	80 ml
½ cup	125 mL	125 ml

(continued)

Volume *(continued)*

U.S. Units	Canadian Metric	Australian Metric
⅔ cup	150 mL	170 ml
¾ cup	175 mL	190 ml
1 cup	250 mL	250 ml
1 quart	1 liter	1 liter
1½ quarts	1.5 liters	1.5 liters
2 quarts	2 liters	2 liters
2½ quarts	2.5 liters	2.5 liters
3 quarts	3 liters	3 liters
4 quarts	4 liters	4 liters

Weight

U.S. Units	Canadian Metric	Australian Metric
1 ounce	30 grams	30 grams
2 ounces	55 grams	60 grams
3 ounces	85 grams	90 grams
4 ounces (¼ pound)	115 grams	125 grams
8 ounces (½ pound)	225 grams	225 grams
16 ounces (1 pound)	455 grams	500 grams
1 pound	455 grams	½ kilogram

Measurements

Inches	Centimeters
½	1.5
1	2.5
2	5.0
3	7.5
4	10.0
5	12.5
6	15.0

Inches	Centimeters
7	17.5
8	20.5
9	23.0
10	25.5
11	28.0
12	30.5
13	33.0

Temperature (Degrees)

Fahrenheit	Celsius
32	0
212	100
250	120
275	140
300	150
325	160
350	180
375	190
400	200
425	220
450	230
475	240
500	260

Index

• *W* •